Mindfulness

A Practical Guide

TESSA WATT

MJF BOOKS
New York

Published by MJF Books
Fine Communications
589 Eighth Avenue, 6th Floor
New York, NY 10018

Mindfulness: A Practical Guide
LC Control Number: 2015957142
ISBN 978-1-60671-331-0

Designed by Lisa Chovnick

Printed in the United States of America.

MJF Books and the MJF colophon are trademarks of Fine Creative Media, Inc.

BG   25   24   23   22   21   20   19   18   17

CONTENTS

AUTHOR'S NOTE

It's important to note that there is much frequently used teaching and research employed in mindfulness. Where I know the source I have been sure to reference it, but my apologies here to the originators of any material if I have overlooked them.

INTRODUCTION

Mindfulness is one of the oldest and most basic skills known to mankind. In its essence, it's as simple as rediscovering the taste of fresh water or the vastness of the sky. It is learning, or re-learning, how to be present, how to be in moment. It can be like stepping out of a grey flat screen mode into a world which is vivid and three-dimensional.

Mindfulness means becoming more aware of what's going on—right here, right now. We can appreciate our lives, instead of rushing through them, always trying to get somewhere else. Being mindful can also help us to be less swept away by our powerful, habitual currents of thought and emotion, which can manifest as stress, depression, negative thinking, anxiety, anger, resentment or self-doubt.

TRAINING IN MINDFULNESS

Mindfulness itself is a way of *being*—a capacity for moment-by-moment awareness—which doesn't belong to any one culture or tradition. But we find that this skill, part of our birthright, has somehow been lost to us; perhaps increasingly so in our speedy 21st-century world. The good news is that we can train ourselves in mindfulness, just as we exercise to keep our bodies healthy.

Mindfulness is about teaching yourself to be more:

- Aware—of your body, your mind and the environment
- Present—in this moment; right here, right now
- Focused—more able to make choices about where you place your attention

- Embodied—being *in* your body; bringing your mind and your body into synch
- Accepting—of yourself and other people.

PRACTICE

Mindfulness training draws on the ancient traditions of meditation and yoga, often incorporating insights from modern medicine and psychotherapy. It involves setting aside time for 'practice'—time when you can literally practise being mindful by bringing your mind back, again and again, to a particular object of attention.

In mindfulness practice you may use one or more of these as your focus:

- Your breath—the physical sensations of breathing
- Your body—in stillness or in movement
- Your senses—such as hearing, seeing and tasting
- Your thoughts—which may include your emotions
- Your experience—whatever arises in your awareness in this moment, including any of the above.

As well as making space for formal meditation, you can bring mindfulness into your life throughout the day. You can use informal practices to help you do this—washing the dishes mindfully, perhaps, or taking a short 'breathing space'. With practice, the mindful approach will slowly seep into your being and you may find yourself naturally being more present and aware in your daily life.

REMEMBER THIS!!! Mindfulness practice can be:

- Formal—such as sitting meditation using the breath as a focus
- Informal—such as making a cup of tea with awareness.

HISTORY

The practice of mindfulness goes back thousands of years. Many spiritual traditions have encouraged presence in the moment as a way to be in touch with our inner selves, or the divine. Buddhism has made mindfulness a core part of its teachings, more so than any other tradition. Buddhist thinkers have taken great interest over the centuries in the way the human mind works, developing methods of training the mind to be more present, focused and aware. The practical techniques used in current mindfulness training come largely from the Buddhist tradition of meditation, along with elements drawn from the more body-oriented Indian discipline of hatha yoga.

Since the 1960s, the political situation in Asian countries like Vietnam and Tibet has sent Buddhist teachers into exile in the West, where they've taken up the challenge of teaching new audiences. Meditation practices which were traditionally done by monks in a forest or monastery have been adapted for busy Westerners with jobs and families. Influential Buddhist teachers have included the Japanese Zen teacher Shunryu Suzuki, the Vietnamese monk Thich Nhat Hanh, the visionary Tibetan Chögyam Trungpa, and of course the well-known Dalai Lama, spiritual leader of Tibet.

But you don't have to be religious, become a Buddhist or believe anything particular to practise mindfulness. Since the 1970s, mindfulness training in the West has developed into structured, secular courses which are increasingly accessible. Mindfulness has spread like wildfire in the public consciousness. In 1979 the American Jon Kabat-Zinn created an eight-week course at the University of

Massachusetts Medical School to help people with difficult conditions such as chronic pain, AIDS and cancer. Without being able to 'cure' them, he discovered that meditation could help them relate to their stress and suffering in a different way. This course of 'Mindfulness-Based Stress Reduction' (MBSR) is now used around the world not only for people with illness, but for many thousands of participants simply wanting to find a way to deal with the normal daily difficulties of life, and to enjoy life more fully.

In the 1990s, mindfulness took its next quantum leap into the world of mental health and psychotherapy when three leading clinical psychologists from the UK and Canada developed Mindfulness-Based Cognitive Therapy (MBCT) as a treatment for people with a history of recurrent depression. MBCT is very similar to MBSR, with more emphasis on how to work with the 'negative thinking' which can lead to depression. Mindfulness has begun to sweep through the profession of psychotherapy, leading to other new therapies like ACT (Acceptance and Commitment Therapy); and many therapists now offer it to their clients as part of their toolkit for mental health.

In this book we'll introduce many of the practices and ideas which are used in mindfulness courses like MBSR and MBCT. We'll also draw inspiration from great mindfulness teachers coming from the Buddhist tradition, who carry with them years of deep training in the practice of meditation.

KEY TERMS There are some key terms that will come up again and again in this book. It's worth taking a moment to acquaint yourself with them now . . .

Meditation is used in this book to refer to a formal practice which helps us train the mind to be more aware and present.

Mindfulness is used to describe a more general approach of being aware of our experience in the present moment—without judging it—which the practice of meditation can help us to develop.

Mindfulness-Based Stress Reduction (MBSR) is an eight-week course that trains participants to be mindful and to relate better to stress, pain and other difficulties.

Mindfulness-Based Cognitive Therapy (MBCT) is similar to MBSR but with elements developed more specifically for people with a tendency to suffer from depression.

SCIENCE

The move of mindfulness into public awareness is thanks largely to an explosion of interest from the scientific and medical communities within the last few decades. Research has demonstrated the enormous benefits of mindfulness practice for our physical and mental health, with new studies out every month. Doctors and counsellors increasingly recommend mindfulness as an approach for patients with depression, stress and anxiety-related ailments. Mindfulness training is also being adopted in schools and workplaces, helping students and employees to be more focused and productive, and less reactive to stress.

Research shows the benefits of mindfulness in many areas:

- **Physical health.** Mindfulness can help us to cope better with a range of conditions, including chronic pain, heart disease and cancer. It's been shown to strengthen the immune system, improving our response to illnesses ranging from flu to psoriasis to HIV.

- **Mental health.** Mindfulness is increasingly being used to help people with recurrent depression, addiction, anxiety-related ailments and general stress.

- **Well-being.** Many participants in mindfulness training have reported greater enjoyment and appreciation of their lives, as well as other benefits like greater self-awareness, greater acceptance of their emotions and increased empathy for other people. Neuroscientists are now backing this up with studies showing that meditation can strengthen areas of the brain associated with happiness, well-being and compassion.

MYTHS AND MISCONCEPTIONS

The kind of meditation we use in mindfulness training is not about going off into altered states, trying to get to some better place. It's not about sitting in the lotus position in flowing white robes on a turquoise beach, as the advertising posters would have it—pleasant though that might be! You're not even trying to get calm and relaxed, or to become a 'better person'. You are befriending the person you already are, and the place where you are sitting, right now. If you do experience any sense of calm, it is not from stilling the stormy weather of life, but from learning to ride its chaotic energy.

Here are some wrong ideas you might have about mindfulness:

- It's about going into an altered state where the mind is completely empty of thoughts
- It's about becoming very calm and not feeling emotions
- You have to become a Buddhist or take up some other religion or cult
- Even if other people can do it, you won't be able to because your mind is too busy.

HOW TO USE THIS BOOK

Mindfulness is about experience, not just words and concepts. To get the most from this book, you'll need to do more than read—you'll need to actually *do* the practices.

- **Take your time.** See if you can resist the urge to rush through to the end and 'get somewhere' quickly. It's better to do the practices thoroughly, and repeat them a number of times, than to think you are 'advancing' by ticking off lots of different exercises.

- **Keep a notebook.** Some of the exercises ask you to write a few lines. You may also like to keep a note of interesting or challenging things which arise in your practice. Writing things down in one place can help you reflect on your own experience and give you a sense of the journey you are taking.

- **Be patient.** Mindfulness is not a quick fix! Don't worry if you don't feel much is happening—there may be more going on under the surface than you think.

WHAT IS MINDFULNESS?

WAKING UP

Mindfulness begins with recognizing that our common experience is *not* very mindful—that we are sleepwalking through much of our daily lives, blind and crashing into things. We stumble from place to place caught in a whirlwind of thoughts, missing what is in front of our noses.

Often the storm of thoughts is not pleasant to be caught up in. We ruminate over what someone said earlier, or what we should have said in reply, or what happened ten years ago, or what we have to do tomorrow. Our minds are exhausting—we may feel exhausted.

The mindful approach is to invite a gap in this endless stream of thoughts and emotions. We train ourselves to wake up; to open a door and let in some fresh air and space. We're not pushing away our experience—quite the opposite. We're allowing ourselves to be present to the energy of our experience, right here, right now. We discover the possibility of waking up to how things are in each moment.

 AWAKE AND AWARE

Take a few minutes to become aware of your experience, right here, right now:

- Feel the weight and texture of the book in your hand.

- Feel the sense of your own body—your feet in contact with the floor, your buttocks on the chair; if you are sitting, feel your torso rising up, your head and shoulders, your arms and hands. Can you feel the movement of your breath somewhere in your body?

- Notice your environment—the space around you, any objects and people, any sounds and colours.

- Notice how you are feeling—are there any thoughts and emotions you are aware of? Are there any bodily sensations? You don't need to change anything, just notice. Spend a few moments opening your awareness to whatever is here in your body, mind and the environment.

AUTOMATIC PILOT

In order to cultivate mindfulness, the first step is becoming aware of our usual tendency to sleepwalk through life. This mode is described as being on 'automatic pilot'. When we're on automatic pilot, we might eat a sandwich at our desk and reach the last crust without having ever actually tasted it. We might come home from work and find ourselves with the key in the door, having forgotten that we meant to stop to buy milk, and having completely missed seeing the blossom trees at the end of the road.

Our tendency to go onto automatic pilot can be particularly unhelpful when we start getting into negative trains of thought. Some small event may trigger us into feeling stressed or depressed, without our even realizing what is happening. Someone pushes in front of us in the queue, and subconsciously we set off on a train of thought about how no one respects us, and how the world is out to get us. Or perhaps a small task goes wrong at work, and before we know it we're convinced we can't finish our project and will lose our job. Most of us have some well-worn grooves into which our thoughts can easily begin to run. A few minutes later we find ourselves in a black mood, without even knowing how we got there.

Through mindfulness, we can recognize when we are on automatic pilot, and have a chance of stepping out into the freshness of the present moment. As we begin to pay attention to what is going on in our body, our mind and our environment, we can see how we get stuck on automatic pilot. By developing mindfulness, we can become more aware of the habits that make us unhappy or stressed, and start to make new choices. We can also become more present, more able to taste the richness of our world and all the little experiences which make up our lives.

A TASTE

One way to get a taste of mindfulness is to start quite literally with that—a practice of tasting. This is a good way to see what it's like when we bring our full awareness to a simple everyday experience.

Mindfulness courses around the world often start with tasting a raisin, a practice which has become traditional since Jon Kabat-Zinn included it in his pioneering clinic in the 1970s. If you don't have a raisin to hand, you can try this with whatever food you have available.

 A TASTE OF MINDFULNESS

- Fetch yourself a couple of raisins, or if you don't have raisins you could use a segment of orange or other small piece of food.

- Look at it. Take the raisin or fruit in the palm of your hand. Imagine you've never seen anything like this before. Pick it up and take a good look at it, with your full attention. Notice the texture, the colour, the shape, the folds and hollows, the light shining on it. Take time to really see it and explore it with your eyes.

- Explore the raisin with your other senses. Give it a squish— perhaps even bring it up to your ear as you do so, to hear if it makes a sound. Notice what it smells like, and if you have any reaction to the smell, maybe in your mouth.

- Notice your thoughts. Whenever your mind wanders off, just be aware of this happening and aware of where your mind goes.

- Taste the food. First bring the object to your mouth, perhaps running it along the lips, noticing any reactions—maybe salivation. When you're ready, place it in the mouth, not chewing yet. Pay attention to the sensations in your mouth, exploring it with your tongue. Finally prepare to chew the raisin, getting it into the right place—taking a bite into it, noticing the taste and texture in the mouth. Without swallowing yet, continue to chew, bringing your full attention to the taste of it.

• Swallow it: be aware first of your intention to swallow, and then actually swallowing the raisin—seeing if you can follow it as it moves down towards your stomach. And are there any aftereffects—how do you feel after the exercise?

• And now, if you have a second raisin or piece of fruit, you might like to do the exercise again, slowly exploring this new object with each of your senses.

How was this exercise for you? Take a moment to reflect on what you've just done, and, if you'd like to, write your thoughts down.

REFLECTING

Here are some responses that other people have had to this exercise:

• It tasted completely different to how I remembered; so much more flavour.

• My mind was really busy—I couldn't keep my focus on the exercise.

• I felt really irritated, and I wanted to go faster.

• I really noticed the texture of it, all the folds and colours. I was surprised that it made a noise when I squished it.

• It reminded me of Christmas and my grandmother's cakes.

• I don't like raisins, so I could only think about how I didn't like it.

Was your experience different from the way you normally eat? Most of us would agree that it's rare to pay this much attention to what's happening when we're eating—to the flavours, textures, colours, and to the reactions going on in our body and mind. Normally we'd cram a handful of raisins in without thinking, or eat them in a bowl of muesli without noticing much about the taste of it.

This usual way of eating is a good example of being on automatic pilot. We go through many of our daily activities without being fully aware of what we're doing. By paying attention to our direct experience in this moment—whether it's a raisin, a cup of tea or a patch of bright sunshine, our lives can become more vivid. We can taste, smell and experience all the small moments that make up our lives, which we so often miss.

PAYING ATTENTION

Jon Kabat-Zinn defines mindfulness in this way:

> *Mindfulness means paying attention in a particular way:*
> *on purpose, in the present moment and non-judgmentally.*

We're always paying attention to *something*, but often not what we choose, as our mind jumps from one thing to another. Through practice we can pay attention:

- **On purpose**, by training ourselves to focus on an object of our choice, such as our left toes, or the movement of the breath
- **In the present moment**, being willing to let go of thinking about the past or the future, coming back to what is here now
- **Non-judgmentally**, being kind to ourselves as we bring our minds back to the focus, over and over, developing gentleness and good humour. We don't judge our experience as 'good' or 'bad', we stay open to it all, just as it is.

 A MINDFUL MEAL

Eat a meal mindfully, in the same way that you ate the raisin (it doesn't have to be quite so slowly!). Put aside doing other activities at the same time, such as listening to the radio, talking or reading. Bring your awareness to the food as you are eating it; the tastes, the textures, the colours—and the act of eating itself.

REMEMBER THIS!!!

- We live much of our lives in a mode which is not mindful, as though we are sleepwalking or on automatic pilot.

- Mindfulness brings us out of automatic pilot into the present moment.

- We can train ourselves to pay attention on purpose, in the present, and without judgment.

- We can use small, simple experiences like tasting our food to begin to understand what it's like to be mindful.

IS THIS THE RIGHT TIME FOR YOU?

Practising mindfulness is a brave thing to do. It means being willing to be alone with yourself—to be present with your own body and mind, without running away or distracting yourself with activities as most of us do. When we let ourselves be still, things we have buried or pushed down can come bubbling up to the surface—perhaps strong feelings or life events we haven't come to terms with. In mindfulness training, we don't generally get too involved in the content of these thoughts and emotions. Instead, as you'll see throughout this book, we let them come up, we notice with kindness how they affect us, and we let them move on.

If you are right in the midst of a very challenging or distressing life situation, such as a bereavement or a deep depression, this may not be the right time for you to start your practice of mindfulness. The emotions may feel too overwhelming for you to be present with them in the way that mindfulness encourages. At this point it may be best to seek professional support from your doctor or a psychotherapist, and continue your exploration of mindfulness when things are a bit more settled in your life. When your mind is more stable, you will be in a better position to learn and practise this new way of approaching things. Mindfulness will then be a skill for life which can help you cope better with difficult events when they arise in the future.

– 3 –

WHY?

What are you doing here? Why are you reading this book instead of a novel or a newspaper? What has piqued your interest in mindfulness and what do you hope to get from it?

It's helpful to have an idea of our intention before we begin a journey. When things are challenging, we can remember our initial inspiration, and find the motivation to go forward. Your intention might be a bit vague—a feeling that something is missing, a general sense of longing, or a curiosity. That's fine. See if you can articulate something about it right now, before you are influenced by reading more about other people's intentions.

 INTENTION

- Sit quietly for a few moments. Bring your awareness into your body. Spend a few moments feeling your feet on the floor, the weight of your body on the seat and your hands wherever they are resting. Feel your spine and head rising upwards.

- Ask yourself, 'Why am I here, reading this book? What do I hope to get from learning about mindfulness?' Notice what first comes into your mind.

- Sit with the question for a few moments. Let it settle in your mind, and see what arises in response. Is there anything deeper under the surface? Are there any half-formed thoughts or feelings that you can put into words?

- Write down your response here or in a notebook where you can find it again:

_____

_____

_____

_____

_____

WHY MINDFULNESS?

Now, have a look at some of the reasons other people choose to take up mindfulness practice. See if any of these motives resonate with you:

- To become more relaxed and calm
- To cope better with stress and anxiety
- To help prevent myself from getting into depression
- To have better concentration and focus
- To cope with chronic pain or illness
- To enjoy and appreciate my life more
- To handle strong emotions more successfully
- To have greater self-awareness and insight
- To be more accepting of myself and others
- To connect with a sense of meaning or something bigger than myself
- To have more sense of space in my life.

Every month new research papers are published on the use of mindfulness in coping with particular physical and mental health issues such as drug addiction, tinnitus or OCD. Other studies focus on specific groups of participants, such as parents, students or prisoners, while still others look at mindfulness in relation to general well-being. *The Mindful Manifesto*, by Ed Halliwell and

Jonty Heaversedge, gives an inspiring overview of the evidence for mindfulness and its benefits. Here are some of the key areas where mindfulness has been shown to be helpful ...

STRESS

Researchers have been interested for some years in the effects of meditation on stress levels, but it was hard to test in a clinical setting. The Mindfulness-Based Stress Reduction course is a good subject for clinical research because of its standardized, replicable format. Numerous studies have now shown that MBSR does what its name says: it reduces stress and helps people cope with it more effectively.

Stress is a natural response of our bodies to threat. As part of our evolution we developed the 'fight or flight response', a state of hyper-arousal in which our body prepares us to fight an attacker or run away to safety. We're no longer often threatened by physical dangers like wild animals, but our nervous system kicks in with the same responses in reaction to modern stresses like work deadlines and traffic jams. We lose the ability to flick the off switch, and find ourselves in a perpetual state of raised heart rate, high blood pressure and pumping adrenaline.

Mindfulness practice has been shown to have a calming effect on the nervous system, helping to switch off the stress response and bring us back into balance. It also trains us to become more aware of stress signals in the body, giving us the chance to respond more effectively. We can take intelligent action rather than reacting blindly by losing our temper, drinking too much, overworking, or whatever else we tend to do.

SPEAKING FROM EXPERIENCE **TESSA (THE AUTHOR)**

'I've always been quite a speedy person—walking quickly, talking quickly. I grew up with severe eczema which meant I was itchy all the time; literally uncomfortable in my own skin. In my twenties I moved from a quiet life in a university town to working as a trainee producer on live national radio. It was exciting but hugely stressful. My eczema got so bad that when I went on holiday in Corsica I couldn't even go swimming. I sat under a fig tree reading a 'teach yourself meditation' book that I had picked up at the airport. I started doing the practices, and I had a glimpse of feeling very different—a sense of coming back inside myself and being content where I was, sitting under that tree.

'Back in London I found a meditation centre, and began to do courses there, and to practise at home. It gave me some stillness in my stressful life, and my itchy skin also calmed down. But as time went on the mindfulness became something much wider and deeper. It seeped into every aspect of my life. I realized how often I was caught up in my repetitive thought patterns—planning and worrying—and that when I let them go there was a whole big world out there. It was a bit like that moment in *The Wizard of Oz*, when Dorothy steps out from black and white into glorious Technicolor.

'It's not that my thoughts and worries have gone away. But I know that at any moment, when I remember, I can drop them and wake up to a world which is much more vivid and spacious. This sense of greater space has also helped me to be less reactive. When a strong emotion like fear or anger starts to rise up in me, I can let myself feel the feelings and allow myself a bit of a gap, without always reacting blindly. If I go for any length of time without doing my mindfulness practice, I can notice the difference—how my thoughts become more claustrophobic and how challenging situations feel a bit more stressful.'

DEPRESSION

In the 1990s, three clinical psychologists—Mark Williams, John Teasdale and Zindel Segal—were developing a new treatment for people with recurrent depression using Cognitive Behavioural Therapy (CBT). They were inspired by Jon Kabat-Zinn's MBSR clinic, and decided to include mindfulness in their programme. What began as a course in CBT which had bits of mindfulness tacked on, eventually became a course with mindfulness as its core, with elements of CBT woven in. Mindfulness-Based Cognitive Therapy (MBCT) has tested very favourably in trials comparing it with other forms of treatment, and is now endorsed in the UK by the National Institute for Health and Clinical Excellence for use with people who've suffered more than two episodes of depression.

If you're prone to depression, you probably have a tendency to 'ruminate'—to get caught up in spirals of obsessive thoughts which are hard to distinguish from facts. Through mindfulness you can learn to stay grounded in the body and to be less caught up in the mind. You can start to see that your thoughts are not reality, and take a step back from them. You can learn to see the early warning signs that a spiral of low mood is starting, and so have a chance of taking a different direction.

The best time to take up mindfulness is not when you are already in the midst of severe depression, but when things are on a somewhat more even keel, when you have the patience and stability to build up skills for your long-term mental health. If you think you may be suffering from depression but have not yet had any advice, it's important to consult your doctor. You may need some professional support such as psychotherapy or medication to help you back into a more healthy state, from which learning mindfulness can be of real benefit to you in the longer term.

PAIN

When Jon Kabat-Zinn started teaching mindfulness at the University of Massachusetts medical school, many of the patients suffered from conditions causing them chronic pain. The aim of such patients learning mindfulness was not to remove the pain, but to teach them a new way of relating to it. Research showed that 65 percent of patients who hadn't responded to conventional medical treatments were less troubled by pain after learning mindfulness. Neuroscientific research is now showing that meditation actually creates changes in areas of the brain which process and regulate pain, and this looks set to be a big area for continued study.

SPEAKING FROM EXPERIENCE **MARION**

Marion is a visual artist who has lupus, a condition where the immune system attacks the body, causing damage in the joints, muscles and other organs. After eight years of intense, erratic pain, she signed up for a mindfulness course.

'I was at a state of desperation. I was at the stage where I thought if the rest of my life is going to be like this I'm not sure I can actually make it. I always thought meditation sounded hippy-ish, not really for someone like me, but at this point I thought, "I've got absolutely nothing to lose."

'I think the first thing I learnt from the mindfulness was how much time I spent not experiencing what I was experiencing, but being in the past or future with it. Spending a lot of time feeling very sad about what I'd lost, and projecting into the future with a lot of fear—"Is this going to get worse? Am I ever going to get well? Am I ever going to be able to work again?" Mindfulness gave me a tiny bit of time in each day when I was actually in the moment, in the now, in a non-judgmental way.

'Then during a meditation I tried going right up to the edge of the pain. I'd done loads of pain management and pain reduction techniques previously—but with the mindfulness it's not about managing it or reducing it, it's about going up to it and saying, "This is how it is in my body at the moment." It's absolutely counter-intuitive, but the way it works is incredibly interesting.

'The way I understand it is that pain happens in a lot of different places in the brain. There's the actual initial nerve sending out an impulse saying you're experiencing pain, and then there's a whole chain of other things that happen around the pain that are maybe to do with anxiety or fear or a whole wide range of emotions. By meditating with those emotions—allowing those emotions to actually be and coming up close to them—I've found that although my pain hasn't gone, my experience of the pain is very different. I would say that it's really dramatically changed my experience of illness.'

ILLNESS

Mindfulness is not a cure for illness, but it's been shown to improve the body's ability to cope with a variety of physical conditions. Stress can weaken the response of the immune system, while evidence suggests that mindfulness can strengthen it:

- A research team gave flu shots to two groups of participants. The group which had trained in mindfulness had a stronger response to the vaccine, producing more antibodies.

- A group of women were offered MBSR after surgery from breast cancer. Their immune systems recovered more quickly than those of the women who were not practising mindfulness.

- Another study measured the effects of mindfulness on people with HIV. The group which had eight weeks of mindfulness training maintained a constant level of CD4 T cells, which play a key role in coordinating the immune system. In the control group without mindfulness training, the cell count dropped over the same period.

HAPPINESS AND WELL-BEING

I learnt to slow down, to appreciate the moment, to breathe.

Dan

I have this small space developing in my life, one that is calm, a place that I can reach for in moments of stress and pain. So I've realized that peace is not something I need to wait for after I have finished my to-do list.

Rebecca

I learnt that I do have a wise and gentle part of myself. The practice helped me to rediscover it.

Alessia

I've begun to understand what 'being in the moment' actually means. It's not just a bumper sticker. Also, I've learnt not to be so hard on myself—or at least started.

Sarah

I've become more accepting of all the bits of me that make me human—sadness, anger, frustration, fear and so on.

Anna

I discovered there is a different way of viewing the world or situations—that sometimes just stopping and observing is the best thing to do. And that anyone can meditate—it's not some special place or state.

Alex

The experience of people who practise mindfulness is now being backed up by science. Within the past few years, neuroscientists have been using MRI technology to look at the brains of people who meditate. The results have been fascinating.

We now know that just as muscles can strengthen with exercise, the brain can strengthen in certain regions according to how we use it. For example, the brains of medical students involved in intense periods of study show changes in the areas important for memory, while jugglers' brains show increased connections in the regions which anticipate moving objects. And now a number of studies have shown that meditators have more activity and grey matter in areas of the brain associated with happiness, well-being and the ability to regulate emotion. Changes have been documented not only in seasoned meditators of many years, but also in participants with just eight weeks of mindfulness practice.

REVIEWING YOUR INTENTION

Now that you've read more about some of the benefits of mindfulness, look again at what you wrote down as your intention. Is there anything you would like to add?

You may find you have one or two intentions which are quite specific—perhaps to become less stressed at work or to cope better with a difficult relationship. You may also have an intention or two which feel broader, or deeper—to feel more at ease or to enjoy life more.

Make any additions or changes you'd like to make, and keep
your written intention where you can find it again later.

JOURNEY WITHOUT A GOAL

Although it's good to have a sense of where you'd like to be heading,
this is not about programming your GPS with a specific postcode
and address, and expecting to arrive in 2 hours 45 minutes.
Mindfulness helps us to open ourselves to a wider and fresher world
of possibilities, and we may find that the journey takes us in unexpected directions. Your experience will be much richer if you can be
open to the changes of landscape, and to revising your intentions as
you go along.

It's also good to relax about monitoring your progress and
expecting to see 'benefits' too obviously or quickly. Paradoxically,
for mindfulness practice to be of any benefit we need to drop our
constant judgment and stop looking for results. Mindfulness is
not a quick fix—we are retraining habits that have been ingrained
in us for years or even decades. Sometimes the practices bring
internal shifts which are slow, subtle and not obvious to our conscious mind until further down the line. One of the hardest
things to grasp is that mindfulness works not by looking for
changes, but by becoming more accepting of who we are right
now. So we cultivate an attitude of non-doing and non-striving,
which is the opposite of what we are used to! We'll talk more
about this in chapter 8.

When participants finish an eight-week mindfulness course,
one of the most frequent comments they make as a recommendation to others is, 'Just do it. Don't judge it, just do the practice.'
You are welcome to decide at the end of the course, or the book,
whether mindfulness is something you find of benefit and want to
carry on with. Meanwhile, see if you can suspend your judgment
and do the practices without worrying too much each time
whether they are doing you any good.

Finally, of course, the journey is your own, and though this book can give you some direction, you have to do the travelling yourself. It's fine to read, but the more you actually practise the exercises, the more you'll get your own feel for the path of mindfulness and where it can take you.

It's good to have an idea of your intention in practising mindfulness. This will help give you the motivation to practise.

BUT

Keep an open mind. See if you can do the practices without constant judgment or looking for immediate benefits.

– 4 –

SPACE

Mindfulness can help us to create space within the rush and busyness of our lives. In fact we talk about 'creating' space but we don't actually have to *create* it—the space is already here, open and infinite. We're creating a gap, in which we can *allow* the space instead of constantly filling it up with our activity.

BEING

What does it mean to be a human being? The mindful answer puts the emphasis on the word 'being'. We are human *beings*, but we have forgotten how to *be*. We have become human *doings*, trapped in a mode of always doing, acting, achieving and keeping busy. When we stop, even for a moment, it can feel frightening and unnatural. Activity and busyness have become our default mode.

In the mid-20th century, when Eastern teachers started bringing the practice of meditation to the Western public, it went against the grain. Here was a practice which encouraged you to sit there, seemingly doing nothing. It appeared self-indulgent and navel-gazing. Early adopters were seen as part of the counter-culture, including literary and musical figures such as Jack Kerouac, Alan Ginsberg and Leonard Cohen.

Meditation has become much more mainstream since then, growing steadily in popularity as thousands of 'ordinary' people have tasted its benefits. When Jon Kabat-Zinn began teaching mindfulness at his Stress Reduction Clinic in the 70s, American truck drivers and grandmothers found themselves sitting cross-legged in silence or twisting themselves into yoga postures; it felt 'un-American', as one participant put it. But it changed their lives.

Patients on the edge of despair learned to stop struggling with their conditions, to reinhabit their bodies and to enjoy life again.

Mindfulness practice allows us time and space to be. It may be setting aside half an hour for the formal practice of meditation. Or it may be allowing a few seconds' gap—a moment of pause.

It's not about spacing out, vegetating or going into an altered state, but *being* with awareness. Being aware of where we are and what is happening, right now. It doesn't mean we can't achieve things. In fact, by training ourselves to shift regularly into this mode of *being*, it's more likely that our *doing* mode will be effective, focused and productive.

BEING VERSUS DOING

The Western Christian tradition is often associated with the Protestant work ethic, with 'doing' and being active. But the Bible contains passages in which Christ encourages his listeners not to worry about material provisions, and celebrates the value of being rather than always doing.

> *Consider the lilies of the field, how they grow;*
> *They toil not, neither do they spin*
>
> Matthew 6:28

More recently, the value of taking time out for being has been encapsulated in bumper-sticker wisdom: 'Don't just do something, sit there!'

PAUSE

The space we create for mindfulness can come in all sizes. There are formal meditation sessions where you set aside time for practice—perhaps for 10, 20, 30 or more minutes a day. Many dedicated practitioners take part in longer retreat sessions lasting for a day, a week, a month, or even several years at a time, like the English-woman Tenzin Palmo, who lived for 12 years in a Himalayan cave.

At the other end of the spectrum, mindfulness practice can be done in the blink of an eye. We can pause at any time in the busy stream of our day, taking a moment to notice where we are. When we find ourselves in fast-forward mode, we can press the pause button. Perhaps just for a few seconds, we can step out of automatic pilot and bring awareness to what's happening here and now in our body, our mind and the environment. Then, without making a big deal of it, we can carry on with our day.

The American Buddhist nun Pema Chödrön is a much-loved meditation teacher and writer. In recent years she has been emphasizing the practice of 'pausing' more and more in her teaching. As she writes in *Taking the Leap*, 'We can always connect with the openness of our minds. We can use our days to wake up rather than go back to sleep. Give this approach a try. Make a commitment to pausing throughout the day, and do that whenever you can.'

 A PAUSE

Stop reading. Take just a few seconds to notice whatever is right here, right now. Your body. Your thoughts and emotions. The environment around you. Any sights, sounds or smells.

Take a few mindful breaths, being aware of the movement of the breath in and out of your body.

Then carry on.

The practice of pausing is not meant to be a substitute for more formal meditation—the two go hand in hand. With meditation we make time to step out of our normal whirlwind of activity and cultivate our ability to be present, to connect with a greater sense of spaciousness. Then, as we train our minds through meditation, we can also let this permeate our daily lives through small and frequent pauses throughout the day. When we become trapped in the claustrophobia of busy thoughts, we can open up to a bigger space, like puncturing holes in a dense cloud so that the sun can shine through.

YOUR PAUSE BUTTON

Pick something that you can use as a trigger or reminder for your 'pause' practice. It could be:

- A sound you hear often in the day, such as a phone, car alarm or siren
- A visual cue, such as a sign or image on your computer or fridge
- An activity you do often, such as washing your hands or sending a text message.

Make a decision that each time you hear or see or do this thing, you'll just pause for a few seconds, notice where you are and what's happening, take a few mindful breaths, and then move on.

Your pause button:

_____

_____

_____

_____

_____

_____

_____

- Mindfulness creates space for 'being' rather than 'doing'.

- If you allow time for being, it will help your doing to be more productive.

- Set aside time for formal meditation practice—even 5 or 10 minutes a day is a good start.

- You can also train yourself to create little spaces, pausing often throughout the day. Use a sound, visual cue or activity as a reminder.

5

BREATH

Breathing is the most basic human function—to know we are breathing is to know we are alive. So, it's not surprising that mindfulness of breath has been practised for millennia.

Awareness of the breath is available to us in any moment. No special equipment is needed—our breath is always with us. Here is a movement which is going on 24 hours a day, most of the time without our noticing it. There is nothing especially mystical about it—we just practise bringing awareness to this most simple and universal activity.

When you bring awareness to your breath, it is *this* breath, in *this* moment—not last year's breath or tomorrow's breath. The breath is closely connected to the body, and also to the mind; it is a link or bridge between the two. When you tune in to your breathing, your body and mind are in synch—you are present. You can train yourself to use the breath as a haven, or an anchor; when you find you are caught up in a whirlwind of thoughts, you can let it go and come back to this natural process of breathing.

MINDFULNESS OF BREATHING

You can do this practice for any length of time—for the first time you could try 5 minutes. Sit on an upright chair with your feet flat on the floor, or cross-legged on a firm cushion.

Taking your seat:

- Come into a posture which feels relaxed and awake, with a tall spine.

- Let your shoulders drop and your hands rest on your thighs.

- Close your eyes or keep them open with a downward gaze, whichever feels most comfortable.

- Feel the weight and gravity of your body. Notice the sensations where your buttocks connect with the chair or cushion, and where your feet or ankles make contact with the floor. Spend a few moments exploring these sensations.

Being with your breath:

- Bring your attention to the movement of your breath, wherever you feel it. There's no need to change the way you're breathing, or do anything special with the breath. Just let it be as it is.

- Tune in to the physical sensations of breathing—not *thinking* about the breath but *being* with it, allowing the breath to breathe itself. See if you can be with the breath all the way in and all the way out. You can imagine you are riding on the waves of your own breath if you find this helpful.

Bringing back your mind:

- You will find that your mind wanders off from the breath— that's not a problem. A mind naturally wanders. You may find yourself daydreaming or worrying, replaying a conversation or running through a shopping list. Whenever you notice your mind has gone off, gently return your attention to the breath.

- If your mind wanders from the breath a hundred times, just bring it back a hundred times. See if you can escort your awareness back to the breath with kindness and good humour. This is the practice: not keeping the mind fixed in one place, but bringing the mind back, over and over. Use the breath as an anchor to bring you back to here and now, to this moment.

Take a moment to write down anything you noticed during your practice of mindful breathing (either here or in a notebook):

_____

_____

_____

_____

IS YOUR BREATH BORING?

In, out, in, out, in, out . . .

You may find your breath somewhat less entertaining than watching the TV or reading a newspaper. Of course if you were in a situation where you found yourself running out of air, unable to breathe, you would suddenly find your breath very interesting indeed!

In mindful breathing, it helps to cultivate a curiosity about your own breath. See if you can be inquisitive, bringing a fresh interest to the breath, as if you had never noticed it before. Here are some things you might like to investigate:

- **Breath in the nostrils**—can you notice the feeling of cool air going in, and warmer air going out?

- **Breath in the torso**—do you feel it moving in the upper chest, in the mid-torso or in the belly? See if you can follow your breath down into the belly, noticing how the walls of the abdomen expand like a balloon on the inhale, and relax back again on the exhale. It may help to put a hand on your belly, so that you can feel the rise and fall of the breath.

- **Qualities of the breath**—does your breath feel long or short? Shallow or deep? Rough or smooth? Can you feel the texture of it? Does it change or stay the same?

- **Inhale and exhale**—what's it like to follow the in-breath in, and then the out-breath out? What happens at the point where the inhale turns into the exhale, and the exhale to the inhale? Does the breath flow straight on, or is there a gap?

- **Breath dissolving**—what happens when the breath leaves your nose or mouth? Do you have a sense of it dissolving and mixing with the space in front of and around you? How far does it go? How does it feel as your breath flows out of the body—perhaps some sense of releasing and letting go?

Remember, you don't have to change anything or manipulate the breath; just be gently inquisitive about each breath—*this* breath, in *this* moment.

MINDFULNESS OF BREATHING: BEING INQUISITIVE

Repeat the mindful breathing exercise from page 31, but this time pick one or more aspects of the breath from the list we just ran through to focus on. Spend a few minutes really feeling the texture of the breath, or the sensations of the breath in the belly. Are there other things you can notice about your breath which are not on this list?

IS YOUR MIND BUSY?

'I can't meditate—my mind is too busy'. This is one of the most common first reactions to the mindful breathing exercise.

When you start to meditate, you may find it shocking how active your mind is. It flits from one thought to another, often without any obvious logic. It may feel like a monkey leaping from tree to tree. You may even think, 'I was looking for calm, but when I started to meditate my mind got busier!' It's more likely that your mind has been this busy all along, but only now are you creating the conditions for noticing the busyness.

In mindfulness we don't see thoughts as a 'problem'—we are not trying to get rid of thoughts to achieve an empty, blank state of mind. Having thoughts is part of who we are as creative, thinking beings. It can be hard to believe this when you start, but the practice of meditation is actually just this: noticing the thoughts, letting them go and bringing the mind back to the focus, again and again. Each time your mind wanders off, it's another opportunity to practise bringing it back.

Mindfulness is not about having a mind that is empty and blank. Your mind will have lots of thoughts, and that is okay!

TAKE YOUR SEAT

The classic meditation posture you see in ancient sculptures is cross-legged on the floor, with the feet tucked up in the lotus position. After years of sitting in chairs and at desks, most of us don't bend that way anymore! That's not a problem—the seated mindfulness practices can be done on a chair, cross-legged on a cushion or kneeling if it's comfortable for you.

A chair:

- Choose a firm chair with an upright back.

- Sit with your feet flat on the floor or place something firm under your feet if they don't reach the floor.

- Ideally, let your spine be self-supporting, sitting away from the back of the chair or with the chair back lightly support- ing you. If it's not comfortable, a cushion in the small of the back may help.

A cushion:

- If you have the chance, you can try sitting on a specially designed meditation cushion; they come in many shapes and sizes.

- Your seat should be firm, not too squishy—try placing a cushion from your chair or sofa on top of large books such as phone books.

- Your ankles can be crossed comfortably, resting on a blanket or mat. Your knees should be a bit lower than your hips. For many of us with stiff hips, this means we need to get our seat quite high up off the ground (perhaps 8–12 inches or more).

Kneeling:

- Some people find it comfortable to kneel, with a cushion under the buttocks and shins on either side of the cushion. You can also buy wooden meditation stools which are used in this kneeling position.

POSTURE

As a child, you may have been told to 'Sit up straight!' As a result, you might even have a secret resistance to the idea of posture. But when we meditate in a sitting position, taking a good posture is the foundation of the practice. Our bodies and minds are connected—when the body slumps, the mind slumps. When the body is uplifted and awake, it encourages the mind to be this way too. Here are some tips for a good posture:

- **Have a firm base**—sit solidly on your seat, feeling the weight of your buttocks on the chair or cushion. Feel the contact of your feet flat on the floor, or the ankles or shins if you are cross-legged or kneeling.

- **Be alert**—your spine is tall, the crown of your head lifting towards the sky. You can imagine sitting like a mountain, or like a monarch on a throne—regal and present.

- **Be comfortable**—your posture is uplifted but not rigid. Let your shoulders relax and your hands rest on your thighs. The front of the body can be soft and open. Let your jaw be loose, and perhaps tuck your chin slightly in. If your eyes are open, look downward a few feet in front of you, with a gaze which is soft and relaxed.

IS BREATHING DIFFICULT?

Some people find mindful breathing difficult because of problems with their breath. It may be a physical issue, or it may be that each time you focus on your breath you start to panic that you can't breathe properly. If this is you, don't worry; it may be good to focus on other mindfulness practices for now, especially bringing your awareness into your body and its sensations. You may find that as you feel more grounded and at home in your body, your breath also starts to feel more comfortable.

 Your breath is available to you at any time as an anchor to bring you back into your body and into the present moment.

MINDFULNESS OF BREATHING—THROUGH THE WEEK

Now that you've tried mindful breathing, see if you can practise it again during the week. You can set aside a few minutes for formal practice—5 minutes, 10 minutes or whatever you can manage.

You can also bring your awareness to the breath at any time during your day, just noticing that you are breathing for a few breaths, and then moving on.

6

BRUSHING YOUR TEETH

Mindfulness practice is sometimes described as being a bit like brushing your teeth. It's something you can do every day as part of your basic mental hygiene. It's better to brush your teeth every day for 5 minutes, rather than for an hour on Sundays. In the same way, it's good to keep the connection with your mindfulness practice by doing a little each day, rather than saving it up for sporadic marathon sessions.

You can also use the act of brushing your teeth quite literally as a chance to practise mindfulness. Instead of mechanically going through the motions while you are busy thinking of other things, you can be aware of your tooth brushing while you are doing it, tuning in to the physical sensations and being aware of your environment. Awareness of a simple daily activity like this can help you bring yourself into the present moment, and offers a practice you can do even at the busiest of times.

 MINDFUL TOOTH BRUSHING

Next time you brush your teeth, see if you can do it mindfully:

- Be aware of putting the toothpaste on the brush, bringing the brush to your mouth, the actions of your hand, sensations in your gums and mouth, the taste of the toothpaste.

- You can also be aware of your environment—any sounds, and objects in your vision, perhaps your face in the mirror.

You don't need to be too precious or self-conscious about it—or become a perfectionist tooth brusher (although your teeth may end up cleaner after paying more attention!). The idea is just to be aware of what you are doing while you are doing it.

Try continuing with this mindful tooth brushing for the next week.

WASHING THE DISHES

You can use other routine activities such as making coffee, taking a shower, chopping vegetables or house cleaning as mindfulness practices. One of the traditional activities mentioned by mindfulness teachers over centuries is that of washing dishes. I remember hearing from childhood the old Zen proverb:

> *'What is the meaning of life?' asks the student.*
> *'Have you eaten your meal?' asks the teacher.*
> *'Yes I have,' replies the student.*
> *'Then go and wash out your bowl,' says the teacher.*
> *At that moment the student is said to have found enlightenment.*

The Vietnamese teacher Thich Nhat Hanh is a great advocate of mindful dishwashing. He says, 'While washing the dishes one should only be washing the dishes'—being completely aware of the washing while you are doing it, and not even thinking about the result. You can try it, enjoying the warmth and soapiness of the water, the satisfaction as you clean things, the reflection of light on the plates.

Bringing mindfulness to daily activities like this brings us out of our rumination into the here and now. It can also help us to shift our feeling of boredom and impatience with so much of what we do in our daily lives, and encourage us to experience more appreciation and enjoyment of the simple tasks which we often perform so mindlessly.

 MINDFUL DAILY ACTIVITY

Choose a routine activity in your daily life—something you do every day, such as taking a shower, washing dishes or making coffee. For the next week, see if you can do it mindfully.

Bring an awareness to the activity each time you do it. If you are washing dishes, be present with washing dishes. Just be aware of what you are doing while you are doing it.

Your choice of 'mindful activity':

_____

_____

_____

_____

_____

So often we go through our week with a feeling of resentment about the 'boring' chores we have to do—rushing to get through them, checking off to-do lists, perhaps trying to do several things at once. Could you appreciate and even enjoy the simplicity of these daily activities?

7

BODY

We might think that mindfulness is all about the *mind*—and yes, becoming familiar with our patterns of mind is part of the journey. But one of the bedrocks of mindfulness practice is the *body*: learning or re-learning how to be fully inside our own body, to be *embodied*. The body brings us into the present moment. As we come back to it, again and again, it anchors us in the here and now. When we are fully aware of the body, our mind and body are synchronized. We are connected, and we are whole.

Our modern Western culture is increasingly disembodied. Many of us sit at computers all day, staring at screens, existing only from the neck up. We *seem* to have a lot of interest in the body—everywhere there are images of sex, of fitness clubs, and of beautiful bodies selling products. But if you reflect on these images, a lot of our culture is about looking at the body from the outside, trying to shape the body into our ideas about how it should be.

When we go running or to the gym or to Pilates class we may push through pain to exert our control over the body. When we eat, how often do we find that 'our eyes are bigger than our stomach' or that we are satisfying cravings that have little to do with what the body really wants or needs?

In mindfulness, we practise feeling the body from the inside and listening to the messages it sends us. All of our experience is registered in the body—the experiences we like, and those that we don't. Our body is constantly clenching, bracing, releasing, opening, softening and closing as we react to our experience in each moment. We resist feeling things that are difficult, and this repeated tightening and bracing can create chronic tension in parts of our body—sometimes in more obvious parts like the shoulders or jaw; sometimes deep in the belly, solar plexus or chest. Often we are unaware of how the body is registering the story of our life and our experience in each moment.

 BODY IN STRESS

- Sit quietly and bring awareness into your body. Feel your feet on the floor and your weight on the chair.

- Think of a stressful situation you've been in—not the most stressful event ever, but something manageable. You might remember giving a presentation, taking an exam, or perhaps a harrowing car journey.

- Take a few moments to imagine the scene. Now notice any sensations in your body. Is there anywhere where you are clenching, bracing or tightening? Perhaps you feel a shakiness, or shallowness of breath, perhaps butterflies in the stomach, or some other sensations? Take note of how your body feels in this scenario.

EMOTIONS IN THE BODY

If we bring awareness to the body, we see there is a close interconnection between our thoughts and emotions and our body sensations. Not just stress, but sadness, anger, joy, desire—whatever we feel—is registered in the body.

Each of these states has its own kind of raw energy, but much of the time we don't allow ourselves to feel it. When we experience fear or anger we may have a sense of discomfort, and immediately we try to get rid of it by pushing it away, ignoring it or reacting in some way—shouting, freezing, running or hiding. By learning to let ourselves feel these body sensations, including the difficult ones, we have the possibility of responding to our experience in a fresh way, rather than falling into our habitual patterns.

WHY PAY ATTENTION TO THE BODY?

- To bring yourself into the present moment

- To connect with your direct experience through the senses, rather than thinking *about* your experience

- To let go of 'thinking' mode and come back to 'being' mode

- To become more aware of your emotions and how they manifest as physical sensations—as you gradually let yourself feel the difficult sensations and emotions, you will discover you *can* handle them and that you don't have to repress them or act them out

- To rediscover the body as a home—a place you can trust and come back to. You can re-inhabit the body and feel its natural qualities of groundedness and stability.

FEELING YOUR FINGERS

This is an exercise to explore the difference between thinking about the body and experiencing it from the inside.

- **Picture your fingers.** Without looking at them, take a moment to visualize them. Imagine the shape of them—are they short and stubby, or long and slender? What do the fingernails look like? Do you have any thoughts about your fingers—perhaps you like them, or dislike them? Take a few moments to see what comes to mind when you think about your fingers.

- **Bring awareness into them.** Let go of *thinking about* your fingers, and see what it's like to bring awareness *into* them instead—to *feel* your fingers from inside.

- **Bring your attention to your left thumb.** Are there any sensations there? Can you feel the contact of the thumb on your thigh, or the book, or wherever it is resting? Is there tingling, or numbness; does it feel hot or cold? Are there any sensations in the tip of the thumb?

- **Now bring your awareness to the other fingers of your left hand.** Can you feel contact between them, or the feeling of air in the gaps? Do they feel moist or dry, cramped or relaxed, heavy or light? Can you feel the fingertips, the fingernails, the joints?

- **Expand your awareness to take in the fingers and thumb of the right hand.** Have a sense of all ten fingers: there's no special way you need to feel, just notice any sensations that are here. Then expand your awareness to take in the whole of your hands, and any sensations in the palms, the backs of the hands, the wrists.

- **Thoughts.** If your mind wanders off during the exercise, that's not a problem. Notice any thoughts that are triggered, and gently bring your attention back again to the hands.

Now let this awareness fade and take a few moments to reflect on the exercise. Did you notice any difference between *thinking* about the fingers, and *feeling* them from the inside? Was it easy or difficult to be present with the direct experience of your sensations?

 Mindfulness helps us to move from *thinking about* the body to *feeling* it from the inside: being fully *embodied*.

THE BODY SCAN

The body scan is a practice which involves bringing our awareness slowly and deliberately to different parts of the body. We're training ourselves to pay attention in a mindful way:

- On purpose—placing our focus where we choose to place it

- In the present moment—noticing whatever sensations are in the body, right now

- Non-judgmentally—opening our awareness to sensations even if they are difficult, and letting them be just as they are.

The purpose is not to become relaxed, or to get into any particular state, but just to bring a friendly inquisitiveness to whatever is here in the body, in this moment.

BODY SCAN: FEET AND LEGS

Here is another exercise to bring awareness into the body. This time you'll also practise 'breathing into' specific parts of the body. Don't worry if this doesn't make sense at first, just play with the idea and see how it feels.

You can do this practice sitting, or lying down on your back—either with legs outstretched or feet flat on the floor and knees up. Take some time after each instruction to explore the physical sensations. It may help to close your eyes after each section, or you could familiarize yourself with the whole exercise and then put the book aside.

- **Settling in.** Start by feeling the weight of your body—notice all the places where you are in contact with the floor (or the chair, if you are sitting). Notice the movement of the breath in your body. You could place your hands on your belly, and bring your awareness to the sensations in your abdomen, rising and falling with each breath.

- **Left toes.** Now bring your awareness down the left side of your body into your left toes, tuning in to any sensations here. What can you feel, if anything, in each of the five toes? Perhaps tingling, cramping, warmth or cold, contact with the sock, or contact with the other toes? Or no sensations, just a feeling of blankness? You don't have to shape your experience in any way, just notice whatever is here in this moment.

    Now imagine or feel you can breathe all the way down your body into your left toes, and then breathe back up from the toes, out through the nose or mouth. Don't strain, but try playing with this for a few breaths—breathing down into the toes, and back out from the toes. Have a sense of the breath and the awareness moving together.

- **Left foot.** On an out-breath, let go of your focus on the toes, and move your attention to other parts of the left foot in turn: the top of the foot, the sole, the heel, the ankle. Notice any sensations of tightness, softness, heaviness, pain—whatever is here. When you're ready, broaden your awareness to take in the whole of the left foot. Now play with the sense of breathing into the whole of the foot, and out again from the foot.

- **Left leg.** Let go of your attention to the foot, and move your awareness slowly through the rest of the leg. Notice any sensations in the lower leg: the bony shin and the fleshy calf. Bring attention to the knee: the kneecap, the muscles and tendons, the soft underside. Move awareness to the thigh, perhaps feeling the heaviness of the big thigh bone, the feeling of contact with clothing. Finally, broaden your focus to having a sense of the whole left leg, as if you were shining a beam of light on the leg from the toes to the top of the thigh. Explore what it's like to breathe into the leg, with a sense of filling the whole leg with breath and awareness.

- **Right leg.** Now take your focus to the right toes, then the right foot, then up through the right leg, as you did with the left. Play with 'breathing into' each region before you move away, imagining the breath flowing into and out from that area.

- **Thoughts.** As with all mindfulness practice, don't worry if your mind wanders off. Each time, just notice your attention has wandered and gently escort it back to the body.

- **Resting.** At the end, spend a few moments resting, bringing awareness back to the sense of the whole body sitting or lying here, and the movement of the breath.

    What was your experience of this body scan practice? Take a few moments to write down anything you noticed during the practice:

_____

_____

_____

_____

Your attention has different settings like a camera: you can have a narrow focus (e.g., your little toe) or a wide focus (e.g., the whole leg).

Mindfulness helps you train this ability to zoom in and out, and to choose what you want to focus on.

BEING WITH DIFFICULTIES

What was your experience of that last exercise? Don't worry if you found it difficult—there is no 'good' or 'bad' way to do this practice. Here are a few of the challenges which often come up when we practise mindfulness of the body:

- *My body feels uncomfortable/painful.* See if you can be gently curious about the discomfort. Can you bring your awareness to the area of any difficult sensations with a kind inquisitiveness? Explore if it's possible to stay with these sensations for a few moments rather than pushing them away or ignoring them. Try 'breathing in' to any areas of intensity, coming up as close as feels possible with your awareness, exploring the edges, and moving away when you need to. Decide for yourself if and when you need to move your body to alleviate the sensation, letting the movement become part of your practice. If there is strong pain, can you notice other parts of the body which aren't hurting? For more on working with difficult sensations, see chapter 13.

- *My mind keeps wandering.* This is natural. The practice is just to keep bringing your attention back, again and again, with good humour.

- *I feel irritated—it's not relaxing.* Whatever emotions come up, can you be inquisitive about them? How does your irritation feel in the body? Is there a place where you can feel it? The aim is not particularly to be relaxed or calm—just to 'be with' your experience whatever it is. If you are irritated, frustrated or bored, that's just your experience right now. See if you can allow it to be as it is. (For more on working with restlessness, boredom and other challenges, see chapter 16.)

 FULL BODY SCAN

The full body scan is usually done lying down, and takes between 25 and 45 minutes. We bring our awareness to each part of the body, most often starting with the left toes and moving all the way up to the crown of the head. The body scan is commonly done with a teacher's voice to guide you, either in a live class, or using recorded audio. You can download a guided body scan at **www.introducingbooks.com/mindfulness**.

It's not easy to do a full body scan while trying to read instructions from a book. But if you'd like to get a feel for it, you can repeat the 'feet and legs' exercise above, and this time continue through the whole body.

- Settle into your body, as in the previous exercise, lying down or sitting in a chair. Feel your weight and the contact with the floor, and the rise and fall of the breath in your abdomen.

- Now begin your scan of the body. In each place, spend a few moments noticing whatever body sensations are here, and exploring 'breathing in' to the different regions. The exact order is not so important, but move as systematically as you can without skipping around too much.

  – Left leg: toes, foot, calf and shin, knee, thigh, whole leg

  – Right side: same as the left

  – Hips, buttocks and pelvic area

  – Back: lower, middle and upper

  – Torso: belly, mid-torso, chest

  – Arms (both together): fingers, hands, lower arms, elbows, upper arms, shoulders

  – Head: neck, back of head, ears, jaw, parts of the face, whole face, top of head.

- At the end of the practice, you can imagine yourself breathing through your whole body, from the crown of your head to the toes and back again. Have a sense of the breath washing through your body, reaching every cell. Finish by resting still for a few minutes, with a sense of the whole body breathing, present and complete.

- When you bring awareness into your body, you are learning to 'be with' whatever is here, including sensations which are uncomfortable. You can train yourself to be gently inquisitive about your sensations and let them be as they are.

- This can help you in stressful situations to 'be with' difficult feelings, rather than reacting, lashing out or running away.

8

ATTITUDE

ACCEPTANCE

One of the most important aspects of mindfulness is the attitude we bring to the practice—an attitude of acceptance or non-judgment. This may be easy to understand intellectually, but is possibly the most difficult thing to practise.

We are always talking to ourselves—we have a running commentary as constant and breathless as the commentator at a football match. But what tone of voice are we using? If you listen to that commentator in yourself, how often is he or she telling you that things aren't as they should be, that you're not as good as you should be, or that something or someone should be different?

In meditation practice, if we look and listen clearly to this internal voice, we may find that we are always giving ourselves a hard time. If our mind wanders, we chastise ourselves. If we are sleepy or irritated or angry, we blame ourselves. Or we turn this criticism outward, blaming the environment, the teacher or the practices for not living up to our idea of how things should be.

In meditation, each time we notice the mind has wandered, the instruction is just to notice and to escort it back to the focus of meditation—with gentleness. This part is crucial. Notice your tone of voice—when you find you've become distracted, do you slap yourself down, or can you develop a kindness to yourself, even a sense of humour? 'Oops, look, there I go again', as a fond grandparent might look with humour on a small child who keeps toddling off and needs to be herded back again and again.

In meditation we have a situation where we can practise speaking kindly to ourselves, and accepting our states of mind, whatever they are. If our mind is busy, it's busy. If we're tired, we're tired. If we're irritated, we're irritated. We can let ourselves feel how we feel.

If we can practise this within the quiet situation of the formal meditation practice, we can start to be more accepting of ourselves in the rest of life, shifting our old habits and softening our tendency to always judge ourselves. By making friends with ourselves, we can also be more friendly and accepting to others (see chapter 17).

SPEAKING FROM EXPERIENCE) SARAH

Sarah is in her 20s and works in events and media. She joined a mindfulness course after a stressful year of work followed by an equally stressful period of being unemployed. 'The thing that encouraged me about mindfulness was the non-judgmental side of it. The most helpful thing was the idea of it being okay to not feel okay. That had real resonance for me. I've had problems with depression and there was a resistance from people like my mother, who'd say, "Oh you just need to eat a good meal!", rather than accepting that this is a real thing that exists.

'So it really helped—the idea of it being okay for you to feel the way you're feeling, and understanding that they're not unique thoughts anyway. The idea that it's okay to feel depressed or sad, rather than doing the British thing of sweeping it under the carpet or trying to fight it—they're both not particularly good strategies for dealing with the problem. If you can find a level of acceptance, then you're on track to deal with it.'

THINK ABOUT IT) ACCEPTANCE VERSUS RESIGNATION

What reaction do you have to the word 'acceptance'? You may have a subconscious revulsion—perhaps it sounds too soft, too caring-and-sharing. You may feel that acceptance is equivalent to 'resignation'—giving up, being a doormat and letting the world trample you down.

This is not the kind of acceptance we're talking about. Acceptance is seeing clearly how things are, and not struggling with that basic reality. It doesn't mean that we can't take action against injustice or wrongdoing in the world. Once we have seen clearly and accepted what is here, then if there are things we can helpfully change, we can take action. In the words of the famous Serenity Prayer:

> *Grant me the serenity to accept the things I cannot change, the courage to change the things I can, and the wisdom to know the difference.*

Mindfulness helps us to allow the space for this natural wisdom to emerge.

ANIMAL TAMING

Mindfulness practice has often been likened to the taming of an animal. The human mind is wild and erratic: it takes skill and discipline to train it, but also patience and kindness.

There's a series of Buddhist pictures, used from the 12th century onward, which depict a young boy herding an ox or bull as a metaphor for this process of training the mind. At first the ox struggles and escapes frequently, and the boy has to put a lot of effort into bringing it under control. Later the ox becomes more gentle and obedient, and the boy is shown riding on its back while playing a flute.

Another metaphor is that of taming a wild horse—not by whipping it into shape, but by becoming familiar with the animal, discovering how to ride its energy, and guiding it back onto the trail when it tries to gallop off. If oxen and horses are rather far removed from your world, you may prefer the analogy of a puppy, bounding with energy, which can gently be trained to heel and to come when it's called. Whatever animal you imagine, it won't be tamed by shouting, but by using a voice that is kind and firm— and this is the tone of voice you can cultivate within your mindfulness practice.

 ANIMAL TAMING

Take a few moments to reflect on how your mind is feeling in this moment. (If you like, practise mindfulness of breathing for a few minutes first.) Is it leaping about from one thing to another, or wandering slowly, or staying still? Does it feel sharp and awake, or dull and heavy? You don't need to judge it as 'good' or 'bad', just notice.

If your mind in this moment were an animal, what animal would it be? A monkey? A wild horse? A sniffer dog? A pigeon? Or perhaps something slower—a snake, a lizard, a slug? Is this a familiar state of mind for you? Are there other animals which might represent your state of mind at other times?

How would you talk to this animal to encourage it—would you coo or cluck or whisper? Or perhaps there's a funny little voice you use when you talk to cats and dogs?

My mind is like:

_____

Next time you find yourself getting a bit too serious or heavy with yourself in your meditation, you could perhaps picture this animal and remember to develop humour and kindness in the way you speak to yourself.

LETTING GO

In nature, things take their own time to unfold—seeds grow, eggs hatch, butterflies emerge, all in their own good time. Likewise our mindfulness practice will take its time to unfold naturally, if we can be patient and open to each moment.

There is a paradox about meditation which is challenging to grasp. We have to put energy and work into the practice, and yet at the same time we have to let go of wanting results or trying to 'get somewhere'. For example, if you are trying to get more calm and relaxed, you are only setting up a struggle, and a feeling that things are not okay as they are. Within the discipline of our practice, we cultivate a kind of 'non-doing'—a willingness to be with things as they are. For control freaks this can be challenging! However, we can start to let go of our need to control everything and trust that our minds and the world are basically okay.

As we become more familiar with our mind, we discover that there are thoughts and feelings we want to cling to. They may be pleasant daydreams, or sometimes the nasty, juicy emotions have the strongest hold on us. In mindfulness, we practise letting go of these thoughts and experiences, whatever form they take, and coming back again and again to the focus of our meditation. As we practise, we may find that we are a little more able to let go of these attachments in the rest of our life. This letting go is a bit like the moment at night when we drop our mental chatter to fall asleep—only now we are practising it while we are awake.

SPEAKING FROM EXPERIENCE) MARION

'The piece of advice I found really useful is that whatever's happening in the practice is what's happening. So if you're completely bored and frustrated and thinking, 'What the f___ is this about?', that's the meditation. That particular meditation is 'I think this is a load of shit, I don't know why I'm even trying.' If you're feeling calm or feeling angry, that's how you're feeling. The practice is just being how you are at that moment. And that's hugely liberating—actually experiencing what's going on without an expectation for it to be different. If you do that a little tiny bit each day, I don't know how it works, but you will find that you feel very different after a while.'

The attitude you bring is a key part of mindfulness. Instead of wanting things always to be different, you let yourself be open to things as they are.

9

FEET

Do you have your head in the clouds? Or are your feet on the ground? We take these as metaphors, but they arise from a common experience which is quite literal and physical.

Take a moment to reflect on the contrast between these states. What does it feel like to 'be in your head', in the highest part of your physical body, with the sense of being caught up in the 'clouds' of your own thoughts? And then how does it feel to be grounded, to literally feel the connection of your feet to the ground, your weight going down into the earth?

In mindfulness, whatever practice you are doing, you begin by 'grounding' yourself, just as a building begins with the ground, the foundation. If you are doing a practice lying down, you can start by feeling which parts of the body are connected to the floor, and by being aware of the weight of your body. In a sitting position, the same thing applies—you can feel your feet on the earth (or your ankles, if you are sitting cross-legged), and the weight of your buttocks on the chair or cushion. If you are standing—doing a movement practice, or even waiting at the bus stop—you can begin by focusing your awareness into the feet.

This contact with the earth brings us into the present moment, and brings us down, down, down . . . out of the bulb at the top of our necks where many of us think we reside, until we can fully inhabit our bodies from the ground up. My own experience is that the simple act of bringing awareness into my feet is one of the most powerful mindfulness practices. It counteracts my tendency to get speedy and 'heady', and I do it many times throughout the day.

MOUNTAIN POSE

- Stand in a simple upright position with your feet hip-width apart, your knees a little bent, your spine tall, the crown of your head lifted, and your shoulders relaxed. In yoga this is called the mountain posture.

- Feel every part of your feet in contact with the floor. Notice the connection of your ten toes, the padded balls of your feet, the outside edges, the arches, the heels. Feel the weight of your body going down through your feet into the earth.

- Try shifting your weight a little to the left and right, front and back. Then find a balanced place at the centre. Feel the sense of stability, and perhaps notice also that you are never completely still—you will likely sense little shifts and movements as you maintain your balance.

- Spend a few minutes tuning in to the sensations in your feet and the feeling of contact with the earth.

MINDFULNESS OF WALKING

The act of walking is a skill which took us weeks or months to learn as a child, perhaps toddling uneasily from one piece of furniture to the next, and falling down. As a species it took us many millennia to get up and move on our hind legs. Yet now we take this process for granted, and do it without thinking. Mindfulness of walking is about bringing our awareness back into this remarkable activity which we do so much in our lives.

Walking meditation can be one of the most enjoyable forms of mindfulness practice, and has the advantage that you can do it without taking extra time out of your day. Any time you need to get from A to B, you can use the act of walking as a way to bring yourself out of your head and into the present moment. You can also do it as a practice in its own right, taking a few minutes out at any time for a mindful walk around the room or around the block.

At first it's good to try mindful walking in a private place where you don't feel self-conscious, and to start at a slow pace to get the feel of it.

MINDFUL WALKING

- Start by feeling the earth beneath your feet. As already discussed, you can feel all the different parts of your feet connecting to the ground, the weight of your body going down, the sense of gravity.

- Now transfer your weight into your left leg, noticing any sensations in your legs and feet as your right leg empties out and weight goes into your left foot. Slowly let your right heel come off the ground, and then the whole of your right foot, tuning in to all the physical sensations in your feet and legs.

- Then take a step forward—feel your right foot move through the air. Place the heel, then the rest of the foot onto the floor, maintaining awareness of the physical sensations as you transfer your weight into your right foot and your left foot empties of weight.

- Continue walking, staying aware of the sensations in the soles of your feet as they make contact with the floor, and of any sensations in the muscles of the legs. Begin very slowly, and then when you feel comfortable you can gradually pick up the pace. You don't have to look down at your feet—they know how to walk.

- When your mind wanders off, just notice this, and gently escort it back to the sensations in your feet and legs. You can use the contact of your feet on the floor as an anchor to bring you back into the present moment, just as we used the breath in sitting meditation.

MINDFUL WALKING: OUT AND ABOUT

- Next time you have a journey to do on foot, bring your awareness to the fact that you are walking. Start by feeling the contact of your feet with the ground and the sensations in your legs as you walk. When you begin, you may find it helpful to have your gaze somewhat downward.

- As your mind becomes more focused on the walking, feel free to raise your gaze and take in the environment around you. Notice the trees, people, shops, sky—whatever is here—while still keeping part of your awareness in your feet. If you find yourself getting caught up in thoughts, it may help to bring your awareness back to a more narrow focus on the feeling of your feet on the ground. As the mind steadies, you can open your awareness again to the sights and sounds around you.

- You can also try different paces—how does the experience change as you walk more quickly? Can you be mindful even when you are hurrying?

Once you have a feel for it, mindful walking can be done at any speed, and you don't need to look like a zombie while you are doing it!

Experiment with walking mindfully for the next day or two. Walking is something most of us do often—commuting to work, going out to the shops, rushing from one meeting to another. Instead of letting yourself be wrapped up in the next thing you have to do, try using it as a chance to come out of automatic pilot and be present for a few minutes.

Mindful walking can provide a sense of space within a busy day, and can leave you feeling calmer and less exhausted when you arrive at your next destination. If you can really bring awareness to this simple act, it will provide a thread of mindfulness which will help you to become more present and awake in your everyday life.

- Bringing awareness into your feet helps you to be literally 'grounded'—to come out of your head and feel your connection to the ground.

- Like the breath, you can use your feet as an anchor, a place you can return your awareness to again and again. Through this simple act you become present inside your own body and awake to where you are right now.

- 10 -

REACTING

We like reactions—a reaction is walking out on us, a reaction is throwing tomatoes at the stage, that's a healthy psychological reaction. I don't care how they react, as long as they react.

Alice Cooper

Whatever we encounter in life, there are three basic reactions we may have: like, dislike and indifference. These instinctive reactions may be so conditioned and habitual that we don't even notice them consciously, yet they dictate how we filter our experience throughout our lives. We have the fresh, direct experience of the world through our senses, and then immediately one of these three will kick in:

- **Attachment**—liking things, craving the things we like, wanting to hold onto the experiences we find pleasant

- **Aversion**—disliking things, pushing away the things we don't like, wanting to avoid the experiences we find unpleasant

- **Indifference**—switching off from the things and experiences that we don't notice or find of interest.

In mindfulness training we are not trying to stop or deny our reactions, but we can become more aware of them, and notice how they affect our mind and body, and our behaviour. We can open ourselves more and more to the direct experience of our world, beyond our habitual reactions. And as we practise, we may find ourselves more able to respond to things in a fresh way, instead of reacting automatically.

SEEING YOUR REACTIONS

Wherever you are—in your house, on a train, in a café—take a few moments to look around. You could scan the scene as if you were a film camera, panning slowly from left to right, and back again. Let your eyes take in whatever is here—objects, people, colours, shapes, textures, light and shade.

See if you can notice your reactions. Are there certain colours, objects or people you feel attracted to—things you naturally like? Are there other things you find unpleasant and would like to push away? Is there a third category of things you feel neutral about, perhaps don't even notice when you first look? You may find your reactions are strong, or they may be subtle—either way, just notice them.

THINGS YOU LIKE

As Julie Andrews sings, we all have our favourite things which make us feel good. However, as we crash through life on automatic pilot, we may find that we're missing out on fully experiencing these moments which make up our life.

 MOMENTS YOU LIKE

- Over the next few days, see if you can notice experiences that feel enjoyable while they are happening. They can be small and simple—drinking a cup of tea, seeing a big full moon, having a laugh with your colleague.

- Notice what thoughts and emotions are coming up. Also notice how you feel in your body. How can you tell that something is enjoyable, pleasurable, an experience you 'like'? Are there signals from your body—perhaps places where you feel a sense of relaxation, or lightness, or other sensations?

- Keep a note of each experience in as much detail as you can:

The experience	How I experienced it
E.g., I arrived home and saw the sun setting at the end of my road.	Thoughts: how beautiful—I'm glad I stopped to notice this. Emotions: happy, peaceful. Body sensations: shoulders relaxed, lightness in my chest, mouth smiling.

This exercise and the next one are inspired by Jon Kabat-Zinn's 'Awareness of Pleasant or Unpleasant Events Calendar' in his pioneering book *Full Catastrophe Living*.

When you begin to notice these little events in your daily life, here are some of the things you can learn about yourself:

- **Your reactions.** Becoming more aware of how the direct experience of your senses is immediately followed by a feeling of liking, disliking or ignoring.

- **Your thoughts, emotions and body sensations.** Noticing how your experience is made up of these different components, which are interlinked and constantly affecting each other. Sometimes you may be more aware of one or another, but usually all are present.

- **How pleasure registers in your body.** How do you know that an event is pleasurable? Can you start to notice the specific sensations which tell you: perhaps a feeling of your chest opening and lightening, your face relaxing, the corners of your mouth turning up, your shoulders dropping down?

- **Appreciating your world.** You may find that your life is full of sources of enjoyment which you haven't been noticing. By the simple act of tuning in to these experiences, your world can become richer and more nourishing.

(You might like to return to this section later on, when you've had time to do the exercise.)

THINGS YOU DISLIKE

You may find it comes more naturally to notice the difficult experiences in your day. The traffic jam, or the meeting where your colleague is rude to you—these things can stick in the mind long after they're over. But can you notice a bit more about what's going on in those moments? What kinds of signals does your body send you when you are experiencing something you don't want to experience?

TRY IT NOW!

MOMENTS YOU DISLIKE

It may be easiest to try this exercise after you've already spent some time with the experiences you like; or you can choose to notice both during the same period.

- During the course of a few days, see if you can notice experiences which are difficult, stressful or unpleasant while they are happening. It might be an argument with your partner, a nerve-racking moment at work, or a crowded ride on the train.

- Notice what thoughts and emotions arise, and how the experience feels in your body. Do you notice any place where there is tension, shakiness or other sensations?

- Write down the details as soon as you can:

The experience	How I experienced it
E.g. Someone pushed in front of me in the queue at the supermarket.	Thoughts: I always get pushed around. I should be more assertive. Emotions: angry and helpless. Body sensations: jaw clenched, stomach tight, shoulders hunched and tight.

When you've done the exercise, here are some things you could begin to be more aware of:

- **Your reactions.** As with the more enjoyable events, noticing how your experience is constantly triggering reactions of liking, disliking and indifference.

- **Your thoughts, emotions and body sensations.** Each experience triggers all of these things. How do they interact?

- **How unpleasant experience registers in your body.** How do you know that you're experiencing something as unpleasant? What can you notice about the specific sensations which tell you this? Perhaps they include a feeling of clenching in the belly or solar plexus, a tightness in the chest or shoulders, a throbbing in the temples or tension in the jaw?

- **Being with difficult things.** You may notice that when you don't like something your body reacts by bracing, clenching, tightening, and generally trying to resist the experience or push it away. This resistance is actually making things worse and is part of what you experience as 'unpleasantness'. By bringing your awareness up close to these difficult sensations—being gently curious about them and giving them your attention—they begin to have less power over you. When your reactions are automatic and unconscious, they can rule the way you think and behave without your knowing it. When you bring these reactions into awareness, they are more able to pass through you and dissipate, without setting off a habitual chain of stress and negative thinking.

THINGS YOU IGNORE

The third type of reaction—indifference—gets less press than the other two but can be just as prevalent in our lives. A friend recently came running out of a cafeteria in tears because a group of people had ignored her. 'I sat down and they wouldn't speak to me—they were talking to everyone else!' Rather than deliberately slighting her, it's likely they just hadn't noticed her—maybe because she was not so interesting to them, or perhaps because they were wrapped up in their conversation.

With more mindfulness we may notice people or things which are right in front of our noses, which we have blanked out without realizing it. When we're indifferent to things it can be easy to switch off from the present moment and withdraw into our thoughts. As mindfulness brings us back to the here and now, we may discover a new richness in aspects of the world which had seemed uninteresting.

REACTING VERSUS RESPONDING

Our reactions to experiences can be subtle or dramatic—and we all have our own style. When the really difficult stuff happens, some of us shout and throw things, and some of us run and hide.

What's your habitual reaction when things get stressful? What do you do when you have a big argument with your partner, or a disaster at work? Have a look at the list below. Do any of these resonate with you?

- Withdraw/hide/run away
- Shout/get angry
- Freeze
- Panic
- Clench my stomach/chest/shoulders/jaw
- Feel hurt/lost/lonely/abandoned
- Blame myself/blame others
- Drink alcohol/drink coffee/eat/smoke
- Overwork/get busy

Take a moment to reflect on which of these words and phrases feels most familiar to you, or choose some words of your own. How do you feel in your body when you're in the midst of this reaction?

As you may have noticed when you were paying attention to moments you dislike, when we experience something difficult, our body resists it by clenching, bracing, tightening and so on. We may feel other symptoms as the body's natural stress response kicks in: increased heart rate and blood pressure, sweaty palms, butterflies in the stomach. All of this feels uncomfortable and we try to get rid of these feelings by lashing out, running away or whatever happens to be our pattern.

In mindfulness, we go against the natural reaction to turn away from these feelings, and instead we turn towards them. We allow ourselves to be with this uncomfortable energy—the adrenaline, the tension, the palpitations. Strangely, as we do this, there's a sense in which the energy of our anger, panic or grief can be allowed to exist and then move on through us, rather than being compounded by our resistance and attempts to get rid of it.

With mindfulness practice, we start to become more aware of our experience as it is happening. This creates a space in which we can have more choice about what we do next. Instead of 'reacting' automatically, we can start to 'respond' more mindfully—less destructively, and more skilfully.

- We are constantly reacting to our experience in three ways: liking, disliking and ignoring.

- We can tune in to our body sensations to become more aware of these reactions as they are taking place.

- Instead of avoiding difficult sensations, we can start to let ourselves feel them. This creates a space in which we can respond mindfully instead of reacting automatically.

11

MOVEMENT

We've begun the practice of bringing awareness into the body in relative stillness—sitting, lying or standing. We've also tried a moving meditation, mindfulness of walking. Now we can extend this to bring our mindfulness into other kinds of movement. As our bodies are naturally in motion for much of the day, movement practices can be a bridge between our formal meditation practice and the rest of our life.

Here are some reasons for practising mindful movement:

- **Being in the body in motion.** As you learn to bring more awareness into your body when it's moving, this can help you to be more present during the many kinds of movement you experience in daily life.

- **Exploring your 'edge'.** You can gently explore your body's natural limits by paying close attention to your physical sensations moment by moment as your body moves. You can play with finding your 'edge', that place where you are coming up to the edge of what's uncomfortable without pushing into it or beyond it. It's a practice of listening to the wisdom of your body, instead of overriding it with your mind. You may begin to see your habits and notice if you have a tendency to strive too hard, or to give up too easily.

- **Being with sensations.** As you explore the edge between comfort and discomfort, you can make your own choice in each moment about how close you want to get to difficult sensations, playing with going a bit further or coming back a bit. This is something you can also start to explore with other kinds of challenging feelings—including intense emotions.

MINDFUL MOVEMENT: STANDING STRETCHES

The purpose of this practice is to bring awareness to the sensations in your body as it moves, and to gently explore the edge of what's comfortable or uncomfortable in each moment. Listen to your own body and don't do anything which is not right for you. If you have any physical problems do check with your doctor or physiotherapist before you do any kind of movement practice. You can perhaps do the movements in your mind, or choose different movements which are okay for you.

- **Mountain pose.** Begin by standing tall, with feet hip-width apart and knees slightly bent. As in the previous mountain pose exercise, feel the connection of your feet to the earth. Let the weight of your body sink into the ground, and the crown of your head lift towards the sky. Have a sense of the space your body is taking up and the space around you—be present.

- **Extending the arms.** Turning your palms away from your body, slowly raise both arms out away from your sides and up towards the sky, remembering to keep breathing. When the arms reach the top, try reaching higher through the fingertips, stretching both sides of the body. See if you can keep the shoulders down and relaxed. Notice any body sensations, and play with finding your 'edge' of comfort.

- When you're ready, slowly lower your arms back down again until they reach your sides, paying attention to the changing sensations on the way down, noticing the muscles being used in this movement. In mountain pose, notice any aftereffects of the stretch.

- Repeat the same motion a few times, less slowly, breathing in as you extend your arms upward, breathing out as you lower them down.

- **Side stretches.** Again breathe in and raise your arms; this time keep them there. Tilt from your waist towards the right, reaching your arms up and over to the right, so you can feel a stretch through the left side of your body. If there's any intensity of sensation, try 'breathing in' to those areas, seeing if you can soften and open up to the sensations. Gently explore your edge, where you are stretching yourself but not straining. Play with that edge, coming up to it, perhaps going a bit further and coming back again—listening to what your body (not your mind) is telling you to do.

- Breathing in, come back to centre and take the stretch to the left side, again exploring your edge. When you're ready, bring your arms back to centre and lower them down by your sides.

- **Shoulder rolls.** Gently lift both shoulders up towards your ears, then forward, then down, then back, making little circles, and remembering to breathe. Notice any places of tension or tightness—not forcing anything, just lubricating the shoulders very gently. After a few rolls, reverse the direction, taking the shoulders up, back, down, then forward, keeping your awareness with the sensations.

- **Mountain pose.** Come back to stillness, and take a few moments to notice the effects of those movements on the body. Feel the connection of the feet to the earth again, the dignity of the upright posture and the sense of being present inside your own body.

Take a few moments to write down anything you noticed during the mindful movement practice:

_____

_____

_____

_____

_____

_____

_____

_____

Visit **www.introducingbooks.com/mindfulness** to download audio for a longer practice of mindful movement.

YOUR REACTIONS

What was your experience of that short movement practice? When we're moving the body there seems to be more happening than when sitting or lying down, so you may enjoy this and feel it's 'easier to focus'. Or you may find that it brings you up close to awareness of your body's limits in a way that feels uncomfortable. Or possibly, if you're used to athletic activity, you may find it frustrating to slow down and pay attention to the more subtle messages of your body sensations.

As with other mindfulness practices, see if you can notice these judgments and then let them go. See if you can open your awareness to the direct experience of the body, beyond what your mental commentary is saying about it.

YOGA

Mindful movement can be practised in many forms, but it helps if the pace is fairly slow so we have time to fully experience the sensations of the body. In mindfulness training we often use yoga postures as the basis for movement practice.

Yoga was developed in ancient India as a form of moving meditation, with the aim of bringing body and mind into synchronicity. In fact the physical postures, known as *asanas*, are only one branch of a comprehensive approach to life which includes ethics and meditation practice. Traditionally the physical sequences are used to calm and focus the energies of the body and mind, preparing the practitioner for the stillness of meditation. Recently, of course, yoga has become popular in the West as a form of exercise, without necessarily being connected to any meditative purpose.

The great early writer on yoga was Patanjali, whose *Yoga Sutras* have been dated to around the 2nd century CE. Patanjali doesn't give detail about what postures to use, but he says that the practice should balance *sthira* (translated as steadiness, firmness or effort) with *sukha* (gentleness, comfort, or ease). In other words, there's a balance we can look for in each moment, between trying too hard and flopping out, and between strength and softness.

By working with relatively slow, careful movements such as yoga sequences, we can take the time to explore this edge within our own body. Instead of competing with ourselves, or trying to match some external image, we can pay attention to the information being given to us by our own physical sensations, finding the right place for our body in each moment.

As well as yoga, there are other traditions of slow, meditative exercise which are excellent to use for mindfulness of movement. These include the Chinese practices of Qigong and Tai Chi, both of which use slow moving sequences to direct the flow of energy in the body. These days almost every town offers classes in yoga or tai chi, and you can also find sequences in audio or video formats. For the purposes of developing your mindfulness of movement, choose a practice which is simple enough that you can focus on your body sensations, rather than trying to follow something which is overly complicated or athletic.

SPEAKING FROM EXPERIENCE TESSA

'I took up yoga when I was working too much on the computer and I started to get repetitive strain injury in my arm—my brother had RSI and told me yoga was the most helpful thing. After a day sitting rigid working on websites, it was a wonderful feeling to get everything moving and flowing again.

'I've always enjoyed outdoor sports but somehow the slower, meditative quality of yoga started to bring me into my body in a way I'd never felt before. I was already a meditator at this point, but over time I noticed a change. I used to talk about *watching* my breath, and it seemed to be something happening mainly up in my head. Now I started to really *feel* the breath moving deep down in other parts of my body like my belly. And when I did walking meditation, I often used to be impatient and want to go faster—now I could enjoy the feeling of all the parts of my foot making contact with the floor with each step, almost like a massage.

'This feeling of being more in my body also affected my

other physical activities. When I swim lengths, I can enjoy the movement of each stroke through the water, rather than getting bored or being off somewhere else in my thoughts. I'm better at tennis—I've discovered my body usually knows where it needs to be on the court, if I can get my mind out of the way. And the best of all, for me, is dancing—when you can stop worrying about other people or how you look, and let the body move the way it wants to move. It's one of the best kinds of moving meditation I know.'

MINDFUL MOVEMENT: YOUR CHOICE

Practise bringing mindfulness into your favourite form of exercise—it could be swimming, going to the gym, running, or dancing around your flat. See if you can bring awareness into your body sensations in each moment, and pay attention to the edges of your physical limits. If you find yourself caught up in thoughts, just notice that and return your awareness to the body.

MINDFUL MOVEMENT: OUT AND ABOUT

It's good to practise mindful movement slowly at first, and to set aside time for some kind of formal practice, so that we can focus on our body sensations without too much distraction. But then we can begin to bring this awareness into our body as we move through our daily lives—whether we're vacuuming or gardening, carrying boxes or pushing a stroller. We can also bring the qualities of mindful movement into other sports and physical activities such as running, tennis, cycling, football or dancing.

Awareness of physical movement, in whatever form, can be a powerful way to bring yourself into the present moment.

12

SOUND

I have often lamented that we cannot close our
ears with as much ease as we can our eyes.

Richard Steele

We live in a noisy world, surrounded by traffic, aeroplanes, music and people, hums and bleeps. You may think of meditation as a welcome escape into blissful silence. And certainly, it can be helpful to find a reasonably quiet place for your practice, where you are not too distracted by constant sounds.

At the same time, it's perfectly possible to meditate with noise around us. When we hear a neighbour shouting or a dog barking, we can let this be part of our awareness. We can even go further and practise mindfulness of sounds, where the field of hearing becomes the main focus of our attention.

 MINDFULNESS OF SOUNDS

- Sitting with upright posture, take a moment to feel grounded. You may like to close your eyes.

- Now turn your attention to sounds. There's no need to go out and hunt for sounds, just allow them to come to you. There may be sounds up close, in your body, in the room, outside or far away.

- Notice the pitch, the texture, the loudness—and the gaps between sounds, silence. See what it's like to be with the direct experience of sound, rather than *thinking about* the sound, as if you were a microphone, just receiving the sounds from wherever they come.

- If your mind wanders, bring it gently back to awareness of sounds. If you find yourself creating a storyline around the sound, see if you can come back to the simple experience of hearing.

- Notice how the sounds come, sometimes stay around for a while, and then go. Sounds arising and dissolving within the wider space of your awareness.

You may notice that sounds trigger all kinds of thoughts, perhaps trying to figure out what they are ('Is that hum the heating or the fridge?'); weaving storylines ('They must be having another party next door . . .') or naming and labelling the sounds ('Clock, washing machine, birds, children . . .'). There's nothing wrong with any of this, but when you notice you're caught up in thoughts *about* the sounds, see what it's like to come back to the direct experience of sound itself.

DIRECT EXPERIENCE VERSUS CONCEPTS

> *In what is seen, there is only the seen*
> *In what is heard, there is only the heard*
> *In what is sensed, there is only the sensed*
> *In what is thought, there is only the thought*

Bahiya Sutta

Through mindfulness of sounds—and indeed any other mindfulness practice—we can notice this difference between *direct experience* and *thinking about* our experience. It's not that the thoughts and concepts are bad; they are useful and necessary for us to function and to be creative. But the direct experience of our senses is always happening here and now, and brings us into the present moment. Reconnecting with direct experience brings us a fresh appreciation of the little things which make up our everyday life. Over a lifetime, our concepts and thought patterns can become narrow, predictable and limited. Direct experience opens us up to a wider and more vivid world.

REACTING TO SOUNDS

Mindfulness of sounds can also be a good training ground for becoming more aware of our reactions to our experience, as discussed in chapter 10. You might notice that you have constant reactions to sounds—some you like, some you dislike, and some you don't mind one way or the other.

You may have a strong physical reaction to some sounds. When you hear a loud, unexpected noise, do you find yourself clenching your stomach, or perhaps bracing your body against the sound in some way? These reactions—to sounds and other stimuli—are happening constantly below the radar of our consciousness. The regular act of bracing, clenching, tightening and so on creates tension in our bodies which we carry around without realizing it. When we bring more awareness to our reactions, as we saw in chapter 10, we may find that they have less hold over us. We are opening up space to other possibilities in the way we relate to our experience.

When we come back to the direct experience of sound, we can try dropping our judgment about it and being curious—what is the texture and pitch? Do the sounds stay the same or change? Are there layers of sound or is it one tone? Try listening this way even to sounds you think you hate, such as traffic. You may find that the sound of traffic, stripped of our judgment about it, has something in common with a sound that we 'like' such as a waterfall or waves on the shore. (Or you may not! There is no right or wrong way to hear things.)

When we have worked in this way directly with sounds, we can use this approach when they come unbidden into other mindfulness practices. For example, we may be practising mindfulness of breath when our flatmate starts making loud clattering in the other room. Instead of letting it trigger us into irritation or anger, we can hear the sounds as just that—sounds. If we do have a reaction, we can notice that—for example, are there any sensations in the body? Then we bring our awareness back to the breath, or whatever is our main focus. We can let the sounds be part of the background, allowing them to be there in our awareness, without needing to fight with them or push them away. This is an excellent practice in cultivating acceptance of how things are, and welcoming our experience as it is, rather than constantly resenting the world for not being the way we want it to be.

MINDFULNESS OF SOUNDS AND REACTIONS

- Repeat the exercise above. This time, also pay special attention to any reactions you may have—'liking' some sounds and 'disliking' others.

- If there are sounds you find unpleasant, notice any reactions you may have in your body—perhaps some tightening or bracing against the sound. You might like to try softening and breathing into the area where there is bracing, and notice if that has any effect on being with the sound. See if you can be especially inquisitive about these less pleasing sounds. Examine the pitch, tone and texture; and notice whether they are constant or changing. Be curious and explore what it might be like to allow the sounds to be as they are.

SOUNDS AND SPACE

Another thing to notice about sounds is the way that they come and go within the wider space of our awareness. Some sounds are close, some right inside our bodies, while some are very far away. We may begin to sense an enormous space, and we may sense that we can rest our awareness in this space. The sounds come and go, but our minds are not the sounds, they are the space in which the sounds arise and dissolve. Our awareness is vast and stretches out in all directions.

This sense of the spaciousness of awareness is one of the crucial discoveries of mindfulness—and although we can point to it with words, it is something that can really only be discovered

through experience. Mindfulness of sounds can be a helpful practice to start getting a feeling of this natural spaciousness of our
minds. We'll talk about this more in chapter 14.

Mindfulness of sounds is a simple practice which can be done
anywhere. You can use this practice to bring your awareness
into the present moment, and to help you to notice:

- The difference between direct experience and concepts *about*
  that experience

- Your constant reactions to your experience—liking, disliking
  and ignoring

- The spaciousness of your awareness in which events like
  sounds come and go.

- 13 -

SENSATIONS

Now, if you like, stop reading for a few seconds. Come out of your head and right down into your body. Feel your feet on the floor, and your weight on the seat. You can do this at any moment, coming back to being in your body.

Western education trains us to put a lot of emphasis on thinking—in Descartes's famous phrase, 'I think therefore I am.' Analysis, logical thinking and scientific reasoning are backbones of our belief system. Our pop songs express a different side of the story—'What a feeling!', 'Feelin' groovy', 'Feelin' it', 'You've lost that loving feeling', 'I feel good'. But what does it mean to feel?

The word 'feeling' can mean both a physical sensation, and an emotional state. In mindfulness training it can be helpful to make a distinction between 'emotions' and 'body sensations'. Sometimes when you're in the midst of a 'feeling' it can be hard to distinguish between what is physical and what is emotional—they are so closely linked. Your anger, fear or desire can be like a weather system moving in—a particular kind of energy which takes you over. But if you can really tune in to how this energy manifests in the body, and be curious about it, it will help you to simply be present with the sensations and not react blindly in your habitual way.

Our culture emphasizes the value of words and concepts, and we're not always so good at experiencing our sensations. How can we become more sensitive to physical sensations, to the messages of our own body? It may help to explore which words might come closest to expressing your physical sensations.

WORDS AND SENSATIONS

- Here are some words about sensations. Read slowly through the list. Are there any which resonate for you? Is there a part of your body which feels like this right now?

  - Hot, cold

  - Tight, loose

  - Moist, damp, dry

  - Soft, firm, hard, brittle, stiff

  - Tense, tight, clenching, bracing

  - Tingling, vibrating, shaking, pulsing

  - Light, heavy, solid

  - Contact, pressure

  - Blank, numb

  - Tender, sore

  - Aching, cramping, painful

  - Dull, sharp

  - Full, empty

  - Open, closed

- Pick a word which resonates for you right now. Your knee is aching? Your neck feels tight? Spend a few moments feeling these sensations. Do they stay the same when you bring your attention to them?

- If you like, repeat this exercise using another word. Feel free to use your own word which is not on this list.

- Pick one of the words which feels familiar to you, and see if you can notice those sensations when they come up during the rest of your day.

Your word or words:

_____

_____

DIFFICULT SENSATIONS

Bringing this level of awareness into the body is not always a comfortable experience. It can be quite shocking to notice how much tension we're holding; how many aches and pains we've been trying to block out. But allowing ourselves to fully experience sensations in the body is a powerful part of our mindfulness practice. Our natural instinct is to push difficult sensations away, to fight with them or avoid them altogether. But in mindfulness we do the opposite, coming up as close to the sensation as feels possible in the moment (as we did in mindful movement) and becoming gently curious about the sensations.

We can train ourselves in opening to whatever is here, even if it is painful. The pain or tension may not go away, but we are no longer losing a lot of energy on fighting with it. Paradoxically, by giving it attention, the chances are the pain may begin to have less hold on us. We may find that it is less solid and less unbearable than we think it is.

It's good to experiment with this approach, but do so kindly. You could try practising first with mildly uncomfortable sensations, aches, itches and so on. If you feel overwhelmed, let go of exploring the difficult sensations and bring your awareness back to the weight of your body, or the movement of your breath. You can come back to the breath as a safe haven, and let yourself be stabilized by its natural movement at any time when other sensations or emotions are feeling too much to handle. Then, from that steady, grounded place, see if you can open to exploring the sensations again.

 MINDFULNESS OF DIFFICULT SENSATIONS

- Settle into a sitting posture which feels dignified and awake. Practise mindfulness of breathing for a few minutes.

- Now expand your awareness around the breathing to a sense of your body as a whole—from your feet on the floor to the crown of your head. Tune in to the feeling of the breath moving through your whole body, reaching every cell.

- Now notice if there are any difficult or uncomfortable sensations in any parts of your body which are calling for your attention. Maybe tension in your neck, aching in your back, tiredness in your legs—or perhaps you have a more intense kind of pain. Instead of avoiding these sensations, see if you can gently bring your awareness up close to this region of intensity. Try coming up to the edges of it, moving away whenever you need to and coming gently back again when you're ready.

- Imagine you can breathe right into this area, carrying your awareness there. You are not trying to get rid of the intensity but to explore what's there by breathing into—and with—the sensations.

- Be curious about the sensations. Do they have a texture, a shape or even a colour? Are they sharp or dull, soft or hard, constant or changing? Are they like metal, or stone, or wood, or textile? Spend a few minutes gently exploring these sensations with your awareness, as much as feels possible.

- When you're ready, widen your awareness to having a sense of the body as a whole, from the feet to the crown of the head. If you've been working with some kind of pain, you could notice now the parts which aren't hurting. Feel the grounded, stable quality of the body. Return your awareness for a few minutes to the breath, and the sense of your body breathing.

Write down anything about your experience during this practice here:

_____

_____

_____

_____

You can incorporate this exercise into any of your mindfulness practices. When you find that strong physical sensations are distracting you, see what happens if you bring a kindly awareness to that region. Let yourself be inquisitive and open to the sensations, rather than pushing them away. Notice if there are other parts of the body where there is any resistance against the discomfort—perhaps a tightening of the shoulders, stomach or jaw? See if you can breathe into and soften around the resistance. Is this resistance or bracing adding an extra layer of pain on top of the original pain? What is left of the discomfort when the resistance is lessened?

SPEAKING FROM EXPERIENCE) MARION

Marion took up mindfulness practice looking for relief from the physical pain caused by her auto-immune condition (see chapter 3). She remembers vividly the first time she tried bringing her awareness up close to the difficult sensations.

'It was absolutely counter-intuitive. It was almost like stepping right up to another person and being an inch away from their nose—going right up to the pain and just being with it, just looking at it, just listening to it, just feeling it; without thinking "I'm trying to reduce this or manage this." Just saying, "This is what's going on in my body at the moment." What I found extraordinary was that after the meditation my relationship to the pain had changed.

'Each time I do a meditation with pain it's completely different. Sometimes I feel like I'm almost wrestling with it, sometimes I'm almost dancing with it, sometimes I'm just chatting with it. Something does change when you go right up to it in a non-judgmental way—not with fear, not with a story. Not even with a story about being brave, not "I'm going to face my pain!"—just seeing what's there.'

TORSO

Do you ever get butterflies in your stomach? Does your heart sometimes ache? Do you ever have a gut feeling?

When we have strong experiences like fear, grief and stress, they tend to register somewhere inside the torso. Deep in the soft central parts of the body, all kinds of sensations are taking place, but often we don't pay attention to them. You may react to difficult experiences in your belly, or solar plexus, or chest. There may be one area which is particularly sensitive for you, or it may vary. If you can pay attention to these sensations, your body can give you early warning signals about how you are feeling in this moment, before your mind becomes fully conscious of it.

Our bodies have strong instincts for self-protection. We armour ourselves against feeling things we don't want to feel, and then this armour gets tighter and tighter—we can't digest properly, we can't breathe fully. The armour can become a kind of iron corset which stops us from relaxing and opening up to the world. Is this true for you? Can you feel a physical difference between being 'open' and being 'closed'?

SENSATIONS IN THE TORSO

- **Mindfulness of breath.** Take up a good sitting posture and practise mindfulness of breathing for a few minutes.

- **Breath in the belly.** Bring your awareness especially into the movement of your breath in the walls of your abdomen, expanding on the inhale, and relaxing back again on the exhale. It may help to put a hand on your belly to feel the subtle rise and fall.

- **Belly.** Tune in to any other sensations in the belly area. Are there sensations of digestion? Feelings of emptiness or fullness? Is there any tightness? Or softness, openness?

- **Solar plexus.** Move your awareness up to the area just under the rib cage; your solar plexus and diaphragm. Can you feel your breath moving here? Notice any sensations: is there bracing, resisting? Or openness, relaxation?

- **Chest.** Bring your focus upward to your chest, and your breath moving here. Inside, do you have any sense of the organs working here: your lungs filling with air, the beating of your heart? What sensations can you notice in this area? Perhaps tenderness, shakiness, softness, openness? Or tightness, holding, numbness? There's no particular way you should feel, just see if you can be gently curious and allow things to be as they are.

- **Early warning signals.** Imagine for a moment a stressful or difficult situation. As you bring this to mind, is there somewhere you can feel a change of sensations in your torso? Perhaps a place where you clench or brace to protect yourself? Is this a familiar feeling? If so, take a note of this as a location where you may get early warning signals in your body. See if you can tune in to this place at other times in your day and notice what is going on here.

- **Mindfulness of breath.** To end the practice, return your awareness to the feeling of your breath moving in your body, and the sense of the whole body, sitting here breathing.

Write down anything which you noticed during this exercise. Is there a particular area which gives you signals that you are feeling stress or difficult emotions?

_____

_____

_____

_____

_____

_____

_____

- You can practise gently opening yourself to intense sensations and being curious about them. By coming towards them instead of pushing them away, they can start to have less hold on you.

- When difficult things happen, you may be reacting to this somewhere in your torso. See if you can tune in to these sensations as an early warning system.

- Notice if there's a different physical feeling of being 'open' to your experience, compared with the feeling of being 'closed'.

– 14 –

THOUGHTS

In practising mindfulness we don't see thoughts as a problem. We can start to make friends with them and see their patterns. We're not trying to get rid of them to achieve an empty mind. They are as natural as waves, coming and going within the ocean of our awareness. But in the normal course of life, we tend to be swept away by our thoughts, experiencing them as more solid and real than they actually are. We buy into them, we believe them, we let them fill up our reality and tell us what to do. We think our thoughts and our selves are the same thing. Through meditation practice, we can start to see that thoughts are not so solid, and that they are not 'us'. We can begin to let go of them, and to loosen their hold on us.

We can practise cultivating a new relationship to our thoughts within any of our mindfulness practices. Each time our mind wanders off, sooner or later we notice that, and gently bring it back to the focus of attention—whether it's the breath, body, sounds or some other focus. We cultivate a kind tone of voice in the way that we do this, so that we don't see thoughts as the enemy. But we can also see through them, and realize that they are insubstantial and impermanent.

SPEAKING FROM EXPERIENCE ISAAC

Isaac is a teacher and consultant in his 40s who meditates regularly:

'It's always really interesting seeing my patterns of thought. It's like a soap opera. You relive last week's episode: "Previously, on Isaac . . . and now, on Isaac." Often there's worry about family, or whether I did a good enough job at work. Sometimes being in love can be quite epic. And there's always emotional baggage connected with other people. Maybe somebody said something in a particular way—"Did they really mean it like that? They just walked off . . . what did I say wrong?"

'Or for me "messing up" is quite a big one. I have this tendency to torture myself with any mistake that I've had the audacity to make, replaying it over and over again, in different permutations. In the end you have to laugh.'

LABELLING THOUGHTS

Some meditation traditions encourage a practice of 'labelling' thoughts. This helps us to be clearer about the difference between when we're caught up in a thought and when we are present with the focus of our meditation. At the very moment when you notice you've been caught, you can say silently to yourself 'thinking', before you return to the breath or other focus. This can be especially helpful when you've been off in a daydream, away with the fairies for some time, and suddenly—here you are again in the room. By acknowledging 'thinking' at this point, you are bringing in an element of precision, and marking the moment of returning to your focus.

In this process, remember not to judge the thoughts as good or bad. Whether you've been thinking about how you'd like to murder your partner, or dwelling in deeply spiritual reflections on the meaning of life, it's all just 'thinking'. You also don't get into analysing your thoughts, although you may notice their flavour a little bit. You may see how some thoughts keep coming back, or how you're tending towards a particular kind of thought such as planning, worrying, or daydreaming. But above all, as you label 'thinking' you are acknowledging your willingness to let go of the thought, however juicy or compelling it may be. There may be another time and place for thinking about this subject, but during the meditation practice, you are willing to come back to simply being present with your body or your breath, here in this moment.

MINDFULNESS OF BREATHING: LABELLING THOUGHTS

- Sit in a comfortable, upright position which embodies dignity and wakefulness. Feel the contact of your feet on the floor and the weight of your body.

- Bring your awareness to your breath. Spend 5 to 10 minutes practising mindfulness of breathing.

- From time to time, and perhaps often, you will notice that your attention has been taken away from your breath. Each time you notice this, say silently to yourself 'thinking', and then return your awareness to your breath. See if you can do this without judgment, cultivating a kindly tone of voice, and even a sense of humour. 'Ah, thinking again!'

- Do this each time your mind wanders, as often as you need. Don't judge the thoughts as good or bad. Each time just label them 'thinking' and return to the breath.

THOUGHTS AS CLOUDS

As we continue our practice, we may become more curious about thoughts: what they are and how they behave. We may find that our awareness is like a big space into which thoughts come and go. Our mind is like a vast blue sky, and the thoughts are like clouds, some of them small and wispy, some of them thick, black and heavy. The clouds may seem to fill the sky, but we begin to understand that we are not the clouds; we are the sky which holds them.

Modern psychology makes a distinction between these different aspects of our mind. We have the process of thought, or cognition, and overseeing this we have meta-cognition. Meta-cognition is the process of knowing about knowing—an awareness that can shine a light on the whole of our experience, including our thinking processes.

This affirms a distinction made by Buddhism, which for centuries has taken a great interest in the workings and processes of the mind. Tibetan Buddhism distinguishes between *sem*, or small mind, and *rikpa*, or big mind, the mind of wisdom. Small mind is the constant chattering as we talk to ourselves, and big mind is the wider field of awareness within which this commentary takes place.

We experience big mind, or *rikpa*, when there are gaps in our chatter. Pema Chödrön likens this to the constant yelping of dogs she experienced during the nighttime in Nepal (small mind) . . . and the deep silence when all the dogs stopped barking for a moment and there was stillness (big mind). As she says, we are not trying to get rid of the dogs, but in meditation we may sometimes find that our mind settles down so that there is just an occasional yip and yap instead of a constant canine cacophony. (At other times the cacophony continues, and we can start to accept the beauty of that too!)

MINDFULNESS OF THOUGHTS

We've practised how to work with thoughts when they appear within our mindfulness practice, taking us away from the object of focus. We can also bring thoughts onto centre stage as the main object of our meditation. This can be a good practice to try after working with mindfulness of sounds, as there is a similar quality to the experience. Just as we notice sounds coming and going within the space of our awareness, we can see how thoughts also come and go within this bigger space of our awareness, arising and dissolving into this space.

Don't worry if this exercise is difficult for you—it's generally considered to be quite a challenging and 'advanced' form of meditation. Just have a go, in the spirit of an experiment. As always, it is good to start the practice by grounding ourselves and being present in the body.

 MINDFULNESS OF BREATH, SOUNDS AND THOUGHTS

- **Breath**. Take a comfortable, wakeful posture and feel your connection to the earth. For the first few minutes, bring your awareness to the movement of your breath in your body.

- **Sounds.** Now when you're ready, move your attention to sounds. Notice pitch, tone, texture, loudness—and gaps between sounds, silence. Notice how the sounds arise and dissolve within the wide space of your awareness.

- **Thoughts.** When you're ready, let sounds fade into the background, and move your awareness to thinking itself. Instead of seeing thinking as a distraction, allow yourself to notice each thought as it arises, perhaps stays around a while, and as it dissolves. It's as if you are the vast blue sky, spacious and clear, and the thoughts are clouds arising in that sky. Some are light and fluffy, some are heavy storm clouds. As best you can, stay present, not trying to do anything with the thoughts. Just be aware of them, and let them come and go.

  You may notice that some thoughts come laden with emotions, heavily charged. If so, can you notice any sensations in the body connected to the emotion? Perhaps you can feel a resistance to feeling this emotion, or thinking this thought—some kind of clenching or tightening in part of the body? As best you can, bring a gentle awareness and curiosity to whatever sensations are here.

- **Breath.** To end the practice, bring awareness back to your breath, and the sense of your whole body sitting here, breathing.

When you finish, you might like to write down anything you noticed during this practice:

_____

_____

_____

_____

_____

What was your experience of this meditation? You might find yourself completely caught in the thoughts, without much sense of any space or 'blue sky' around them. Or you might have the opposite experience—suddenly when you are asked to pay attention to thoughts, none appear; your mind is blank. If that's the case, isn't that interesting? Can you rest in this experience of space, without thoughts, however momentary?

There is no right or wrong thing for you to experience. But by experimenting with turning our awareness directly to thoughts, we can encourage ourselves to be curious about their nature. We can start to get a glimpse of how our mind works, and see that the constant stream of images and conversations it throws up are no more substantial than the changing scenes of a movie on a screen. We may find ourselves swept up into the scene with the actors, but each time we can notice that and come back to our seat right here in the cinema. The more we do this, the more we may find that through all the dramas and storylines we are able to hold our seat.

THOUGHTS ARE NOT FACTS

The practice of looking clearly at our thoughts is an important part of Mindfulness-Based Cognitive Therapy, which was developed especially to help people with a history of depression. When we get into a state of depression, we have a tendency towards 'rumination': thought processes which go around and around, and can be very unhelpful. There may be a chain reaction of thoughts, which starts with something small and leads us inexorably forward into deeply negative thoughts about ourselves and our lives.

For example, we make a mistake at work and we think:

'I don't know what I'm doing.'
'I can't get this done on time, I can't do this project.'
'Everyone knows I'm useless.'
'I'm going to get found out and lose my job.'
'I'll be out on the streets, I won't be able to get
another job, I'll be penniless, I'll lose my home and
security, I'll die poor and lonely . . .'

Most of us have our own version of this snowballing thought process, which leads each time to our own deepest worries or fears. It's a well-worn groove we can easily slot into, and once we're on that track, we travel on automatic pilot from the slightest trigger to the grim conclusion. Often these thoughts are subconscious, or only semi-conscious. A small event or remark can set off a reaction, and we find ourselves moments later feeling heavy and bleak, without being fully aware of what's happening. By bringing more awareness to the situation, we have the opportunity to interrupt our habitual reaction and create a chance for something fresh and different in our response.

CHAIN OF THOUGHTS

- Take a good posture, feel grounded, and spend a few moments in mindful breathing.

- Imagine a difficult scenario in your life at the moment—perhaps a conflict in your workplace, or a challenging relationship, or a worry about money. Choose something which is manageable, not too overwhelming. Bring your awareness to any emotions and body sensations which arise as you picture this situation.

- Now bring your attention to your thoughts. Is there a 'snowball' of thoughts that you experience in this situation? Write down the sequence of thoughts that come to you. Are there any familiar worries or fears coming up? See if you can notice any 'chain reaction' of one thought triggering another, as in the example above.

- Most of us find that there are certain underlying fears which are particularly familiar to us; dark thoughts we find ourselves arriving at, no matter what the specific scenario. Your particular version might be 'I'm useless', or 'Nobody loves me', or 'Everyone is against me', or 'I can't do anything right'. Take a moment to think about whether there are particular thoughts like this which feel familiar to you.

My chain of thoughts:

_____

_____

_____

_____

_____

_____

_____

SEEING THOUGHTS AS THOUGHTS

Mindfulness-Based Cognitive Therapy offers some suggestions about how we might work with these unhelpful and destructive thoughts when we become aware of them. We can bring them into the bright light of day and challenge them, asking ourselves questions about the thoughts, such as:

- Am I making assumptions?
- Am I blaming myself for something which isn't my problem?
- Am I expecting something unrealistic from myself?
- Am I turning something small into a catastrophe?
- Is there another way of looking at this? How would a good friend advise me to look at it?

These can be helpful strategies, and the act of challenging negative thoughts is an important method used in Cognitive Behavioural Therapy (CBT). You may like to research and develop this approach further, particularly if you have a tendency to depression. And in general, if you find that a lot of thoughts and emotions are coming up which are hard to handle on your own, it could be good to find a friend who can help you talk it through—or perhaps look into some further support from a counsellor or therapist.

Whether we are depressed or just feeling a bit low, it can be very useful to bring our negative thoughts into the light of day, and to challenge them with practical questions like the ones above. However, the core teaching of mindfulness in relation to thoughts is very simple: see thoughts as thoughts; as mental events, no more or less. We begin to understand that the thoughts are not facts, and the thoughts are not us.

Through our training in formal mindfulness practice, we show ourselves willing again and again to see our thoughts as thoughts, and let go of them. We discover that we have a much vaster awareness—the 'big mind' which we can come back to and rest in at any time when the chattering and yelping of 'small mind' is overwhelming us. This can slowly begin to have a powerful effect on the way we relate to our minds and thoughts in daily life.

SPEAKING FROM EXPERIENCE **ANTHONY**

Anthony was in his 50s working in a stressful job as a hospital chaplain and going through a marriage breakdown when he joined a mindfulness course.

'My wife was saying that she wanted us to separate, and it was very shocking and upsetting. My experience is that when things are stressful I find it very easy to get taken out of myself into worry about what's going to happen. A lot of the time the thoughts are quite condemnatory and judgmental. The circling thoughts take me out of myself—in a sense I lose myself. Mindfulness brings me back to my centre, to me.

'The practice helped me to come to new thoughts about what I should do in the situation. The usual thoughts go round and round in my head, but these other solutions seem to come almost physically from deep inside me. The mindfulness practice allows things to shift in a way that normal thinking never does.'

SPEAKING FROM EXPERIENCE) DEBBIE

Debbie, now in her 40s, has been practising mindfulness for almost 20 years:

'I used to get depressed, but since I started mindfulness I don't go into depression in the same way. I used to ruminate— I'd have negative feelings on top of negative feelings. If, for example, I thought "I'm lonely", I'd then add "I'm lonely and I haven't got a boyfriend, I'm never going to get a boyfriend, I'll always be on my own . . ." and so on. I'd go into rumination and there's the snowballing effect.

'Since then I've started to catch that quite quickly. So if I'm doing my practice I'm able to go, "Aha, it's this thing again!" So I cut through it before I go off into depression. I remember the first time I started actually catching myself having thoughts at the time I was having them—that was a bit of a eureka moment. I'd be feeling really overwhelmed but then have a watcher, another part of me able to see these things and have some space.'

IF YOU REMEMBER ONE THING Through mindfulness practice we can learn to let go of our thoughts and see that they are not as solid and real as we usually think they are.

15

BREATHING SPACE

PRACTISING BREATHING

We've been exploring mindfulness in different forms, and tasting a variety of practices. But if you'd like to deepen your experience, it's good to settle on one practice and try it regularly for a period of time. That way you can become familiar with the practice, and at the same time discover that it is different every time; each moment is unique, and therefore each session is unique.

Mindfulness courses like MBSR and MBCT normally begin with practices which focus on body sensations—the body scan and mindful movement. Through this approach, participants can develop their experience of being more grounded in the body, more fully embodied. These exercises are usually done with guidance from a teacher (in a classroom, or at home on audio), and sessions usually last about 30 minutes or more.

If you're just starting out on your own without a class, you may find that mindfulness of breathing is the simplest technique for you to develop first as a regular practice. You can do it on your own without audio or other guidance, and you can do it for any length of time and in almost any location. It helps if you can set aside at least 5–10 minutes each day for this practice, perhaps building up to 20–30 minutes as you feel comfortable.

As you make a connection with the mindful breathing practice, you are linking in with one of the oldest and most prevalent forms of meditation in the world. It is simple to explain, but seasoned meditators practise it for decades and still find something new to explore. You're tuning in to the act which keeps you alive, and developing an anchor for your awareness which is available to you at any moment, until the day you take your last breath.

⭐ TRY IT NOW! MINDFULNESS OF BREATHING: THIS WEEK

See if you can practise mindfulness of breathing every day for the next week (see chapter 5 for instructions). You could aim to practise for 5–10 minutes, or longer if you feel inspired. You may find it helpful to set a timer so you don't have to keep looking at your watch. If you don't think you have enough time one day, see if you can sit down for just 2 minutes!

Keep a diary and make a short note—even just a word or phrase—about what you notice during the practice each time. If you're finding it difficult, look at chapter 16, where we discuss different kinds of challenges and how to work with them.

Monday	
Tuesday	
Wednesday	
Thursday	
Friday	
Saturday	
Sunday	

THREE-STEP BREATHING SPACE

As well as setting aside formal time for mindfulness of breathing, you can also take a 'breathing space' at any time in your day. This is a way to step out of automatic pilot and reconnect with the present moment.

We already introduced a short breathing space in chapter 5,

which we called a pause. We just stopped for a moment and took a few conscious breaths, and then moved on.

The three-step breathing space is an extension of this pause, taking a bit more time and bringing more awareness into the process. It is sometimes called the three-minute breathing space, but it doesn't have to be three minutes—it could be 30 seconds, a minute, or longer. It's a way to bring formal meditation practice into everyday life.

THREE-STEP BREATHING SPACE

Take a moment to come into an upright posture—sitting or standing, eyes open or closed, as you wish. There are three parts to the instructions.

Part 1: Awareness. Ask yourself: 'What's happening in this moment for me? What thoughts, emotions and body sensations am I experiencing right now?' Don't start analysing in a big way—just feel in your body what's going on, and be present. See if you can acknowledge and accept any difficult feelings just as they are, even if they're unwanted.

Part 2: Breathing. Now bring your attention to your breath. Gently direct your full focus to the physical sensations of breathing. Experience each in-breath and each out-breath. Let the breath help you to focus your awareness and bring you into the present.

Part 3: Expanding. Expand your awareness around the breath to the sense of your whole body, as if your whole body is breathing. Have a sense of the space your body takes up, and the space around you too—your environment. Let your awareness include any sensations you are feeling, even if they're difficult. Hold everything in this wider space of your awareness. See if you can let this sense of space and awareness be with you as you continue your day.

This is a version of a very commonly used mindfulness exercise which was originally published in *Mindfulness-Based Cognitive Therapy for Depression* by Zindel V. Segal, J. Mark G. Williams and John D. Teasdale.

That sequence of instructions is like an hourglass—a wide focus, followed by a narrow focus, followed by a wide focus.

Part 1: awareness (wide focus)

Part 2: breathing (narrow focus)

Part 3: expanding (wide focus)

You can do this breathing space exercise wherever you have a few moments—sitting on a train, standing in a queue or waiting for the kettle to boil. As you become familiar with it, you can use this practice during stressful situations. At first though, it's good to practise regularly at more predictable times, so you can get used to it. Then it will be a tool that's available to you when you need to create space in moments of stress.

BREATHING SPACE: OUT AND ABOUT

Pick an activity you do regularly a few times a day—it could be waiting for a bus, making coffee, or waiting for your computer to start up. Use this as a reminder to practise the three-step breathing space. See if you can do it a few times a day until it becomes familiar to you.

Your reminder:

_____

_____

_____

_____

_____

_____

_____

 The breath can become a powerful tool for bringing your awareness into the present moment. To develop this:

- Set aside formal time to practise mindfulness of breathing.

- See how you can bring the 'breathing space' into your daily
  activities.

16

CHALLENGES

Mindfulness practice sounds simple. Just sit down and follow your breath, or lie down and pay attention to different parts of the body—how hard can that be? But for most of us, these seemingly simple practices are surprisingly difficult. Chances are that when you first begin, you will think you are a bad meditator. You may think that everyone else can do it except you. Wrong! We all have challenges which come up in our practice. We get bored, frustrated, irritated, sleepy, angry . . . and this is all a natural part of the process.

If you find mindfulness difficult, don't be discouraged. For thousands of years meditators have been experiencing similar obstacles, and have written encouragement, suggestions and 'antidotes'. No matter how difficult our experiences, there are ways to work with the problems and learn from them. Often facing up to these challenges is the way we learn the most about ourselves and the patterns of our minds. As we see our habits more clearly, we can gradually open up to fresh ways of experiencing the world.

SPEAKING FROM **EXPERIENCE** AARON

Aaron is an actor and writer in his 30s.

'When you start meditating, at first you think it's brilliant because it calms you down. Then you can come to this place where you suddenly realize how noisy your brain is—you see all your thoughts and your emotions. Your watcher becomes stronger, and it can be a bit overwhelming. The noise in your head feels like a waterfall. The best advice I had is, just keep going, stay with it. You can find every little excuse not to—"What shall I have for lunch?". . . "I've got to go and call my dad". . . but just stay with it.'

RESTLESSNESS

It's very common to feel restless when we first start to meditate. You feel twitchy, you want to get up and move, even run right out of the door. You may feel like a child who's been told to sit still and wants to rebel.

See if you can just be with this restless feeling, without acting on it. Where do you feel the restlessness in your body? Is there a sensation in the legs, arms or hands of wanting to move? Is there an itchiness, shakiness, vibration, or tension somewhere? Can you be curious about this restless energy and how it manifests in your body?

SLEEPINESS

We often find when we meditate that we are much more tired than we realized. We start the practice and are overcome by drowsiness, even drifting into sleep. Don't give yourself a hard time about it. Instead of setting up a feeling of struggle, see if you can practise an attitude of non-judgment, accepting the sleepiness as how things are in this moment.

You can encourage a greater sense of wakefulness by making sure you have an upright posture, with your spine tall and self-supporting. Feel the solid connection of your feet to the floor and your weight on the cushion or chair. If you find that sleepiness is your dominant challenge, try practising at a different time of day. It may also be that your body is sending you a message that you need more sleep!

BOREDOM

Our lives are normally so full of entertainment—we can hardly take a five-minute train journey without turning on the iPod, texting a friend or reading a newspaper. No wonder, when we take all this away, it can seem very boring. This boredom can manifest as restlessness, feeling twitchy and wanting to move; or as a dull, flat sort of boredom, just spacing out and losing interest.

When you notice boredom, see if you can rekindle your natural inquisitiveness. For example, can you be more curious about the object of meditation? If you're working with mindfulness of breath, are you taking for granted that each breath is the same? (*'Yeah, breath. I know what that is already, nothing interesting about breath.'*) See if you can approach each breath as something unique, paying attention to the texture and other qualities of the breath, as listed in chapter 5. Remember there is no special way to breathe; you are simply bringing curiosity to this breath, in this moment.

You can also direct your curiosity to the feeling of boredom itself. How does your body feel when you are bored? Are there any physical signs and sensations of boredom? Are there other emotions under the boredom? For example, sometimes 'boredom' is covering up things we don't want to feel, such as fear or sadness. See if you can be gently curious about what's really here, rather than taking your boredom at face value. As you develop this curiosity, you may find that the practice is much richer and more interesting than you realized.

PAIN AND DISCOMFORT

Back pain, stiff shoulders, sore knees, ankles falling asleep—all manner of aches and pains can arise during your practice. Sometimes they become so distracting you can think of nothing else.

One possibility is that you actually need to change your posture—perhaps the height of your seat is wrong for you, or you're holding your arms in a way that puts tension in your shoulders. If this is the case, see if you can make the changes mindfully, rather than just shifting around. Make a decision to move, then move with awareness, and tune in to how the change affects your body sensations.

If the discomfort is not something you can alleviate, another option—which takes some courage—is to bring your awareness right up close to the discomfort, and kindly investigate what is here. Is it sharp or dull, constant or changing? See chapter 13 for an exercise on working with difficult sensations. The pain may not go away, but you can alter your relationship with it—instead of fighting with it, you can start to make some sort of friendship with it, or at least a more peaceful co-existence. You may notice how your struggle with the discomfort creates extra layers of pain, and explore if it's possible to soften in those places of bracing and resistance.

LAZINESS

This is a challenge which can keep us from even sitting down to meditate. We intend to get up early, but we hit the snooze button. We plan to meditate after supper, but we end up watching TV. We set aside time for mindfulness but we get caught up in emails. We can find a lot of other activities we need to do instead of practising. Sometimes this looks like busyness but it can simply be another form of laziness. (There may also be other ingredients like fear which are involved here, so see if you can be gently curious about why you're finding it so hard to get round to your practice.) And then sometimes when we *do* sit down to practise, we may find that we let ourselves space out, without investing much effort in the session.

When this happens, there's no need to be hard on ourselves— we can just make a fresh start, and reconnect with our inspiration to practise. Take a moment to think about why you are doing this. Remember what inspired you to try this, and what you would like to get from it. You could look again at the intention you wrote down in chapter 3. A fresh sense of inspiration can help to overcome our natural procrastination and avoidance tactics.

DOUBT

'What am I doing here? This is a waste of time. I'm hopeless at this. I'm doing it wrong. I'm not getting anything from this.' You're likely to have all kinds of doubts, whether about mindfulness as an approach, or about your own ability to practise it.

If doubts arise during your practice, see if you can recognize that they are thoughts just like any others. Instead of buying into them, recognize them as distractions from the practice you have committed yourself to doing in this moment. See if you can let them go, returning your focus to the object of meditation.

Make a decision to 'suspend your disbelief' for this time while you are practising. You've decided to give mindfulness a go, and you know that it's not a quick fix, and that there will be challenges. So, see if you can drop the commentating voice which constantly judges things to be good or bad, useful or without use—just get on with doing the practice right now as best you can!

SADNESS

We're used to thinking of sadness as a problem. When someone asks how you are, you are supposed to smile and say 'fine'. But it's part of life to feel sad; we live in a world where things change, where friends and family get ill, where partners leave us, and where ultimately we all die! To feel sadness is very human. Even our most joyful moments can contain sadness, as we know that nothing can last forever. When we hear a piece of music or see a sunset that is so beautiful it makes us want to cry, we may not be sure if it's joy or sadness, as the two feelings are so intertwined.

Often we armour ourselves against feeling sadness, closing off our hearts from the rawness of this emotion. In meditation we can gently let ourselves be more open to the experience of sadness. Chögyam Trungpa writes about 'the genuine heart of sadness' which comes from allowing ourselves to be tender and open. This is part of what it means to be more fully human, more awake and alive.

You can be gentle with yourself in this process of allowing in feelings that you might normally bury. But don't feel that sadness is a problem—it is a sign that you are opening up and softening. Being willing to experience your own sadness also helps you to be able to be with the sadness of others, and not to require the people in your life to be constantly jolly and 'fine'.

SPEAKING FROM EXPERIENCE) AARON

'If you're the kind of person who has trouble growing up, I think meditation really helps turn you into an adult. Being an adult is about connecting with the world and taking responsibility for stuff. That means feeling and being open to things. And that's what meditation helps you to do—it helps you have the presence and the ability to stay open in difficult situations, situations of suffering. It has slowly changed me and allowed me to be present. When friends' parents have died or something like that, I'm much more able to stay present and not just run away and eat pizza and play computer games which is my general survival tactic.'

EMOTIONS

Sometimes you may be surprised by what arises when you're meditating. You're just sitting there minding your own business and *whoosh*; you are swept up in a strong emotion such as anger, lust, desire, grief, or jealousy. There may be a difficult situation in your life right now which is an obvious cause, or it may be an old feeling which seems to well up out of nowhere.

When you feel a strong emotion like this, see if you can reconnect as fully as possible with your sense of being present in your body. Feel your feet on the ground, and your bum on the seat. You could have a sense that the weight of your body tethers you to the earth, and keeps you from being swept away by the force of the emotion. You can also reconnect with the texture of your breath, and its rhythmic movement.

Then see if you can be curious about the nature and quality of the emotion. When you feel this anger or jealousy, are there sensations anywhere in the body which accompany it? Perhaps a resistance or bracing in the torso somewhere; a shakiness in the chest, a tightness in the throat, or a clenching in the belly?

Normally when we feel an emotion we are very caught up in the story we are telling ourselves—'Then I did this, and then she said that, and then you did this.' See if you can let go of the story-line and feel the raw energy of the emotion. Does it have a location in the body? Does it have a texture, a shape?

Don't worry if this feels impossible—it's not an easy practice to drop our 'thinking' about a particular situation, and be present with the energy of the 'feeling'. But just by sitting there on your cushion or chair, experiencing your anger without shouting or throwing things, chances are you are doing something more valuable than you realize. So often we act out strong emotions, or we repress and bury them. Here you are allowing them to be there, letting them unfold in their own way. You may find that they are less solid than they seemed, and that by giving space to the emotions you make them more able to dissipate, or at least to flow and move through you rather than holding you in a fixed and stony grip.

Emotions, like thoughts and sensations, are changing all the time. Instead of fighting them, or trying to hold on to them, we can let them move through us like the changing weather. As always, be gentle in this process, and if it all feels overwhelming, come back to the movement of your breath, or whatever focus you are working with, as an anchor for your awareness.

FEAR

Fear may not always be instantly recognizable as fear. You may find yourself fidgety, restless; maybe there is a buzz of adrenaline, like when you've had too much coffee; or feelings of doubt and irritation about what on earth you are doing here. If we can be gently curious, we will often find that beneath other feelings like impatience or boredom, there is fear. We are scared of this silence and space. We are scared of sitting here so intimately with ourselves, with nothing to entertain or distract us. It may feel like a great void, with nothing to hang on to.

The good news is that great meditation teachers see this fear as something extremely important and valuable. Chögyam Trungpa writes that 'because we possess such fear, we are also potentially entitled to experience fearlessness. True fearlessness is not the reduction of fear, but going beyond fear.' We can teach ourselves to recognize fear, and to let ourselves feel it. Through this practice, the fear lessens its unconscious power over us, and we are able to open up to the world and to aspects of our experience we may have been shutting down.

Our natural instinct is to push fear away, or deny it, but that only increases its hold on us. As with other experiences, mindfulness encourages us to be curious about it—to let ourselves feel its energy. We can do this by noticing what is going on in the body. Where is the fear located? Are there body sensations? See if you can allow the sensations of fear, without feeling you need to change anything. Remember you can 'breathe in' to any sensations which are difficult.

'Feel the fear and do it anyway', as Susan Jeffers's popular book title puts it. But as with everything in mindfulness practice, we need to do this gently. If you experience fear that feels overwhelming, don't feel you have to barge straight into it. Let yourself come up to the edges of it, and explore it in your own time. Be kind to yourself. If things feel unmanageable, you can return your attention to a safe haven such as your breath or your body.

Don't feel you need to identify and label your fear as being 'about' anything in particular. Meditation practice may bring up some of our most basic, nameless fears such as the fear of non-existence. The busyness of our daily activity is constantly confirming us in how we define ourselves. When we stop that activity or slow it down, we may be frightened of somehow losing ourselves, of no longer existing. At the bottom may even be the fear of death itself—the final non-existing—which we rarely confront. But there is no need to get into too much analysis. Instead, mindfulness practice encourages us to accept the fear as a natural part of being alive, and to let it be here.

If you have started mindfulness practice, even a little, it's worth congratulating yourself on your own bravery. It takes courage to be still with nothing but yourself and whatever emotions and fears may arise. You may think of bravery as diving off a high board or going into battle or making a speech. But possibly one of the bravest acts we can do is to sit down on our bottoms and 'do nothing'. Each of these small acts of bravery may slowly help us to be more courageous in our interactions with the world as we go through our lives.

- Real fearlessness is not being without fear, but 'going beyond' fear by acknowledging its presence.

- When you notice fear coming up, see if you can tune in to any physical sensations with gentle awareness—and allow them to be here.

SITTING MEDITATION: WORKING WITH CHALLENGES

- Practise mindfulness of breathing for 5 to 10 minutes. Or if you prefer, you could work with another focus such as sounds.

- During this practice, notice if there is a tendency towards one or more of the experiences described in this chapter—and if so, which ones.

- At the end of the practice, take a moment to reflect on what was your major challenge. Are you tending to drift off into sleep? Do you feel restless or full of anger?

- Is this a common experience for you, or is it particular to this session? What other difficulties have you encountered in your practice so far?

- Read again about the challenges which feel most familiar to you, and the suggestions for how to work with them. See if you can put this into practice the next time you meditate.

- If you like you could even repeat this exercise right now and try out the suggestions for how to work with whichever challenge is most dominant in your practice.

Your biggest challenge(s) when you practise:

_____

_____

_____

_____

_____

_____

If you don't feel you have any particular challenges, that's fine! You can return to this chapter at any point when you are finding the practices difficult.

See if you can begin to train your mind to be aware of the state it is in. You can start to develop a vigilance about what arises. You can be gently curious about any states of mind you are experiencing, and what lies underneath them. Whatever the challenge, the first step is being clear about what is going on—then you can see how best to work with it.

17

KINDNESS

SPEAKING FROM EXPERIENCE **MARION**

'Since I started practising mindfulness, a few people have commented that they're finding me very gentle. The more I spend time coming up close to who I am, the more I think it's changed the way I look at other people. It's not that I would have said I wasn't an empathetic person before, but I think that my empathy is more authentic now. I'm so aware of the hidden emotions in myself behind each consciously experienced emotion. I also think I'm getting a bit gentler in terms of my judgments of other people—I'm seeing other people as more complex groupings of emotions. It's all stuff that I knew intellectually before, but there's a difference between talking about something intellectually and really experiencing it.'

Most of us are very hard on ourselves. As we've noticed already in our practice, no matter how confident we may seem, we often have an internal voice which is critical and hard to please. If we are unforgiving to ourselves, we may find we are also hard on other people. Likewise, the more we can be kind to ourselves, the more genuine kindness we can show to others.

We might think that kindness is a personality trait which we either have or don't have—we all know people who seem to be naturally sweet and generous, and we may think 'that's not me'. We may even pride ourselves on being a bit spiky, a bit tough. But we all know there have been times when we've made ourselves and others unhappy by being irritable, angry or sullen in a situation where we could have been more generous and forgiving. Mindfulness practice shows us that we all have an innate capacity for kindness; we just need to create the right conditions for it to flourish and flow. This is not a one-shot deal, but a lifelong process of opening up to ourselves and other people, as we are, with all our quirks and imperfections.

The writer and teacher Pema Chödrön tells a story in *Taking the Leap* which she says was circulating after the September 2001 bombings in New York. A Native American grandfather was trying to explain the existence of violence and cruelty to his grandson. He said it was like he had two wolves fighting in his heart: one angry and one kind. The grandson asked who would win this fight between the wolves, and the grandfather answered, 'The one I choose to feed'. Pema encourages us to recognize that it's up to us, in each moment, to choose whether to 'feed the right wolf'.

In mindfulness training, we can practise 'feeding the right wolf' by paying attention to the tone of our inner voice. As we've discussed throughout this book, no matter what formal practice we are doing, we can develop a tone of greater kindness in the way that we bring ourselves back to the focus of meditation each time. When you find yourself getting frustrated with the busyness of your mind, or other experiences, see if you can develop gentleness and humour in the way you usher your mind back to its focus, like a dog-lover herding a wayward puppy. This is an important retraining of your internal voice which will slowly seep into the rest of your life.

You can also work more directly with practices which cultivate your compassion for yourself and others. These practices are known in Buddhism as 'maitri' practices, from the Sanskrit word *maitri* which can be translated as compassion, friendliness or loving-kindness. Do take these practices gently—they can sometimes bring up a lot of emotions. Or you may feel the opposite: a bit of a blank. Don't worry if you don't feel the words you are saying, just try it out as an experiment without expecting to feel anything in particular.

It's good to always 'sandwich' a practice like this with simple mindfulness of breath at the beginning and end. We start with awareness of breath and body to ground ourselves and create a sense of stability within which the loving-kindness practice can take place. If you feel overwhelmed at any point, just come back to your breath and let yourself be steadied and soothed by its natural rhythm.

LOVING-KINDNESS MEDITATION

1. **Mindfulness of breath.** Sit in an upright position, feel your connection to the ground, and practise a few minutes of mindfulness of breath. When your mind feels somewhat steady, you can begin the loving-kindness practice.

2. **Yourself.** Now bring an image of yourself to mind, as if you could see yourself standing right in front of you. Have a sense of sending yourself good wishes, warmth and kindness. You could imagine giving yourself a warm blanket, a cup of tea, or whatever would make you feel happy and loved. You can say to yourself, either in these words, or your own words:

   > May I be safe
   > May I be happy
   > May I be free from suffering
   > May I be at ease

   Spend a few minutes feeling the essence of these words, and generating these feelings of loving-kindness for yourself. You may find this challenging and emotional, or awkward and artificial—don't worry, just have a go and see what it feels like. See if you can bring kindness and gentleness to whatever arises for you. You are welcome to stay with generating kindness for yourself for the rest of the practice, as this is usually the area we need to work with most. Remember to return to mindfulness of breath for the last few minutes of the meditation.

3. **A person you love.** If you'd like to carry on, now let this image of yourself fade, and bring to mind someone you find easy to love and wish well for. It could be a child, friend or relative, but make it someone for whom your feelings are not too complicated; it could even be a dog or cat. Visualize this person or creature in front of you, send them feelings of compassion and kindness, and again say these words, or just

feel the essence of them: 'May they be safe, may they be happy, may they be free from suffering, may they be at ease.' Spend a few minutes visualizing this person you love and generating good wishes for their happiness.

4. **A neutral person.** Now let that person fade in your mind's eye, and bring to mind somebody neutral; someone you don't know very well, and don't have strong feelings for or against. It could be a neighbour, or someone who works in the shop where you buy your newspaper. Bring their image in front of you, and see what it's like to generate the same feelings of wishing them well. Repeat the process from step 3 with this neutral person in front of you. Feel free to stop after this stage and return to mindfulness of breath.

5. **A difficult person.** If you'd like to continue, let this neutral person fade and now bring to mind someone who is a bit difficult in your life. Don't pick the *most* difficult person, but perhaps someone you have a slightly challenging relationship with, and may find it hard to wish well for. Picture this person in front of you and repeat the same process. See what it feels like to generate warmth and compassion for this person.

6. **All four people.** Now let this person fade, and bring all four of the people in front of you, in your mind's eye: yourself, the person you love easily, the neutral person and the difficult person. See how it feels to send out good wishes and compassion to all of these people equally, saying to yourself, 'May we be safe, may we be happy, may we be free from suffering, may we be at ease.' Is it possible to send out this loving-kindness with equanimity for all of these people, yourself included?

7. **All beings.** If it feels right for you, as a final stage you can let these four people fade into the background, and imagine yourself extending these feelings of kindness beyond this immediate circle, out into the neighbourhood and the city—to all the people you know and don't know. Expand as far as your imagination will let you, out to the country, the globe—to people suffering from war and natural disasters, illness and unhappiness. Send out these wishes for all people and beings: 'May we be safe . . . may we be at ease.'

Then let go of this contemplation, and rest for a few moments noticing any sensations in the body. How does it feel when you've been generating these feelings of compassion and kindness?

8. **Mindfulness of breath.** Return your awareness to the movement of your breath. Spend a few minutes regrounding yourself in the physical sensations of your breath moving in your body.

As we mentioned above, the loving-kindness practice can be challenging and emotional. Some of us find it hard to wish kindness for ourselves—maybe it feels selfish. Or we may find it too difficult to generate good wishes for the neutral and difficult people. If this practice feels too uncomfortable, don't force it; feel free to come back to explore it again at some other time.

You may like to write down something about your experience of this practice:

LOOKING AFTER YOURSELF

As you start to bring mindfulness into your daily activities, you could become more aware of how you spend your time. Are you showing kindness to yourself in your daily life? How often do you sit too long at the computer without a screen break, as if in a hypnotic trance? How often do you forget to eat properly, or to go outside on a sunny day? We can all get caught up in activities and habits which deplete our energy, and neglect to do the things which we know are nourishing.

When we become more mindful, we can notice if we're not looking after ourselves properly, and show some greater kindness to ourselves during the course of our day. There's an exercise used in MBCT which can help us to see this more clearly. (The original version of this exercise is published in *Mindfulness-Based Cognitive Therapy for Depression* by Zindel V. Segal, J. Mark G. Williams and John D. Teasdale.)

 MINDFULNESS OF YOUR DAY

- Make a list of the things you do in a typical day. If you don't have a typical day, pick any recent day. Write the list in some detail, e.g., *wake up, make tea, have a shower, listen to the news, eat breakfast*, and so on.

- When you're finished, look at the list and put a letter beside each activity:

  N = Nourishing: things which increase your energy, nourish you, help you feel awake and alive

  D = Depleting: things which drain your energy, deplete you, make you feel less awake and alive.

  (There may be some activities which can be either, so it's fine to put both.)

- Now have a good look at your list and notice what seems interesting, or surprising. Are there a lot of nourishing activities, or more draining ones? Are there some things which can be either, depending on the attitude you bring to them—if so, what makes the difference? Do you find it difficult to be kind to yourself and do the things that you know are energizing and nourishing?

- Reflect on your list and see if there is anything you could change. There may be some things you don't have control over, but is there a way you could do more of the nourishing activities and fewer of the depleting ones? What would those be? Make a note of one or two things you would like to change:

One way we can start to be more kind to ourselves is to keep creating little spaces in our day, where we can notice what we're doing, and change direction if we need to. We began this process with the short 'pause' in chapter 4, and continued this with the 3-step 'breathing space' in chapter 15. Now we can revisit the breathing space, adding a few more details about how we can use it in times of stress or busyness.

BREATHING SPACE: CREATING A CHOICE

If you are very busy or stressed, you may find it's hard to do even such a short practice without getting distracted. It can help to talk yourself through the process, using your internal commentator as a way of directing your focus. Begin with an awake and dignified posture—sitting or standing.

Part 1: Awareness. Ask yourself: 'What's happening for me right now?' It may help to say to yourself, 'My stomach is clenched', or 'I'm feeling really irritated', or 'I'm worrying that I can't do this job on time'. Let yourself acknowledge any difficult feelings and allow them to be here.

Part 2: Breathing. Bring your full attention to a very specific focus: the movement of your breath. It may help to say to yourself, 'Breathing in, breathing out'—or even to count the breaths up to 5 or 10. Often when we're stressed our breath gets shallow, so you may also find it helpful to see if you can let your belly relax and feel the movement of your breath down in the belly area.

Part 3: Expanding. Expand your awareness so that as well as feeling the sensations of breathing, you are also aware of your body as a whole, including any sensations in it. Allow any difficult feelings to be here too—you could say to yourself, 'It's OK to feel this way.' Have a sense of your body and the space around you too. See if you can allow this sense of space to be with you as you move back into your day.

And what next? As you finish your breathing space, ask yourself—what's the best thing for me to do in this moment? How can I look after myself? It could be that you need to carry on with whatever you were doing, and if that's the case, can you do it with mindfulness, being present? Or is this the moment to do something nourishing for yourself? Perhaps make a cup of tea, get some fresh air, or talk to a friend? Instead of getting stuck on automatic pilot, use the breathing space as a moment to have a choice about what to do next, and to be kind to yourself.

This exercise is adapted from one in *Mindfulness-Based Cognitive Therapy for Depression* by Zindel V. Segal, J. Mark G. Williams and John D. Teasdale.

Mindfulness helps you to develop a kindness and friendliness to yourself which will naturally start to extend to other people. This can happen:

- Through any of the formal mindfulness practices, as you start to let go of judging yourself, and let things be as they are

- Through loving-kindness practices where you can explore what it's like to generate warm feelings for yourself and others

- Through being mindful of your activities and doing things which energize and nourish you during the day.

18

SLOWING DOWN

It's possible to be mindful at any speed—you can be sure an Olympic sprinter is completely focused and present for those 10 seconds it takes to run the 100 metres. We can be mindful when we're running, skiing, cycling or salsa dancing, and we can enjoy the feeling of speed in its right place. But we all know there are times when speed becomes mindless, and when 21st-century life seems to be one big race. We find we're unable to appreciate life because we're rushing through it, with one eye always on the clock.

Since the Industrial Revolution, we've been living by the creed that faster is better, with industry and business leading the way. But in recent years, an alternative viewpoint has been developing in the form of the 'slow movement'—not one organization, but a number of different groups and advocates suggesting it's time for a cultural shift. Journalist Carl Honoré became a spokesperson for slowing down after an epiphany when he found himself speed-reading bedtime stories to his two-year-old son. His book *In Praise of Slow* is not about living life at a snail's pace, but finding the right speed for everything we do: what musicians call the *tempo giusto*.

The slow philosophy is essentially about bringing mindfulness into our daily life—being present to what's going on in each moment, rather than rushing through doing too much at once, and always thinking of the next task. Evidence shows that working excessive hours and not taking breaks does not actually make us more productive—billions are lost each year in the costs of work-related stress. By allowing more space in your day, and varying the pace, you can be more creative and productive, as well as having time to enjoy life more.

This chapter draws on the ideas of Slow Down London, a group (including this author) which has been working on ways to encourage a saner pace of life in one of the world's big cities.

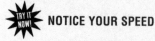 **NOTICE YOUR SPEED**

- For the next few days, see if you can be more aware of your pace at different times during the day. Are you going fast or slowly? Are you at the right speed for the task you are doing in this moment? Sometimes we do need to hurry, but check—if you are rushing, do you need to be?

- It may be helpful to pick one activity or signal which you use as a reminder to do a speed check. It could be each time the phone rings, each time you boil the kettle, each time you wash your hands. This is just like the 'pause' we've already been practising, but you could also bring awareness to the pace you're going at, and notice if it's time to slow down or take a break.

- Write down your signal here:

_____

- Don't feel you need to make a judgment or feel bad about your speed—just train yourself to notice. If you find you have an internal speed demon, see if you can develop a sense of kindness and humour towards it!

ONE THING AT A TIME

As we try to do everything faster, we're meant to be proud of our ability to multitask. Our electronic technology seems to encourage doing 5 or 10 things at once: juggling email, web searching, instant messaging, writing documents, taking phone calls, texting, listening to music, watching a video and eating a sandwich at our desk.

But research has started to show that this constant switching of attention from one task to another is actually hugely counter-productive. Each time we let ourselves be distracted from working on a task to answer an email, it takes time and energy to switch focus, and then to return our attention to the original task. One study at the University of London in 2005 found that workers distracted by email and phone calls suffer a fall in IQ more than twice that found in marijuana smokers! Another American study in 2007 claimed that extreme multitasking costs the US economy $650 billion a year in lost productivity.

Apart from the fact that we actually get less done, multitasking can leave us feeling jittery, unfocused and exhausted. By contrast, doing one task at a time, mindfully, can be more satisfying and less depleting of our energy. Unitasking: it's the new multitasking! As Lord Chesterfield wrote in the 1740s:

> *There is time enough for everything in the course of the day, if you do but one thing at once, but there is not time enough in the year, if you will do two things at a time ... The steady and undissipated attention to one object, is a sure mark of a superior genius; as hurry, bustle, and agitation are the never-failing symptoms of a weak and frivolous mind.*

UNITASKING

This week, practise doing one thing at a time, especially in the way you use technology.

- Next time you sit down at your computer, make a pact with yourself to do one thing at a time. Switch your email off, and check it once an hour, or less if that's practical. If you're working on a task, turn off other distractions like instant messaging and Facebook.

- If you want to listen to radio or watch TV, really listen or watch rather than doing other things at the same time.

- When you use your phone, see if you can give the other person your full attention for the duration of the call.

- While you are eating, set aside other activities, and just eat.

SLOW ACTIVITIES

The word 'slow' has been adopted in a number of fields as a byword for paying more attention to quality and substance, as opposed to fast, take-away, throw-away culture. Slow Food is a growing movement which arose in Italy, and which supports traditional cuisine and regional products. Slow Travel encourages taking the train, bus or boat instead of flying, and enjoying the journey not just the destination. Slow Cities (or Cittaslow) is a network which celebrates the special qualities of each town, and resists homogenization. The slow philosophy has a lot in common with environmentalism, encouraging us to be more aware of the ecological and social impact of wanting everything to be fast and convenient.

Practising mindfulness doesn't mean you have to sign up to any of these slow movements, but you may find some ideas here that are worth exploring. For example, there may be days when a quick take-away is in order, but sometimes you might find it satisfying to visit the local farmers' market and take time to cook a meal, or to engage in a slow, traditional activity which uses your hands, such as painting, knitting, baking, gardening or carpentry. Many of us spend our days in our heads—thinking through problems, sitting at computers, attending meetings. There is something about doing things with our hands which can bring us into the present moment. It feels soothing and refreshing after a day of mental activity, and we feel once again embodied.

 SLOW ACTIVITY

This week, find one activity which helps you slow down and be mindful—hopefully something which you also enjoy! Here are some ideas, but you may have others. If you already do some of these things, you could pick something new, or bring the activity into your life at a different time. For example, if you normally garden at the weekend, could you head outside on a weekday evening after work instead of flopping in front of the TV?

- Cook a meal from scratch, being mindful of the whole process, from shopping to chopping vegetables to eating.

- Write a letter. Find a nice pen and stationery, if you can, or just use what's to hand. Sit down and write to a friend or family member. It doesn't matter what you write. Post it and imagine their surprise. When was the last time you wrote or received a letter that wasn't business mail or a bill?

- Do something with your hands: digging, painting, knitting, playing an instrument or building some shelves. If you have children, try playing with their modeling clay or making a castle with Lego. (Or feel free to go out and buy something playful and childish for yourself!)

- Take a walk somewhere different. Look up and around. Be like a tourist in your own city, noticing the cafés, churches, shops, architecture and people.

- Write down your slow activity:

_____

_____

_____

_____

 Mindfulness doesn't mean doing everything at a snail's pace, but you may feel less exhausted and depleted if you can consciously:

- Notice your speed.

- Do one thing at a time.

- Make space for some activities you enjoy which can help you to slow down and be mindful.

- 19 -

ME

*True happiness, we are told, consists in getting out of one's self;
but the point is not only to get out—you must stay out; and to
stay out you must have some absorbing errand.*

Henry James

What is your first thought when you get up in the morning? The
meditation master Sakyong Mipham suggests it is likely to be
a version of 'What about me? Will I get what I want today?'
This is a mantra that we learn to recite subconsciously throughout
our day.

This 'What about me?' mantra doesn't actually make us happy,
because it's based on a false version of reality. We see ourselves as
the centre of the universe, and we are constantly disappointed and
resentful that the universe doesn't give us exactly what we want.
At the times when we stop worrying about getting what we want
and are able to think of the bigger picture—including the needs of
other people—we may paradoxically feel more cheerful.

This doesn't mean that we can't look after ourselves properly,
or that it's selfish to have a nice hot bath or take a weekend break.
Even if we are not the centre of the universe in the way we imagined it, we are still walking around with a mind and body which
are unique and worth taking care of. As we discussed in chapter
17, we can cultivate a kindness to both ourselves and other people.

However, a lot of what we do for ourselves is not always
making us happier. We try to get what we think will make us feel
happy and safe: the new job, the nice flat, the beautiful partner.
But we are never satisfied and always wanting something else.

As we practise mindfulness, we may start to notice how, by trying to protect this 'me', we often isolate ourselves from others, and cut ourselves off from our own experience. We create an idea of how things should be, and then we get stuck with our version of things and miss something much more interesting. We try to make ourselves a little nest which feels safe, but it starts to get airless and claustrophobic. We rerun the same old stories, and replay the same old scenarios. But because it feels familiar, we're scared to come out.

It's like we're stuck in a motel room under a smelly old duvet, eating stale chips and watching bad reality TV. We've pulled all the curtains closed and there's no light. But then we open the curtains a crack, and then the window. We discover there's a fresh breeze blowing and warm sea air. Slowly we start to open up all the windows until sunlight and fresh air come flooding in. Eventually, we might even take down all the walls, and find we're standing under a huge sky.

In our mindfulness practice we can start to see our habitual patterns of thought and behaviour more clearly. We can let in some fresh air and discover that there's a whole big world out there, and we don't always have to relate to it and react to it in the same old ways—and that shockingly, mercifully, we are not at the centre of it! There are lots of other 'me's walking around out there too. Of course we know this, but do we *really* know it?

MANY 'ME'S

- Sit in a place where other people come and go—it could be a café, a bus or train, or a waiting room.

- Watch the people as if you are a novelist or film director who wants to include them as characters, and needs to understand them. Use your imagination. What kind of a day are they having? What is going on in their minds? What kind of thoughts and emotions are they experiencing?

- Pay special attention to the people you don't find immediately interesting or attractive. Why does that guy look so sullen and sour? What might be the reason for his unhappiness—

perhaps he's just lost his girlfriend, or had a fight with his father? Or maybe he missed his train and is late for a meeting? Or his cheese sandwich was stale?

- If it feels right, you can also see what it's like to generate a sense of wishing them well, as in chapter 17: 'May they be safe, may they be happy, may they be free from suffering, may they be at ease.' If that feels too much, just notice them with the awareness that, like you, each of these strangers has a whole world of thoughts and feelings going on inside.

- 20 -

SOCIETY

As mindfulness becomes more mainstream, people who have found it important in their own lives are naturally turning outwards and looking at how to bring it into their environment. How could we create a more mindful society—and what would that look like?

Some of the most exciting and successful projects have been focusing on how we can teach mindfulness skills from an early age. In schools in Vancouver, Canada, four-and five-year-old children begin their day with a few minutes of mindful breathing. They are taught how to calm themselves in moments of stress, and to listen to their emotions. They draw pictures of their brain, and talk about which parts are used in processing their emotional reactions.

In Tonbridge in the UK, schoolboys aged 14 and 15 take part in an eight-week mindfulness course designed specifically for adolescents. At the end, most of them say they are likely to keep using the techniques, especially as a way of coping with the pressures of exams and sports events.

Increasingly, mindfulness is being brought into education, health care, and many kinds of organizations and workplaces. Prisoners are being offered mindfulness training to help cope with their anxiety and frustration, and to develop 'emotional intelligence'. Lawyers are coming to mindfulness courses to improve their listening skills, clarify their thought processes, and deal with the intense emotions that can come up in the courtroom. Business people are learning mindful leadership as a foundation for better decision making and communication. Parents are discussing ways to be more mindful in their family life and the way they interact with their children.

The way mindfulness is taught may have a different flavour and focus, according to the different needs of teenagers or lawyers or corporate leaders. But in the end it's all about learning to be more present and aware in an increasingly hectic world. And not only being present when we're sitting alone in meditation, but also when we are relating to other people.

SPEAKING AND LISTENING

We've talked about mindfulness as a way of allowing more space in our lives—creating gaps in our mental chatter and busyness. In our contact with other people we may also find there is normally not much sense of space. We react to each other in habitual ways; we jump in on what the other person is saying to make our own point, and we feel frustrated at speaking without being heard. We may find it hard even to hear ourselves—to hear the voice of what feels true rather than what we think we are supposed to say.

As you practise mindfulness, there's a natural spaciousness which may begin to seep into the way you are with other people. You can also practise intentionally bringing mindfulness into moments of communication.

- **Listening.** When you are listening, just listen, with your undivided attention—not planning what you are going to say next. If you drift off into other thoughts, gently bring yourself back to what the other person is saying.

- **Speaking.** When you are speaking, try allowing space— taking a 'pause' at any time. See if you can let whatever you say next emerge from that spaciousness rather than from a feeling of hurry and jumble.

- **Silences.** When no one is speaking, can you let it be that way? Are you always the one who jumps in to make conversation? If so, can you see what happens if you don't?

Let us not look east and west for materials of conversation, but rest in presence and unity. A just feeling will fast enough supply fuel for discourse, if speaking be more grateful than silence. When people come to see us, we foolishly prattle, lest we be inhospitable. But things said for conversation are chalk eggs. Don't say things. What you are stands over you the while, and thunders so that I cannot hear what you say to the contrary.

Ralph Waldo Emerson

 SPEAKING AND LISTENING

This is an exercise to do with a friend or partner. It's just about bringing some of the same qualities you bring to your meditation practice into your interaction: being present, open and without judgment.

Pick a question you would both like to answer—it could be something you choose yourselves, or one of the following:

- What is difficult for you in your life right now?

- What does it feel like to be in your body?

- What do you long for in your life?

- What are you frightened of?

- What helps you to be present and what stops you from being present?

Choose one person to ask the question and listen to the answer; then reverse the roles. Take about five minutes for each speaker.

While you are the listener, don't speak—you don't even need to keep nodding and gesturing in response. Just listen with openness and without judgment.

When you are speaking, pause as often as you like and trust that words will emerge. (Or if you find you don't want to speak at all, that would also be fine!)

When you've finished, take a few minutes to share what the experience was like. If it feels right you could repeat the exercise with another question, or even the same question again—you may be surprised to find something different emerging each time.

SPEAKING FROM EXPERIENCE ISAAC

'The funny thing about mindfulness is that once you've had the taste of it, it's difficult to switch off. There's nothing more annoying than when you're in the middle of an argument and you know that at that point you're being really, really unreasonable! When you practise mindfulness there's an opportunity for you to either switch on and engage with other people, or switch off. The gift that mindfulness gives us is that when you make that decision to either switch on or switch off, you are fully aware of it. You might deny it or make excuses, but you do know it!'

21

STILLNESS

Peace and calm. We long for it—in our modern life it's a valuable commodity. We gaze at advertising billboards showing a gleaming white beach and a turquoise sea. A woman in flowing white sits cross-legged with her eyes closed and a serene expression on her face. We want some of that! And so we spend lots of money on candles and aromatherapy oils, spa treatments, relaxation tapes, and *The Little Book of Calm*.

Not everyone believes in calm. Economist Todd Buchholz wrote a book called *Rush: Why You Need and Love the Rat Race*. He argues that we thrive on busyness, and that people who sit back and relax are miserable. We must all have friends or colleagues who'd agree with him—people who've built their lives on never stopping, and who work seven days a week; or else fill their weekends and evenings with activity which keeps them just as busy as on their working days. Or maybe we are those people ourselves!

Mindfulness is not necessarily about buying in to either of these caricatures. Yes, we do need to set aside time for 'doing nothing', or at least for doing the kind of nothing we cultivate in the meditation practices. But that doesn't mean we can't also thrive in a busy environment, and enjoy the buzz of the urban 'work hard, play hard' life. If we give ourselves times of space and stillness, this will help us to ride the waves of chaos when we need to.

EQUANIMITY

The popular image of 'calm' can seem also to imply a person without emotions—serene and detached in all situations. But this is not the aim of mindfulness. We're not trying to get rid of all the fire and passion in life; to become boring, indifferent, or uncaring towards others. We're not denying our feelings—on the contrary, we can let ourselves feel the extraordinary power and energy of emotions. However, by being more aware and present to them, we don't let ourselves get swept around by them so much, and knocked into automatic, habitual reactions. It's like we're able to be at the eye of the storm, and not uprooted and blown around by the gale-force winds.

We could describe this quality as 'equanimity': a sense of inner balance or equilibrium which means we're not so easily blown off course by our reactions. Pema Chödrön says, 'To cultivate equanimity we practise catching ourselves when we feel attraction or aversion, before it hardens into grasping or negativity.' So it doesn't mean we don't feel, but we can create enough space to make a choice about what we do next, and how we act on those feelings.

Think of yourself as a surfer on the crest of a huge wave, or a rider on a bucking bronco. The surfer, or rider, is in relative stillness amidst a great whoosh of movement. How can you hold your balance in a similar way? This is one of our challenges in life: to have some sense of stillness and stability within our dynamic and constantly changing experience. To be able to dance, as T. S. Eliot puts it, 'at the still point of the turning world'.

MEDITATION: STILLNESS, STABILITY, SPACE

We've mentioned throughout this book that our meditation practice is not about trying to get calm, or aiming for any particular state of mind. This only sets up a struggle, wanting ourselves to be somehow different. If we do experience any feeling of increased calm, it's the kind of calm which comes from allowing things to be as they are, including sometimes accepting that at this moment we're not feeling very calm!

The natural world gives us some powerful images of what it might mean to embody stillness within flux and change, and stormy weather. Mountains and sky have already come up during the book as metaphors to use in our mindfulness practice, but now we can meditate or reflect on them a bit more. We can also bring these images to mind at any time in the middle of a chaotic day, and just for a moment have a sense of embodying these qualities ourselves.

MEDITATION: MOUNTAIN

- Sit with good posture, and spend a few moments in mindfulness of your body and breath.

- Picture a mountain in front of you—either one you've seen, or one you can imagine. See the enormous size and majesty of the mountain, with its broad base in the earth, and its peak rising above the clouds.

- Now have a sense of bringing this mountain into your own body, with your base rooted in the earth, and your peak rising skyward. Feel the strength, stability and unwavering quality of the mountain. You can also feel your breath moving, like a gentle breeze.

- Imagine the seasons passing on the mountain: autumn, with its rain and winds; winter, bringing snow and sleet; spring, when the snows melt and flowers grow; summer, bringing the heat of sun onto the rocks. Take a few moments to imagine each season and the changing weather it brings. Throughout all these changes, the mountain remains present and unwavering.

- Spend some time feeling the mountain in yourself, a sense of stillness and rootedness through all the storms and difficulties of life. See if you can bring something of this mountain quality into the rest of your day.

MEDITATION: SKY

- Settle into your meditation posture and practise mindfulness of breathing. Feel grounded in your body and breath. Let yourself be aware of any thoughts coming and going like clouds.

- Now picture a grey, rainy day. The clouds above you are thick and heavy, and fill the whole sky. They seem to be endless; they weigh you down.

- Then imagine yourself on a plane, taking off. The houses and cars are getting smaller below you. You enter the clouds, and everything is blank for a few moments. Then suddenly you burst into sunshine and blue sky. Picture the brightness of the blue, the whiteness of the clouds below you, and the relief— the blue sky has been here all along, and is always here.

- You can let the plane dissolve in your imagination and have a sense of just being up there above the clouds—perhaps you have a soft, firm white cloud as a seat. Let your mind open to the brilliance of the blue sky and the limitless space.

- Now rest your mind, with this feeling of space and sky. At the same time, you have a real sense of being in your body, feeling its weight sitting here, and your breath moving. When you're ready to finish, see if you can carry some of this feeling of space and vastness into the next moments of your day.

SPEAKING FROM EXPERIENCE TESSA

'When I was a child I was awed by the idea of space. I used to visit the city planetarium regularly, and watch light shows about the stars and galaxies. I remember making up a song on my guitar about my frustration that I would never know the answers to my questions about the universe.

'As I got older I stopped thinking much about space, and left it to the boys to read science fiction and watch *Star Trek*. But more recently, whenever I'm away from city lights, I've started looking more at the stars, and relearning the constellations. My husband developed an obsession with the spacecraft which were launched in the 70s. It was in the news that *Voyager 1* is now reaching the outer edges of our solar system, after travelling for 34 years and covering over 17 billion kilometres. As it heads for interstellar space, it will apparently take at least 40,000 years to reach the next star, in the constellation Ursa Minor. That's how much space is out there, between our Sun and the next little pinprick of light, just one of billions and billions of stars stretching throughout the universe.

'You can hardly begin to imagine the vastness of this space! It might feel overwhelming, but I find it strangely comforting. I tend to think I have to look after everything, or the world will fall apart. When I remember this limitless space, it seems to put it all in perspective. If I notice I'm feeling overwhelmed, I look up and

connect with the sky, and the feeling of space stretching outwards, and it feels like a fresh breeze comes into the situation.'

 You can have a sense of stillness and equanimity within the
chaos of everyday life. Remembering the vastness of the sky
or the stability of a mountain can help you to embody these
qualities.

22

WHERE NEXT?

As you come to the end of this book, hopefully you have a taste of what mindfulness is about. It might be a raisin-sized nibble, or a few juicy mouthfuls, depending especially on how much you've been trying out the exercises. So what do you think? Do you feel any inspiration to pursue this further?

 INTENTION: GOING FORWARD

- Take a few moments to feel grounded in your body and bring awareness to your breath.

- Reflect on your experience of reading this book and doing some of the practices. Is there anything you have discovered for yourself that you would like to remember? Write down your thoughts, either here or in a notebook. Something you discovered from exploring/practising mindfulness so far:

_____

_____

_____

_____

- Bring your mind back to your original intention. Why were you interested in mindfulness? If you wrote something down in chapter 3, you could look at this again. Is this still your intention going forward, or has anything changed? Would you like

to develop your mindfulness practice further, and if so, why?
Your intention going forward:

_____

_____

_____

Reasons why you'd like to practise mindfulness (or if not,
reasons why not):

_____

_____

_____

FINDING A TEACHER

Books can be a good introduction, but mindfulness is really an
oral tradition. The practices we do have been passed from teacher
to student for centuries, with each new teacher adding the flavour
of their own insight. If you're serious about mindfulness, it's
important to have the support of a live teacher. This is someone
who can share their own understanding of the practices, and can
help you to articulate your own experience and to see more clearly
what you can learn from it. They should be a person who has a
regular mindfulness practice themselves, and who has been
trained to support other people's practice through friendly questioning, listening and responding.

YOU ARE NOT ALONE

While mindfulness practices do encourage us to be alone with ourselves, it's also extremely helpful to practise with other people. Sitting in silence in a group is surprisingly powerful. And you can learn a lot from discussing your practice with others. Sometimes they will say something which resonates; sometimes they will come from a completely different angle to you. In either case this can help to clarify your own experience. You can find fellow practitioners by joining a course, or by connecting with a local meditation centre.

The eight-week courses known as MBSR (Mindfulness-Based Stress Reduction) and MBCT (Mindfulness-Based Cognitive Therapy) are widely recognized by the international medical community, and research shows their many benefits for health and well-being (see chapter 3). A structured course like this can help you to embed the practices in your daily life, with the support of a teacher and a group. MBSR and MBCT are very closely related, and participants don't usually experience a big difference between the two—you may find the choice is made by which one is offered near you. If you have an ongoing mental health issue such as depression or anxiety disorder, then MBCT can offer you more specific help working with negative thought patterns, and courses are run by clinical psychologists trained to work with depression. Mindfulness teachers normally offer an assessment process before you sign up, so you can discuss with them whether their course is the right one for you at this time in your life.

Another way to deepen your experience is to find a local meditation centre or group. Many Buddhist centres offer regular meditation sessions where you can practise with other people, without having to sign up to any beliefs or become a Buddhist. There are other faith-based organizations such as Christian churches which run meditation sessions, as well as secular groups of mindfulness practitioners. You'll need to research the organization to avoid anything cultish, and be discriminating about the kind of meditation that is practised. Some forms of meditation may be more about going off into an altered state, or serving a particular 'higher purpose'. Without denigrating these traditions, if it's *mindfulness* you're interested in, ask yourself if the meditation supports the purposes of mindfulness discussed in this book. Does it help you to be more aware and present? More embodied? More accepting of yourself and others?

If you don't have a course or group near you, another option is to go for a big feast of mindfulness all in one go, by travelling to a retreat centre. Every Western country has places where you can learn to meditate for a weekend, a week or more, often in beautiful countryside settings. Some retreats are relaxed and sociable; others take a more monastic approach, with early rising and a rule of silence. This can be a wonderful opportunity to discover what happens when you let your mind and body really slow down and settle in one place.

SPEAKING FROM EXPERIENCE TESSA

'For me, one of the best things about practising mindfulness has been the connection with other people. When you're meditating you really need to be with other people who find it normal to sit on their bum in silence for hours at a time. When I first started meditating, all my friends were in their 20s and 30s working in the media. I came to the meditation centre and there were people of all ages and backgrounds—nurses, actors, lecturers, gardeners, builders, policemen, business people and students. It felt refreshing. I was very wary of anything cultish, but I relaxed when no one seemed to be interested in converting me to anything.

'When you spend time meditating, people seem to soften up and become more open and relaxed with each other. I used to size people up to see whether they were a good advertisement for meditation. Then at some point it clicked that there wasn't a type of person they were going to become. They were each just more and more themselves. Jim was very Jim, Isaac was unique in his Isaac-ness and Debbie was increasingly Debbie. That was a great relief—that I could relax into being Tessa.'

INSPIRATION

We're bombarded daily by images and words encouraging us to be mindless—free newspapers with gossip about celebrities we'll forget five minutes later, billboards which steal our attention with their slogans, and TV which can leave us hypnotized on the sofa. How do you escape from all that to make space for meditation?

You can counteract this by seeking out books, audio and video which inspire you to meditate and remind you why you practise. There are books which offer practical guidance, including a few which will take you step-by-step through an eight-week mindfulness course. You can also take inspiration from great meditation masters and teachers from different traditions, each with their own way of putting things which can bring a fresh viewpoint—as you read, suddenly something goes *ping* inside you. Poetry, music and visual art can also remind us to be mindful. Artists often capture the essence of the present moment—its simplicity and magic.

YOUR OWN PRACTICE

It's lovely to read and talk about mindfulness, and you may think 'Yes that's great, I sign up to that!' However, there's no substitute for actually doing the practice! Words can only point in the vague general direction—you have to experience it in your own body and being. Think of your practice as a small plant you've been given to look after. You need to water it daily rather than letting it dry out for ages, and then hoping to revive it with a drenching. If you keep watering you may find it surprises you by producing unexpected fruit or a vivid blossom.

Time. See if you can find a regular time of day which works for you. Some people like the freshness of the morning; others feel more relaxed in the evening. Some people even manage to find a quiet meeting room at work in their lunch break. Experiment in your own life, and then see if you can create a habit.

- **Place.** Create a physical space for your practice. It may just be a small corner of your room, but see if you can find a place to meditate which isn't full of clutter or dirty laundry. You could have a plant or picture to inspire you. See if you can create a little space which calls invitingly for you to come and practise your mindfulness.

- **Keeping a record.** Keep a diary of your practice. Just making a quick note each day can help you to see more clearly when you are keeping up your practice or letting things drop off, and what effect that has on your state of mind.

- **Any little helps.** It's better to practise for 10 minutes a day than for a marathon session once in a blue moon. Even two or three minutes of practice can help you reconnect with the sense of being present.

SPEAKING FROM EXPERIENCE AARON

'I've found that for me it helps to get up in the morning and do it first thing. I have breakfast, brush my teeth, have my shower—feel comfortable with myself. Then I sit down and meditate. One of my teachers said that for him not meditating is like not brushing his teeth. After a while I do feel like my brain has bad breath if I haven't been meditating. And it doesn't feel good to go out with a messy mind, to go out there and meet other people with my bad breath brain.'

SPEAKING FROM EXPERIENCE ISAAC

'It was a great discovery for me, finding out that it was easier for me to do at night, just before I went to sleep. Rather than my head hitting the pillow and having thoughts running right the way through, I found the thoughts would already have exhausted themselves if I meditated first.

'There've been moments when things in my life were getting heavy, where I've felt there was just so much I had to get a grip on, I didn't have the time to meditate. Actually, it's these times when you really need to meditate. Those five minutes—if I'm able to do it in the maelstrom—make all the difference. There's a part of me that thinks "If I meditate now I'm not going to do it properly, am I? I'm all over the place." The point is just to "come as you are". You don't have to be in a particular state for you to start—you can just do it at that point.'

WHERE NEXT?

Would you like to explore mindfulness further? If so, take a few moments to reflect about practical next steps. Will you find a course? Read another book? Set aside time for daily practice? What sort of challenges do you think may come up, and how could you work with them? Write down your thoughts here or in a notebook.

Your next steps (e.g., course, book, meditation centre, regular practice):

_____

_____

A formal practice you will try to do regularly for the next month (e.g., mindful breathing, body scan, mindful movement):

_____

_____

When you will practise (e.g., morning, lunchtime, evening, whenever you can):

_____

An informal practice you will try to do regularly for the next month (e.g., mindful tooth brushing, pausing, mindful walking to work):

_____

_____

What are likely to be your obstacles or challenges to practising?

_____

_____

What would help you with these challenges?

_____

_____

One word or phrase which will help you remember why you'd like to practise mindfulness:

_____

AS THINGS ARE NOW

Quick now, here, now, always—

T. S. Eliot

It could be easy to think of mindfulness as a self-improvement plan. Most of us tend to think there's something wrong with us, or our lives, and one day we will fix it. But mindfulness is not about striving to be better. We can let go of this idea that things need to be different from how they are right now. Yes, it helps if we can put a bit of energy and thought into making space for mindfulness practices. But we're creating space within which we can stop doing and striving, and simply be here, just as we are.

You could feel overwhelmed by life's busyness and give yourself a hard time for not being more mindful as you go through your day. But none of us are walking around being mindful and awake at every moment. It's a constant movement in and out of awareness: opening, closing and opening again to the vividness of our experience.

Each time you are 'mindless' is another opportunity to be mindful again—each time you can enjoy your rediscovery of the present moment. 'Oh look!' Here we are again—back in the 'now' at any moment. You're off in a long boring conversation in your head, and suddenly you're brought back by the bright green of a tree, the hot water of the shower, the taste of a strawberry. The more you were off in the clouds, the more you can take delight in coming back.

> *He who binds to himself a joy*
> *Does the wingèd life destroy*
> *But he who kisses the joy as it flies*
> *Lives in eternity's sun rise.*

William Blake

We can't hold anything still. The shower will be over, the strawberry will be eaten, and a new 'now' will come along to take its place. Sometimes the now is difficult and challenging, sometimes surprising and magical. May your mindfulness practice help you to be at ease with now, whatever it may bring!

LIST OF PRACTICES

We have worked with a lot of exercises in this book. Many of them are variations on a theme—starting with a basic practice like mindful breathing, and revisiting it with a different focus or emphasis. Once you've got a flavour of these different possibilities, it would be good to choose just one or two practices to get familiar with and explore in more depth.

SITTING MEDITATION

Mindfulness of breathing (p. 31)

Mindfulness of breathing: being inquisitive (p. 34)

Mindfulness of sounds (p. 75)

Mindfulness of breathing: labelling thoughts (p. 91)

Mindfulness of breath, sounds and thoughts (p. 92)

Working with challenges (p. 113)

Loving-kindness meditation (p. 117)

Meditation: mountain (p. 141)

Meditation: sky (p. 141)

MINDFULNESS OF BODY

Body in stress (p. 44)

Feeling your fingers (p. 45)

Feet and legs (p. 46)

Full body scan (p. 49)

Words and sensations (p. 82)

MINDFULNESS IN DAILY LIFE

FURTHER RESOURCES

BOOKS

MINDFULNESS IN DEPTH

*These books will help you to go further into mindfulness practice
as it is taught in the MBSR and MBCT programmes.*

*Full Catastrophe Living: Using the Wisdom of Your Body and Mind to Face
Stress, Pain and Illness,* by Jon Kabat-Zinn (Delta, 1990)
This influential book presenting mindfulness and its benefits for
health and well-being is by Jon Kabat-Zinn, creator of the Mindfulness-
Based Stress Reduction programme.

Mindfulness: A Practical Guide to Finding Peace in a Frantic World, by
Mark Williams and Danny Penman (Piatkus, 2011)
Professor Mark Williams, one of the founders of Mindfulness-
Based Cognitive Therapy, takes you through an eight-week mindfulness
programme, including a CD for guided practice.

Mindfulness-Based Cognitive Therapy, by Rebecca Crane (Routledge,
2009)
This book provides a clear and thorough outline of the key theoretical
and practical features of MBCT, mainly for use by mindfulness teachers
and therapists.

*Mindfulness-Based Cognitive Therapy for Depression: A New Approach to
Preventing Relapse,* by Zindel V. Segal, J. Mark G. Williams and John
D. Teasdale (Guilford Press, 2002)
This seminal work on MBCT is mainly for use by mindfulness
teachers and therapists. For a book written more for the general public,
see the next title by the same authors and Jon Kabat-Zinn.

The Mindful Way through Depression, by Mark Williams, John Teasdale,
Zindel V. Segal and Jon Kabat-Zinn (Guilford Press, 2007)
    A guide to mindfulness, including CD, for anyone who has struggled
with depression, written by the founders of Mindfulness-Based
Cognitive Therapy.

*Wherever You Go, There You Are: Mindfulness Meditation for Everyday
Life,* by Jon Kabat-Zinn (Piatkus, 1994)
    This book by Jon Kabat-Zinn is less about medicine and health
(compared with his earlier *Full Catastrophe Living*) and more of a
personal and poetic guide to the practice of mindfulness.

MINDFULNESS, MEDITATION
AND INSPIRATION

*These are guides to mindfulness, meditation and life by writers
and teachers from a range of backgrounds and traditions.*

Get Some Headspace, by Andy Puddicombe (Hodder & Stoughton, 2011)
    A practical guide to meditation by a clinical consultant and former
Buddhist monk who suggests that ten minutes a day of practice can
have life-changing effects.

In Praise of Slow, by Carl Honoré (Orion, 2005)
    Journalist Carl Honoré explores the rise of slow movements in food,
workplaces, medicine, urban planning and other areas—challenging the
idea that faster is always better.

*The Mindful Manifesto: How Doing Less and Noticing More Can Help Us
Thrive in a Stressed-Out World,* by Dr Jonty Heaversedge and Ed
Halliwell (Hay House, 2010)
    An inspiring overview of mindfulness research and practice, offering
a vision of a more mindful society.

The Miracle of Mindfulness, by Thich Nhat Hanh (Rider, 1991)
    The Vietnamese monk Thich Nhat Hanh, one of the West's most

popular Buddhist teachers, encourages meditation practice through gentle anecdotes and exercises.

The Power of Now: A Guide to Spiritual Enlightenment, by Eckhart Tolle (New World Library, 1999)
     This best-selling book is too 'New Age' for some, but many readers have been inspired by Tolle's vision of how to become more fully present.

Ruling Your World, by Sakyong Mipham (Shambhala, 2007)
     A guide to developing contentment and confidence in daily life, from the leader of the Shambhala international network of meditation centres; son of Chögyam Trungpa.

Seeking the Heart of Wisdom: The Path of Insight Meditation, by Jack Goldstein and Jack Kornfield (Shambhala, 1987)
     An introduction to Insight Meditation, which brings the teachings of Theravada Buddhism (rooted especially in Southeast Asia) into an accessible context for Westerners.

Shambhala: The Sacred Path of the Warrior, by Chögyam Trungpa (Shambhala, 2007)
     The Tibetan meditation master Chögyam Trungpa teaches how to live a life of fearlessness and goodness based on the Shambhala teachings, named for a legendary enlightened kingdom.

Taking the Leap: Freeing Ourselves from Old Habits and Fears, by Pema Chödrön (Shambhala, 2010)
     American Buddhist nun Pema Chödrön teaches how to break free of destructive patterns in our life by learning to stay present and open.

Turning the Mind into an Ally, by Sakyong Mipham (Riverhead, 2004)
     Sakyong Mipham writes with clarity about how to strengthen our minds and bring peace to our lives through the practice of meditation.

When Things Fall Apart: Heart Advice for Difficult Times, by Pema Chödrön (Shambhala, 2000)
> Pema Chödrön teaches with her usual humour and compassion on how to work with painful situations and emotions.

WEBSITES

Be Mindful
www.bemindful.co.uk

The Mental Health Foundation hosts a site with a wealth of information about mindfulness, including a directory where you can find current courses offered by teachers across the UK.

Be Mindful Online
www.bemindfulonline.com

A four-week online course run by the Mental Health Foundation and presented by Tessa Watt and Ed Halliwell. It features video lessons, guided audio, and interactive exercises.

Being Mindful
www.beingmindful.co.uk

The author is co-director of this small London-based organization which offers MBSR courses, sessions for workplaces, and mindfulness coaching.

The Center for Mindfulness in Medicine, Health Care and Society
www.umassmed.edu/content.aspx?id=41252

This organization, based at the University of Massachusetts Medical School, grew out of Jon Kabat-Zinn's pioneering Stress Reduction Clinic, and is the home of MBSR. On the website you can find mindfulness programmes in North America, and information on the Center's research into mindfulness in health care.

The Centre for Mindfulness Research and Practice
www.bangor.ac.uk/mindfulness

Based at Bangor University in Wales, this centre is a leading provider of professional mindfulness training. It also offers public courses including a distance learning programme, in which you can follow an eight-week course supported by weekly phone calls with a teacher. The website also has guided mindfulness meditation CDs for sale.

Gaia House
www.gaiahouse.co.uk

This site gives information on Insight Meditation retreats in the Buddhist tradition, based in Devon, UK.

Mindful
www.mindful.org

This lively website features stories and commentary about mindfulness and 'mindful society'. There is news of projects in schools, hospitals, offices, campuses, prisons and so on, as well as updates on scientific research, and articles on practical subjects like mindful parenting.

Mindfulness-Based Cognitive Therapy (UK)
www.mbct.co.uk

The official UK website of MBCT contains information and links to other resources.

Mindfulness-Based Cognitive Therapy (North America)
www.mbct.com

A good starting point for MBCT resources in North America.

Mindfulness Meditation Practice CDs and Tapes
www.mindfulnesstapes.com

Here you can order CDs and tapes recorded by MBSR founder Jon Kabat-Zinn.

Mindfulness Research Guide

www.mindfulexperience.org

A resource providing information on the scientific study of mindfulness, including publications, measurement tools and research centres.

Oxford Mindfulness Centre

www.oxfordmindfulness.org

The Oxford Mindfulness Centre is a charity working to research and promote the therapeutic use of mindfulness. On this site you can download academic papers on the use of mindfulness for working with specific mental health challenges such as bipolar disorder, suicidal behaviour and eating disorders.

Shambhala

www.shambhala.org

An international network of meditation centres rooted in the Buddhist tradition but offering meditation evenings and courses open to all, in over 170 locations worldwide.

Slow Planet

www.slowplanet.com

A home for blogs and articles about the slow movement—in technology, design, work, parenting, travel and so on—run by Carl Honoré, author of *In Praise of Slow*.

Slow Down London

www.slowdownlondon.co.uk

As well as articles specific to London, this site offers ideas and inspiration for slowing down and appreciating life wherever you live.

ACKNOWLEDGEMENTS

I'd like to thank all my teachers and friends on this journey into mindfulness and meditation over the years. In particular, enormous thanks go to my mindfulness mentor Cindy Cooper for her generosity and wisdom in reading and commenting on my drafts of this book. Thank you Cindy for all your support and encouragement!

I'd like to express my deep appreciation to my Being Mindful colleague Debbie Johnson for her friendship, partnership and 'heartfulness'. Special thanks to Ed Halliwell for sharing his inspiration to make the benefits of meditation more widely known. I'm grateful to my wonderful Slow Down colleague Deepa Patel for always reminding me what it means to embody the practice in our lives. Thank you to the many dedicated teachers at Shambhala, especially my meditation instructor Jim O'Neill, and of course our inspiring teacher Sakyong Mipham Rinpoche.

Many thanks to Duncan Heath at Icon Books for inviting me to write this book, and to Harry Scoble for his careful and sensitive editing. I'm grateful to Professor Mark Williams for his advice, and my friend Anna Janmaat for her kind feedback. Thank you to the people who have shared their own experiences of mindfulness for this book: Marion, Sarah, Isaac, Anthony, Debbie and Aaron. I'd also like to thank the participants in my courses at Being Mindful, for bringing their fresh experience to the practices and always teaching me something new.

I'm grateful to my brother Nicholas Watt for introducing me to yoga, and my father, Frank Watt, for encouraging me to write from an early age. Thanks to Frank and Emily for sharing Three Ponds

Farm, my favourite place for meditation practice and mindful swimming.

Finally my huge thanks to my family, Richard, Katrina and Tanya Woolley, for giving me the space and time for practice, and for all their love and support.

May you be safe, may you be happy, may you be free from suffering, may you be at ease.

ALSO BY JANET MALCOLM

Diana and Nikon

Psychoanalysis: The Impossible Profession

In the Freud Archives

The Journalist and the Murderer

The Purloined Clinic

THE SILENT WOMAN

The
Silent Woman

SYLVIA PLATH *&*
TED HUGHES

by

JANET MALCOLM

Alfred A. Knopf

NEW YORK

1994

THIS IS A BORZOI BOOK
PUBLISHED BY ALFRED A. KNOPF, INC.

Copyright © 1993 by Janet Malcolm
All rights reserved under International and Pan-American
Copyright Conventions. Published in the United States by
Alfred A. Knopf, Inc., New York, and simultaneously in Canada
by Random House of Canada Limited, Toronto.
Distributed by Random House, Inc., New York.

Originally published, in different form, in *The New Yorker.*

Owing to limitations of space, all acknowledgments for permission to reprint
previously published and unpublished material will be found on page 211.

Library of Congress Cataloging-in-Publication Data
Malcolm, Janet.
The silent woman : Sylvia Plath and Ted Hughes /
by Janet Malcolm—1st ed.
p. cm.
ISBN 0-679-43158-6
1. Plath, Sylvia.   2. Women poets, American—Biography—History and
criticism.   3. Women poets, American—20th century—Biography.
4. Executors and administrators—Great Britain.   5. Biography as a literary
form.   6. Hughes, Ted, 1930- .   7. Canon (Literature)   I. Title.
PS3566.L272Z776   1994
811'.54—dc20
[B]   93-33848
CIP

Manufactured in the United States of America
FIRST EDITION

To Gardner

The reporter and the reported have duly and equally to understand that they carry their life in their hands. There are secrets
for privacy and silence; let them only be cultivated on the part
of the hunted creature with even half the method with which
the love of sport—or call it the historic sense—is cultivated
on the part of the investigator. They have been left too much
to the natural, the instinctive man; but they will be twice as
effective after it begins to be observed that they may take their
place among the triumphs of civilisation. Then at last the game
will be fair and the two forces face to face; it will be "pull devil,
pull tailor," and the hardest pull will doubtless provide the hap-
piest result. Then the cunning of the inquirer, envenomed with
resistance, will exceed in subtlety and ferocity anything we today conceive, and the pale forewarned victim, with every track
covered, every paper burnt and every letter unanswered, will,
in the tower of art, the invulnerable granite, stand, without a
sally, the siege of all the years.

—HENRY JAMES, "George Sand" (1897)

Liz Taylor is getting Eddie Fisher away from Debbie Reynolds,
who appears cherubic, round-faced, wronged, in pin curls and
house robe—Mike Todd barely cold. How odd these events
affect one so. Why? Analogies?

—SYLVIA PLATH, *Journals*, September 2, 1958

PART ONE

I

TED HUGHES wrote two versions of his foreword to *The Journals of Sylvia Plath*, a selection of diary entries covering the years between 1950 and 1962. The first version (the one that appears in the book, published in 1982) is a short, lyrical essay constructed on a single Blakean theme— the theme of a "real self" that finally emerged from among Plath's warring "false selves" and found triumphant expression in the *Ariel* poems, which were written in the last half year of her life and are the whole reason for her poetical reputation. In Hughes's view, her other writings—the short fiction she doggedly wrote and submitted, mostly unsuccessfully, to popular magazines; her novel, *The Bell Jar*; her letters; her apprentice poems, published in her first collection, *The Colossus*—"were like impurities thrown off from the various stages of the inner transformation, by-products of the internal work." He writes about a remarkable prefigurative moment:

> Though I spent every day with her for six years, and was rarely separated from her for more than two or three hours at a time, I never saw her show her real self to anybody— except, perhaps, in the last three months of her life.
>
> Her real self had showed itself in her writing, just for a moment, three years earlier, and when I heard it—the self I had married, after all, and lived with and knew well—in that brief moment, three lines recited as she went out through a doorway, I knew that what I had always felt must happen had now begun to happen, that her real self, being the real poet, would now speak for itself, and would

3

throw off all those lesser and artificial selves that had mo-
nopolized the words up to that point. It was as if a dumb
person suddenly spoke.

Hughes goes on to say that "when a real self finds language, and manages to speak, it is surely a dazzling event."
However, because the *Ariel* poems reveal little about the "in-
cidental circumstances or the crucial inner drama" that produced them, he pauses to reflect that "maybe it is this very
bareness of circumstantial detail that has excited the wilder
fantasies projected by others in Sylvia Plath's name." Publication of the journals, he feels, will presumably lay some of
these fantasies to rest, but he does not elaborate on how they
will do this; he merely notes that they record Plath's "day to
day struggle with her warring selves" and are to be exempted
from his overall characterization of her prose writings as
"waste products." Hughes ends his three-page essay with a
revelation that is so unexpected and so abrupt that one
doesn't immediately take in its significance:

> The journals exist in an assortment of notebooks and
> bunches of loose sheets. This selection contains perhaps a
> third of the whole bulk, which is now in the Neilson Library
> at Smith College. Two more notebooks survived for a while,
> maroon-backed ledgers like the '57-'59 volume, and contin-
> ued the record from late '59 to within three days of her
> death. The last of these contained entries for several
> months, and I destroyed it because I did not want her chil-
> dren to have to read it (in those days I regarded forgetfulness
> as an essential part of survival). The other disappeared.

The second version of the foreword, published in *Grand
Street* in 1982 and, three years later, in an anthology of writ-

ings about Plath called *Ariel Ascending*, edited by Paul Alexander, is considerably longer, denser, and more complex; it hasn't the elegant single-threadedness of the first version. It is as if Hughes looked at his first version and cast it aside as one of the too simple and too pretty false starts that a writer must make as a necessary part of finding out what he wants to say. (You could even call it a throwing off of impurities.) In his second foreword Hughes puts his revelation about the lost journals at the very beginning:

> Sylvia Plath's journals exist as an assortment of notebooks and bunches of loose sheets, and the selection just published here contains about a third of the whole bulk. Two other notebooks survived for a while after her death. They continued from where the surviving record breaks off in late 1959 and covered the last three years of her life. The second of these two books her husband destroyed, because he did not want her children to have to read it (in those days he regarded forgetfulness as an essential part of survival). The earlier one disappeared more recently (and may, presumably, still turn up).

We note that Hughes has made two changes. In one he holds out hope that the "disappeared" journal may eventually reappear (inviting the speculation that the journal is in fact, and may always have been, in his hands). In the other, and more crucial, change he has himself disappeared: "I destroyed" now becomes "her husband destroyed." Hughes can no longer sustain the fiction—on which all autobiographical writing is poised—that the person writing and the person being written about are a single seamless entity. In his second foreword Hughes needs to spell out his awareness of the discontinuity between the observing and the observed self: the observed self ("her husband") represents the interests of the

Hughes children, who must be protected from destructive knowledge, whereas the observing self—whom he calls "we," as in "We cannot help wondering whether the lost entries for her last three years were not the more important section"— represents the interests of the reader, who wants to understand the relationship between the *Ariel* poems and the poet's life. The publication of Plath's journals was evidently undertaken to elucidate this relationship. But "her husband" 's destructive act has made a kind of mockery of the enterprise, since the very journals that would cast light on the *Ariel* poems—the journals written while the poems were being composed—are the ones he destroyed and lost. This is the conundrum that Hughes must solve in his second foreword, and this is why he has, with helpless honesty (which an unsympathetic reader could mistake for evasiveness), divided himself into—you could even say lost himself in—the two selves, neither one "true" or "false," that allegorize the impossibility of his situation as both editor and destroyer.

In the course of his second foreword Hughes makes a Houdiniesque escape from the trunk he has stuffed himself into and has had thrown in the river. As he writes of a mysterious, urgent, hermetically sealed process of psychological rebirth going on within Plath, from which the *Ariel* poems came and to which the surviving journals are a key, the warring roles of the destructive husband and the irked editor quietly recede. The jarring designations "her husband" and "we" are heard less and less frequently, and a new figure, a serene critical intelligence, enters the essay and firmly takes charge of its purposes, riveting us with the suspenseful, elating narrative of Plath's poetic emergence. By the end of the essay, the problem of the missing journals is a dot on the distant horizon. Hughes has been able to lead us away from it because he led us up to it. When he made his confession at the end of his first version, it was as if he had suddenly rolled an impassable boulder into the reader's path. By beginning his second version with the boulder in place, he is able to propose ways of getting around it: by acknowledging difficulty, by resisting the temptation to minimize it, by moving sideways.

Life, as we all know, does not reliably offer—as art does— a second (and a third and a thirtieth) chance to tinker with a problem, but Ted Hughes's history seems to be uncommonly bare of the moments of mercy that allow one to undo or redo one's actions and thus feel that life isn't entirely tragic. Whatever Hughes might have undone or redone in his relationship to Sylvia Plath, the opportunity was taken from him when she committed suicide, in February of 1963, by putting her head in a gas oven as her two small children slept in a bedroom nearby, which she had sealed against gas fumes, and where she had placed mugs of milk and a plate of bread for them to find when they awoke. Plath and Hughes were not living together at the time of her death. They had been married for six years—she was thirty and he was thirty-two when she died—and had separated the previous fall in a turbulent way. There was another woman. It is a situation that many young married couples find themselves in—one that perhaps more couples find themselves in than don't—but it is a situation that ordinarily doesn't last: the couple either reconnects or dissolves. Life goes on. The pain and bitterness and exciting awfulness of sexual jealousy and sexual guilt recede and disappear. People grow older. They forgive themselves and each other, and may even come to realize that what they are forgiving themselves and each other for is youth.

But a person who dies at thirty in the middle of a messy separation remains forever fixed in the mess. To the readers of her poetry and her biography, Sylvia Plath will always be young and in a rage over Hughes's unfaithfulness. She will never reach the age when the tumults of young adulthood can be looked back upon with rueful sympathy and without anger and vengefulness. Ted Hughes has reached this age—he reached it some time ago—but he has been cheated of the peace that age brings by the posthumous fame of Plath and by the public's fascination with the story of her life. Since he was part of that life—the most interesting figure in it during its final six years—he, too, remains fixed in the chaos and confusion of its final period. Like Prometheus, whose ravaged liver was daily reconstituted so it could be daily reravaged, Hughes has had to watch his young self being picked over by biographers, scholars, critics, article writers, and newspaper journalists. Strangers who Hughes feels know nothing about his marriage to Plath write about it with proprietary authority. "I hope each of us owns the facts of her or his own life," Hughes wrote in a letter to the *Independent* in April, 1989, when he had been goaded by a particularly intrusive article. But, of course, as everyone knows who has ever heard a piece of gossip, we do not "own" the facts of our lives at all. This ownership passes out of our hands at birth, at the moment we are first observed. The organs of publicity that have proliferated in our time are only an extension and a magnification of society's fundamental and incorrigible nosiness. Our business is everybody's business, should anybody wish to make it so. The concept of privacy is a sort of screen to hide the fact that almost none is possible in a social universe. In any struggle between the public's inviolable right to be diverted and an individual's wish to be left alone, the public almost always prevails. After we are dead, the pretense that we may somehow be protected against the world's careless malice is abandoned. The branch of the law that putatively protects our good name against libel and slander withdraws from us indifferently. The dead cannot be libelled or slandered. They are without legal recourse.

Biography is the medium through which the remaining

secrets of the famous dead are taken from them and dumped out in full view of the world. The biographer at work, indeed, is like the professional burglar, breaking into a house, rifling through certain drawers that he has good reason to think contain the jewelry and money, and triumphantly bearing his loot away. The voyeurism and busybodyism that impel writers and readers of biography alike are obscured by an apparatus of scholarship designed to give the enterprise an appearance of banklike blandness and solidity. The biographer is portrayed almost as a kind of benefactor. He is seen as sacrificing years of his life to his task, tirelessly sitting in archives and libraries and patiently conducting interviews with witnesses. There is no length he will not go to, and the more his book reflects his industry the more the reader believes that he is having an elevating literary experience, rather than simply listening to backstairs gossip and reading other people's mail. The transgressive nature of biography is rarely acknowledged, but it is the only explanation for biography's status as a popular genre. The reader's amazing tolerance (which he would extend to no novel written half as badly as most biographies) makes sense only when seen as a kind of collusion between him and the biographer in an excitingly forbidden undertaking: tiptoeing down the corridor together, to stand in front of the bedroom door and try to peep through the keyhole.

Every now and then, a biography comes along that strangely displeases the public. Something causes the reader to back away from the writer and refuse to accompany him down the corridor. What the reader has usually heard in the text—what has alerted him to danger—is the sound of doubt, the sound of a crack opening in the wall of the biographer's self-assurance. As a burglar should not pause to discuss with his accomplice the rights and wrongs of burglary while he is jimmying a lock, so a biographer ought not to introduce doubts about the legitimacy of the biographical enterprise. The biography-loving public does not want to hear that biography is a flawed genre. It prefers to believe that certain biographers are bad guys.

This is what happened to Anne Stevenson, the author of a biography of Sylvia Plath called *Bitter Fame*, which is by far the most intelligent and the only aesthetically satisfying of the five biographies of Plath written to date. The other four are: *Sylvia Plath: Method and Madness* (1976), by Edward Butscher; *Sylvia Plath: A Biography* (1987), by Linda Wagner-Martin; *The Death and Life of Sylvia Plath* (1991), by Ronald Hayman; and *Rough Magic: A Biography of Sylvia Plath* (1991), by Paul Alexander. In Stevenson's book, which was published in 1989, the cracking of the wall was all too audible. *Bitter Fame* was brutally attacked, and Anne Stevenson herself was pilloried; the book became known and continues to be known in the Plath world as a "bad" book. The misdeed for which Stevenson could not be forgiven was to hesitate before the keyhole. "Any biography of Sylvia Plath written during the lifetimes of her family and friends must take their vulnerability into consideration, even if completeness suffers from it," she wrote in her preface. This is a most remarkable—in fact, a thoroughly subversive—statement for a biographer to make. To take vulnerability into consideration! To show compunction! To spare feelings! To not push as far as one can! What is the woman thinking of? The biographer's business, like the journalist's, is to satisfy the reader's curiosity, not to place limits on it. He is supposed to go out and bring back the goods—the malevolent secrets that have been quietly burning in archives and libraries and in the minds of contemporaries who have been biding their time, waiting for the biographer's knock on their doors. Some of the secrets are difficult to bring away, and some, jealously guarded by relatives, are even impossible. Relatives are the biographer's natural enemies; they are like the hostile tribes an explorer encounters and must ruthlessly subdue to claim his territory. If the relatives behave like friendly tribes, as they occasionally do—if they propose to cooperate with the biographer, even to the point of making him "official" or "authorized"—he still has to assert his authority and strut about to show that he is the big white man and they are just the naked savages. Thus, for example, when Bernard Crick agreed to be George Orwell's authorized biographer he first had to ritually bring Orwell's widow to her knees. "She agreed to my firm condition that as well as complete access to the papers, I should have an absolute and prior waiver of copyright so that I could quote what I liked and write what I liked. These were hard terms, even if the only terms on which, I think, a scholar should and can take on a contemporary biography," Crick writes with weary pride in an essay entitled "On the Difficulties of Writing Biography in General and of Orwell's in Particular." When Sonia Orwell read excerpts from Crick's manuscript and realized the worthlessness of the trinkets she had traded her territory for (her fantasy that Crick saw Orwell exactly as she saw him, and viewed her marriage to Orwell exactly as she viewed it), she tried to rescind the agreement. She could not do so, of course. Crick's statement is a model of biographical rectitude. His "hard terms" are the reader's guarantee of quality, like the standards set by the Food and Drug Administration. They assure the reader that he is getting something pure and wholesome, not something that has been tampered with.

When Anne Stevenson's biography arrived, it looked like damaged goods. The wrapping was coming undone, the label looked funny, there was no nice piece of cotton at the top of the bottle. Along with the odd statement about the book's intentional incompleteness, there was a most suspicious-looking Author's Note on the opening page. "In writing this biography, I have received a great deal of help from Olwyn Hughes," Stevenson said. (Olwyn Hughes is Ted Hughes's older sister and the former literary agent to the Plath estate.) "Ms. Hughes's contributions to the text have made it almost a work of dual authorship. I am particularly grateful for the work she did on the last four chapters and on the *Ariel* poems of the autumn of 1962." The note ended with an asterisk that led to a footnote citing exactly which poems Olwyn Hughes had done work on. As if all this weren't peculiar enough, the Author's Note in the published book differed from the Author's Note in the galleys sent to reviewers, which read, "This biography of Sylvia Plath is the result of a three-year dialogue between the author and Olwyn Hughes, agent to the Plath Estate. Ms. Hughes has contributed so liberally to the text that this is in effect a work of joint authorship."

Anne Stevenson apparently had not subdued the natives but had been captured by them and subjected to God knows what tortures. The book she had finally staggered back to civilization with was repudiated as a piece of worthless native propaganda, rather than the "truthful" and "objective" work it should have been. She was seen as having been used by Ted and Olwyn Hughes to put forward their version of Ted Hughes's relations with Plath. Hughes has been extremely reticent about his life with Plath; he has written no memoir, he gives no interviews, his writings about her work (in a number of introductions to volumes of her poetry and prose) are always about the work, and touch on biography only when it relates to the work. It evidently occurred to no one that if Hughes was indeed speaking about his marriage to Plath through Stevenson this might add to the biography's value, not decrease it.

II

WHEN I first read *Bitter Fame*, in the late summer of 1989, I knew nothing of the charged situation surrounding it, nor was I impelled by any great interest in Sylvia Plath. The book had been sent to me by its publisher, and what aroused my interest was the name Anne Stevenson. Anne had been a fellow student of mine at the University of Michigan in the 1950s. She was in the class ahead of me, and I did not know her, but I knew of her, as the daughter of an eminent and popular professor of philosophy and as a girl who was arty—who wrote poetry that appeared in *Generation*, the university's literary magazine, and who had won the Hopwood award, a serious literary prize. She had once been pointed out to me on the street: thin and pretty, with an atmosphere of awkward intensity and passion about her, gesticulating, surrounded by interesting-looking boys. In those days, I greatly admired artiness, and Anne Stevenson was one of the figures who glowed with a special incandescence in my imagination. She seemed to embody and to have come by naturally all the romantic qualities that I and my fellow fainthearted rebels against the dreariness of the Eisenhower years yearned toward, as we stumblingly, and largely unsuccessfully, attempted to live out our fantasies of nonconformity. Over the years, I watched Anne achieve the literary success she had been headed toward at Michigan. I had begun to write, too, but I did not envy or feel competitive with her: she was in a different sphere, a higher, almost sacred place—the stratosphere of poetry. Moreover, she had married an Englishman and moved to England—the England of E. M. Forster, G. B. Shaw, Max Beerbohm, Virginia Woolf, Lytton Strachey, Henry James, T. S. Eliot, D. H. Lawrence—and that only fixed her the more firmly in my imagination as a figure of literary romance. When, in the mid-seventies, I read Anne's book-length poem *Correspondences*, a kind of novel in letters, a chronicle of quiet (and sometimes not so quiet) domestic despair over several generations, my vague admiration found a sturdy object. The book showed Anne to be not only a poet of arresting technical accomplishment but a woman who had lived, and could speak about her encounters with the real in a tough, modern woman's voice. (She could also modulate it into the softer tones of nineteenth-century moral thought.)

The years passed, and one day a poem by Anne Stevenson appeared in the *Times Literary Supplement* entitled "A Legacy: On My Fiftieth Birthday." Anne was now a grand literary lady. Her poem was full of poets and editors and critics and friends and children and dogs, and its tone of intimate allusiveness evoked a society of remarkable people meeting in each other's burnished houses and talking about literature and ideas in their quiet, kind English voices. I briefly considered writing Anne a note of congratulation and identifying myself as an old Michigan schoolmate—and didn't. Her society seemed too closed, sufficient unto itself.

More years went by when I didn't hear or think about Anne Stevenson; then *Bitter Fame* brought her into my imaginative life again. I read the early chapters about Plath's childhood and adolescence and college years with pangs of rueful recognition—the three of us were almost the same age—and with a certain surprise at the accuracy and authority of Anne's evocation of what it had been like to be a young person living in America in the 1950s. How did Anne know about it? I had placed her far above and beyond the shames and humiliations and hypocrisies in which the rest of us were helplessly implicated. Evidently, she knew about them all too well. "Middle-class teenage Americans in the 1950s subscribed to an amazing code of sexual frustration," she writes, and continues:

Everything was permissible to girls in the way of intimacy except the one thing such intimacies were intended to bring about. Both partners in the ritual of experimental sex conceded that "dating" went something like this: preliminary talking and polite mutual inspection led to dancing, which often shifted into "necking," which—assuming continuous progress—concluded in the quasi-masturbation of "petting" on the family sofa, or, in more affluent circumstances, in the back seat of a car. Very occasionally intercourse might, inadvertently, take place; but as a rule, if the partners went to the same school or considered themselves subject to the same moral pressures, they stopped just short of it.

When writing of how Plath, in her senior year at Smith, daringly matriculated from petting to sleeping with her boyfriends, and deceived her mother about her activities, Anne is moved to observe: "Many women who, like myself, were students in America in the 1950s will remember duplicities of this kind. Sylvia's double standard was quite usual, as was the acceptable face she assumed in letters to her mother. My own letters home of the time were not dissimilar."

The early chapters of *Bitter Fame* pulled me back into a period that I still find troubling to recall, precisely because duplicity was so closely woven into its fabric. We lied to our parents and we lied to each other and we lied to ourselves, so addicted to deception had we become. We were an uneasy, shifty-eyed generation. Only a few of us could see how it was with us. When Ted Hughes writes about the struggle of Plath's "true self" to emerge from her false one, he is surely writing about a historical as well as a personal crisis. The nineteenth century came to an end in America only in the 1960s; the desperate pretense that the two World Wars had left the world as unchanged as the Boer War had left it was finally stripped away by the sexual revolution, the women's movement, the civil rights movement, the environmental movement, the Vietnam War protests. Sylvia Plath and Anne Stevenson and I came of age in the period when the need to keep up the pretense was especially strong: no one was pre-pared—least of all the shaken returning G.I.'s—to face the post-Hiroshima and post-Auschwitz world. At the end of her life, Plath looked, with unnerving steadiness, at the Gorgon; her late poems name and invoke the bomb and the death camps. She was able—she had been elected—to confront what most of the rest of us fearfully shrank from. "For good-ness sake, stop being so *frightened* of everything, Mother!" she wrote to Aurelia Plath in October, 1962. "Almost every other word in your letter is 'frightened.'" In the same letter she said:

> Now stop trying to get me to write about "decent coura-geous people"—read the *Ladies' Home Journal* for those! It's too bad my poems frighten you—but you've always been afraid of reading or seeing the world's hardest things—like Hiroshima, the Inquisition or Belsen.

But Plath's engagement with "the world's hardest things" came only just before she killed herself. (Robert Lowell wrote in his introduction to *Ariel*, "This poetry and life are not a career; they tell that life, even when disciplined, is simply not worth it.") The history of her life—as it has now been told in the five biographies and in innumerable essays and critical studies—is a signature story of the fearful, double-faced fif-ties. Plath embodies in a vivid, almost emblematic way the schizoid character of the period. She is the divided self par excellence. The taut surrealism of the late poems and the slack, girls'-book realism of her life (as rendered by Plath's biographers and by her own autobiographical writings) are grotesquely incongruous. The photographs of Plath as a vac-uous girl of the fifties, with dark lipstick and blond hair, add to one's sense of the jarring disparity between the life and the work. In *Bitter Fame*, writing with the affectionate asperity of a sibling, Anne Stevenson draws a portrait of Plath as a highly self-involved and confused, unstable, driven, perfectionistic, rather humorless young woman, whose suicide remains a mystery, as does the source of her art, and who doesn't add up.

As I read the book, certain vague, dissatisfied thoughts I had had while reading other biographies began to come into sharper focus. It was only later, when the bad report of the book had spread and I had learned about some of the circumstances of its writing, that I understood why it gave the sense of being as much about the problems of biographical writing as about Sylvia Plath. At the time, I thought that it was Sylvia Plath herself who was mischievously subverting the biographer's project. The many voices in which the dead girl spoke—the voices of the journals, of her letters, of *The Bell Jar*, of the short stories, of the early poems, of the *Ariel* poems—mocked the whole idea of biographical narrative. The more Anne Stevenson fleshed out Plath's biography with quotations from her writings, the thinner, paradoxically, did her own narrative seem. The voices began to take over the book and to speak to the reader over the biographer's head. They whispered, "Listen to me, not to her. I am authentic. I speak with authority. Go to the full texts of the journals, the letters home, and the rest. They will tell you what you want to know." These voices were joined by another chorus—that of people who had actually known Plath. These, too, said, "Don't listen to Anne Stevenson. She didn't know Sylvia. I knew Sylvia. Let me tell you about her. Read my correspondence with her. Read my memoir." Three of these voices were particularly loud—those of Lucas Myers, Dido Merwin, and Richard Murphy, who had written memoirs of Plath and Hughes that appeared as appendixes in *Bitter Fame*. One of them, Merwin's, entitled "Vessel of Wrath," rose to the pitch of a shriek. The memoir caused a sensation: it was deplored because of its intemperateness.

Dido Merwin couldn't stand Plath, and had waited thirty years to tell the world what she thought of her former "friend," depicting her as the unbearable wife of a long-suffering martyr. According to Merwin, the wonder was not that Hughes left Plath but that he "stuck it out as long as he did." After the separation, Merwin writes, she asked Hughes "what had been hardest to take during the time he and Sylvia were together," and he revealed that Plath, in a fit of jealous rage, had torn into small pieces all his work in progress of the winter of 1961, as well as his copy of Shakespeare. Merwin also recalls as if it had happened yesterday a disastrous visit that Plath and Hughes paid her and her then husband, the poet W. S. Merwin, at their farmhouse, in the Dordogne. Plath "used up all the hot water, repeatedly helped herself from the fridge (breakfasting on what one had planned to serve for lunch, etc.), and rearranged the furniture in their bedroom." She cast such a pall with her sulking (though her appetite never diminished, Merwin notes, as she tells of balefully watching Plath attack a fine foie gras "for all the world as though it were 'Aunt Dot's meat loaf'") that Hughes had to cut the visit short. Anne Stevenson was heavily criticized for giving an "unbalanced" idea of Plath by including this venomous portrait in her biography.

In fact, where Anne Stevenson made her mistake of balance was not in including such a negative view of Plath but in including such a subversively lively piece of writing. The limitations of biographical writing are never more evident than when one turns from it to writing in another genre; and when, led by a footnote, I turned from the text of *Bitter Fame* to Dido Merwin's memoir I felt as if I had been freed from prison. The hushed cautiousness, the solemn weighing of

"evidence," the humble "she must have felt"s and "he probably thought"s of biographical writing had given way to a
high-spirited subjectivity. Writing in her own voice as her
own person, fettered by no rules of epistemological deport-
ment, Dido could let rip. She knew exactly how she felt and
what she thought. The contrast between the omniscient narrator of *Bitter Fame*, whose mantle of pallid judiciousness
Anne Stevenson was obliged to wear, and the robustly intemperate "I" of the Merwin memoir is striking. Merwin's portrait of Plath is a self-portrait of Merwin, of course. It is she,
rather than Plath, who emerges, larger than life, from "Vessel
of Wrath," and whose obliterating vividness led readers into
their error of questioning Anne Stevenson's motives.

III

THE FIRST of the bad reviews of *Bitter Fame*—a powerful harbinger—appeared in the September 28, 1989,
issue of *The New York Review of Books* and was by the English
writer A. Alvarez. Alvarez was a logical choice to review *Bitter
Fame*. He was one of the first people in England to recognize
Plath's talent and, as poetry editor of the *Observer* in the sixties, he had published several of her poems. In 1971, he had
himself written a memoir of Plath; it appeared as the first
chapter of *The Savage God*, a book he wrote about suicide, and
it was the first account in print to give details of Plath's death.
Like Dido Merwin's memoir—like every memoir—Alvarez's
is a work of autobiography, though what Merwin does naïvely
and unwittingly he does artfully and consciously. He works
his recollections of Plath into a kind of allegory of suicidal
drive; the depression and disorder of his own life (he tells us
he swallowed forty-five sleeping pills a decade earlier) are

fused with and metaphorized by the last act of her life, when she gambled with fate—as Alvarez characterizes it, and as he himself did—and lost. Alvarez argues, giving chilling details, that Plath meant to be found and saved, and that she died only because of a freakish series of accidents. His argument is compelling and horrifying.

But it is a second narrative, a sort of sub-allegory, that gives Alvarez's memoir its high verve and also its status as a foundation text of the Plath legend. This is the narrative of the flow of power between husband and wife—the story of how, during the two years of his acquaintance with Plath and Hughes, Alvarez watched power go from one to the other, like water poured from one pitcher into another. At first, the husband was the full vessel. "This was Ted's time," Alvarez writes about Hughes when he first met him, in London, in the spring of 1960; Hughes's second book of poems, *Lupercal*, had just appeared and Alvarez thought it "the best book by a young poet that I had read since I began my stint on the *Observer*." Alvarez goes on to describe the poet himself: "He was a tall, strong-looking man in a black corduroy jacket, black trousers, black shoes; his dark hair hung untidily forward; he had a long, witty mouth. He was in command." In contrast, he says, Plath was just a banal little housewife, "briskly American: bright, clean, competent, like a young woman in a cookery advertisement." Alvarez didn't notice her very much then. He reports an embarrassing moment when, as he and Hughes were going out the door (the two of them would take walks or go to the pub, while Plath stayed home), Plath shyly stopped him and mentioned a poem of hers that he had accepted for publication in the *Observer* the previous year. At first, Alvarez didn't know what she was talking about—he simply didn't connect the bright, clean housewife with the world of poetry, and hadn't known that her writing name was Plath. Later that year, when Plath's first book of poems, *The*

Colossus, was published in England, Alvarez reviewed it for the *Observer.* "It seemed to fit the image I had of her: serious, gifted, withheld, and still partly under the massive shadow of her husband," he writes in his memoir. He praised Plath's poems for their technical proficiency but felt that something was being held back: "Beneath most of the poems was a sense of resources and disturbances not yet tapped."

Alvarez went to America to teach for a term, and when he returned to London, in February of 1961, his relationship with the couple attenuated: "Ted had fallen out of love with London and was fretting to get away; Sylvia had been ill— first a miscarriage, then appendicitis—and I had my own problems, a divorce." When he saw them next, in June, 1962, they were living in Devon, in Court Green, an old manor house with a thatched roof and a cobbled courtyard and a big wild garden and orchard, next to a twelfth-century church. It was now Sylvia's time, Alvarez reports:

> They had had a new baby in January, a boy [Nicholas], and Sylvia had changed. No longer quiet and withheld, a housewifely appendage to a powerful husband, she seemed made solid and complete, her own woman again. Perhaps the birth of a son had something to do with this new confident air. But there was a sharpness and clarity about her that seemed to go beyond that. It was she who showed me around the house and the garden; the electric gadgets, the freshly painted rooms, the orchard . . . were *her* property.

And Ted: he "seemed content to sit back and play with little Frieda [his two-year-old daughter], who clung to him dependently." Alvarez adds, a little nervously, "Since it appeared to be a strong, close marriage, I suppose he was unconcerned that the balance of power had shifted for the time being to her."

By the fall of 1962, the strong, close marriage had failed, and Hughes had moved back to London. Plath remained in Devon with the children, travelling to London from time to time on literary business. She began to visit Alvarez regularly in his studio, a converted stable in Hampstead, and read to him from her new work. Alvarez was now more Plath's friend than Hughes's. He parts the curtain and permits us a glimpse of himself and Plath in the studio:

> [It] was beautiful in its crumbling way, but uncomfortable; there was nothing to lounge on—only spidery Windsor chairs and a couple of rugs on the blood-red uncarpeted lino. I poured her a drink and she settled in front of the coal stove on one of the rugs, like a student, very much at her ease, sipping whiskey and making the ice clink in her glass.

The poems that Plath read to Alvarez were the poems that are now taught in literature courses—"Ariel," "Lady Lazarus," "Daddy," "The Applicant," "Fever 103°," the bee poems, "A Birthday Present"—and their destructive and unforgiving force, he reports, so shook him that to maintain his equilibrium he resorted to small, picky criticisms; one that he now particularly regrets was of a line in "Lady Lazarus," which Plath took out at his suggestion. After the reading of the poetry and Alvarez's criticism of it, the talk would become more personal. "Perhaps because I was also a member of the club," Alvarez writes, Plath told him about her first suicide attempt, in the summer of 1953 (she, too, had swallowed a bottleful of sleeping pills), and about a more recent incident of driving her car off the road. Another bond between the critic and the poet was Plath's admiration of an introduction Alvarez had written for a Penguin anthology called *The New Poetry*, "in which," he says, "I had attacked the British poets' nervous preference for gentility above all else, and their avoidance of the uncomfortable, destructive truths both of the inner life and of the present time."

However, the relationship between the critic and the poet did not go where it seemed to be going. Alvarez backed off from Plath. "She must have felt I was stupid and insensitive. Which I was," he writes of their last meeting, on Christmas Eve of 1962, less than two months before her death. "But to have been otherwise would have meant accepting responsibilities I didn't want and couldn't, in my own depression, have coped with." By this time, Plath, too, had left Devon for London, and was living on Fitzroy Road in a flat that Alvarez found chillingly orderly and austere. She had invited him for dinner, but he was engaged elsewhere and only stopped in for a drink. "When I left about eight o'clock to go on to my dinner party, I knew I had let her down in some final and unforgivable way. And I knew she knew. I never again saw her alive."

Alvarez's memoir set the tone for the writing about Plath and Hughes that was to follow; it erected the structure on which the narrative of Plath as an abandoned and mistreated woman and Hughes as a heartless betrayer was to be strung. Although Alvarez is extremely discreet and gives no details of Hughes and Plath's separation—about which, in fact, he knew a great deal—it is not hard to read his self-castigation as a veiled accusation against Hughes, whose rejection of Plath was, after all, much more profoundly final and unforgivable. The ordeal of Ted Hughes could be said to date from the publication of Alvarez's memoir in *The Savage God* and its serialization in the *Observer*. Hughes was immediately aware of the destructive power of the piece, and he succeeded in getting the second half of the memoir pulled from the *Observer*, but he could do nothing about its appearance in *The Savage God*, or about its subsequent influence.

Once the plot of the suicidal poetess and her abandon-
ment by the man with the witty mouth was released into the
world, there would be no end to the variations played on it,
or to Hughes's burial alive in each of its retellings. When *Bitter Fame* appeared, declaring that it would "dispel the posthumous miasma of fantasy, rumor, politics, and ghoulish gossip"
that was feeding Plath's "perverse legend," it was hardly surprising that the book was not greeted with open arms. The
world likes to hold on to its fantasy, rumor, politics, and
ghoulish gossip, not dispel them, and nobody wanted to hear
that it was Hughes who was good and Plath who was bad.
The pleasure of hearing ill of the dead is not a negligible one,
but it pales before the pleasure of hearing ill of the living.
Given the task of reviewing a book whose declared object was
to dismantle the narrative that he himself had set in motion,
Alvarez could hardly have been expected to look upon it fa-
vorably. He raked over *Bitter Fame*, and when he was finished
there were three bad guys where previously only one had
stood: to Ted Hughes were now added Anne Stevenson and
Olwyn Hughes. An ancillary narrative was born of Alvarez's
review—the narrative of the corrupt biographer and the evil
sister.

IV

THE ground had been prepared for this narrative by the
biography of Plath written by Linda Wagner-Martin, a
professor of English then at Michigan State University. The
chief interest of this book, which is written in a style as
blandly unpretentious as a young girl's diary ("Dick had gone
to Florida during spring break, he and Perry had just taken a

trip to Maine, and now he was going to Arizona. In contrast, she stayed in Wellesley and mowed the grass"), is its preface, in which Wagner-Martin boldly speaks out about her unhappy dealings with the Plath estate:

> When I began researching this biography in 1982, I contacted Olwyn Hughes, who is literary executor of the Sylvia Plath estate. Olwyn was initially cooperative, and helped me in my research by answering questions herself and referring me to others who could be of assistance. As Olwyn read the later chapters of the book, however, and particularly after she read a draft of the manuscript in 1986, her cooperation diminished substantially. Olwyn wrote me at great length, usually in argument with my views about the life and development of Plath. Ted Hughes responded to a reading of the manuscript in draft form in 1986 with suggestions for changes that filled fifteen pages and would have meant a deletion of more than 15,000 words.
>
> Of necessity I continued to correspond with Olwyn Hughes in order to obtain permission to quote at length from Plath's works. But on every occasion Olwyn objected to the manuscript, frequently citing Ted Hughes's comments (although, as mentioned earlier, Ted Hughes refused to be interviewed directly for the book). I did make many changes in response to these comments. However, the requests for changes continued, and I concluded that permissions would be granted only if I agreed to change the manuscript to reflect the Hugheses' points of view. When I realized that this tactic would continue indefinitely, I had to end my attempt to gain permission to quote at length if I was ever to publish this book. As a result of this circumstance, I have had to limit quotations. Consequently, this biography contains less of Plath's writing than I had intended. The alternative would have been to agree to suggestions that would have changed the point of view of this book appreciably.

In his review of *Bitter Fame* Alvarez quotes this passage, holding it up as the "typical" experience of unauthorized biographers of Plath. He commends the plucky Linda Wagner-Martin for standing up to the estate and writing "a mildly feminist but otherwise careful and evenhanded account of the life" (note the "but"), and rendering an "admiring and forgiving" portrait. The supine Anne Stevenson, in contrast, is censured for caving in under the pressure of the evil sister and writing a book that Alvarez sees as "more than 350 pages of disparagement." Of the Dido Merwin memoir in the appendix, Alvarez writes that it is "a work of sustained and quite astonishing venom and what is most tasteless about it is not that it should have been written about someone who can no longer defend herself but that it should be published in a biography commissioned and approved by the Plath estate." As in his own memoir of Plath, Alvarez once again presents Ted Hughes as a recessive figure, about whom he elaborately speaks no ill but who is damned by his very recessiveness. Since "Ted Hughes has steadfastly refused to be involved in the biographical wrangling," Alvarez writes, Plath, the defenseless dead woman, has been left abandoned to the mercies of the cruel Olwyn. Once again, Hughes has evaporated when Plath needed him most, and once again Alvarez has stepped in to play the role of Plath's champion and (as it proved) Hughes's nemesis.

What Alvarez left delicately unsaid but hovering in the air was quickly picked up by other reviewers of *Bitter Fame* and run into the ground. In one of the crassest of the post-Alvarez reviews, in the November 10, 1989, *Independent*, Ronald Hayman wrote, "At the core of this vindictive book are two strategies. One is to lay the blame for the breakup of the marriage squarely on Sylvia Plath by depicting her behaviour as so consistently outrageous that no husband could have put up with it for long, while Ted Hughes is characterised as patient, generous, warm, innocent, reluctant to be unfaithful. The other strategy is to undermine her poetic achievement by representing her verse as negative, sick, death-oriented, and comparing it unfavorably with his." Hayman complained:

> There is also very little about Assia Wevill, the woman for whom Ted Hughes left Sylvia Plath. We are given the impression that the only relevant conversations between husband and wife were two in which Plath ordered Hughes out of the house, and we are told Assia said her affair with him would never have begun "had Sylvia behaved differently." This conflicts with the impression formed by many of the people who knew them, and it ignores the account given in a privately published memoir by Professor Trevor Thomas, who lived in the flat underneath and was the last man to see Sylvia alive. Calling Assia a Jezebel, a scarlet woman, she told the professor [Assia] had stolen her husband.

Hayman continued:

> Nor is there any reason to doubt [Thomas's] account of meetings with Ted Hughes, who blamed him for locking the front door, "so they couldn't get in and save my wife." On the day of the funeral a party was held in the flat with records and bongo drums. Later on, Assia, whom [Thomas] describes as "a very beautiful woman," told him that Hughes had been so distressed that "some of us decided to have a party to surprise him and cheer him up when he got back home."

"Fantasy, rumor, politics, and ghoulish gossip" are represented here in their most unconstrained and ugly guise. As it happens, there is every reason to doubt Trevor Thomas's account, and when Ted Hughes challenged its veracity before an organization called the Press Council he was upheld (the *Independent* published a correction and apology), and when he brought legal action against Thomas he similarly prevailed. (Thomas died on May 27, 1993.) But the harm was done— or redone. The narrative of the faithless, heartless Hughes and his Jezebel could not be dislodged. *Bitter Fame*, far from altering the old image of Hughes, only entrenched it further in the public imagination. The patient got sicker from the attempted cure. The doctors (who had already quarrelled, as doctors do in hopeless cases) withdrew in disarray. Deep pathologies of biography and of journalism began to fuse, and to engender virulent new strains of the bacillus of bad faith. As a susceptible member of the journalist tribe myself, I began to feel the early symptoms of infection: the familiar stirrings of reportorial desire.

In December, 1989, I wrote to Ted Hughes, in care of his sister (as I had been told to do by his publisher), and asked him for an interview, saying, among other things, that I thought of the Plath biographical situation as a kind of allegory of the problem of biography in general. By return post I received a long letter from Olwyn Hughes. I read it in wonder and awe. We all move through the world surrounded by an atmosphere that is unique to us and by which we may be recognized as clearly as by our faces. Some of us, however, have thicker atmospheres than others, and a few of us have an atmosphere of such opacity that it hides us entirely from view—we seem to be nothing but our atmosphere. Olwyn Hughes is like this. Her letter was that of a person so intensely preoccupied and so passionately aggrieved that she simply could not be bothered to explain what she was talking about. She just hurtled headlong into her subject, "the myth of Sylvia Plath," and I was left to follow her or not—it was all the same to her. She wasn't there to persuade me; she was there to once again set down what she *knew* to be true. Olwyn wrote:

> Your letter of 3 December came to me—and I thought a few points listed below could be useful to your proposed article. I'm forwarding your letter to Ted.
>
> I don't quite know what the peculiar biographing of Plath is an allegory for. Personally, after the ravages of the myth I am no longer astonished (as I once was) by—say—the Pasternak Soviet Writers' Union "trial," or the formation of any Nazi-type group that sees the whole of existence in its own patently cranky terms. People are monstrous, stupid, and dishonest. If there is a bandwagon, the most unexpected people are only too happy to close down eyes, ears, and brain and get on it. . . .
>
> The myth was created by the following amalgam: Sylvia's own version of herself and her situation, and of other situations after the separation. This was dictated by her paranoid mechanism (or whatever was wrong with her), perfected in small ways over the years. Toward the end, her remarks about others were little more than lies, designed to elicit maximum sympathy and approval toward herself. PLUS her mother's attitude throughout. Endlessly supportive of what she knew to be a frail craft during Sylvia's life, she continued this after her death: one must only see Sylvia's "best side." This sentimentalizing hypocrisy, forgivable in a mother, was largely supported by Ted Hughes, if only in silence, as he greatly pitied Mrs. Plath and the hammering she took after publication of *Bell Jar* and some of the poems. It's my belief that if Mrs. Plath had said, when Sylvia died, "She suffered from mental illness, but was a marvellous person and I loved her" the myth would never have happened. Unfortunately, Mrs. Plath was ashamed of the mental illness—it has never been made clear, for instance, just how very ill Sylvia was with her first breakdown. . . .
>
> Then came the glowing memoirs—those of Al Alvarez,

Elizabeth Compton (now Sigmund), and Clarissa Roche particularly. All had in common that their friendship with Plath had been slight. (Though she had real interest in Alvarez, they met only half a dozen times.) As no other of Plath's friends would talk to the flood of journalists, would-be biographers, etc., etc., these three—the ladies particularly—had the field to themselves, from Butscher's biography up to the present one. Roche and Sigmund now pronounce regally on anything to do with Plath as her great friends. . . .

Stevenson's is certainly the first biography worthy of the name. Linda Wagner-Martin's was much improved, though much thinned down, by my requiring her to substantiate the unbelievable . . . rubbish she had in earlier drafts. Because she finally published when I was still awaiting a "final draft" there are new gobbets, as well as shadows from this earlier nonsense, still in her book. . . .

What has been amazingly lacking is any human feeling for the people who had the tragedy of Sylvia's death at first hand as part of their own lives—Aurelia, Ted, and her children. It's totally changed my entire attitude to people. An extraordinarily interesting experience, following it all, but finally horrifying and unforgivable.

If I was surprised by the length and vehemence of Olwyn's letter, I was not surprised by the fact of hearing from her rather than from Hughes. Of course, I thought. Over the years that Ted Hughes has been trying to escape from his narrativizing pursuers, his sister has done just the opposite. As literary agent of the Plath estate, a position she assumed in the mid-sixties and resigned from in 1991, Olwyn has had dealings with everyone who has wanted to write about Plath, presenting herself as a kind of Sphinx or Turandot before whom the various supplicants must appear—and invariably come to grief. She is also famous for her letters to editors and for the comments she regularly makes to journalists following the appearance of new writings about Plath and Hughes; these, too, display her strange fierceness and discursiveness. Her two roles fit uneasily together: Sphinxes and Turandots don't usually write letters to editors or talk to journalists. They bar, they forbid, they slay; they don't volunteer. After three and a half years of acquaintance with Olwyn—of meetings, telephone conversations, and correspondence—I cannot say I know her much better than I did when she first appeared to me in her letter. But I have never seen anything in her of the egotism, narcissism, and ambition that usually characterize the person who welcomes journalistic notice in the belief that he can beat the odds and gain control of the narrative. Olwyn seems motivated purely by an instinct to protect her younger brother's interests and uphold the honor of the family, and she pursues this aim with reckless selflessness. Her frantic activity makes one think of a mother quail courageously flying into the face of a predator to divert him from the chicks scurrying to safety. The journalist whose talons are closing around her cannot but be stirred by the woman's fierce loyalty and love—and cannot help wondering about the emotions of the man for whom she is sacrificing herself, as he observes it from his cover.

V

IN 1971, in *The New York Review of Books*, Elizabeth Hardwick wrote of Plath that "she has the rarity of being, in her work at least, never a 'nice person.'" Hardwick put her finger on the quality that so arrested readers of *Ariel* when it first came out (in England in 1965, and in America in 1966), and continues to arrest us today. Plath's not-niceness is the outstanding characteristic of the *Ariel* poems, it is what sets her apart from the other so-called confessional poets of the fifties and sixties, it is the note of the "true self" that Hughes celebrates. Her status as a feminist heroine has in large part derived from this tone. Women honor her for her courage to be unpleasant. "Every woman adores a Fascist," Plath wrote in "Daddy"—meaning a male Fascist. But women have adored Plath for the Fascist in her, for the "boot in the face" that, even as she writes of male oppression, she herself viciously administers to readers of both sexes. Though *The Bell Jar* hasn't the art of the late poems, its tone is still bracingly not-nice. (Had she lived, Plath might have developed into a first-rank novelist; *The Bell Jar* might have been to her mature fiction what "The Colossus" is to her mature poetry.) The novel is an indictment of the fifties in America. It chronicles the breakdown and suicide attempt and "recovery" of its heroine, Esther Greenwood, and is narrated by Esther in a voice that has all the disdain of the voice of *Ariel*, if not its chilly beauty and authority. The book has a surface puerility, a deceptive accessibility: it reads like a girls' book. But it is a girls' book written by a woman who has been to hell and back and wants to revenge herself on her tormentors. It is a girls' book filled with poison, vomit, blood, and volts of electricity (the electrocution of the Rosenbergs and Esther's horrifyingly powerful shock treatments are mordantly linked), and peopled by creepy men and pathetic older women.

The Bell Jar is a fictionalized account of Plath's own breakdown and shock therapy and suicide attempt in 1953, and Plath did not want the originals of her unlovely characters—particularly her mother—to read the book. Esther's mother is rendered with deft mercilessness. "My mother took care never to tell me to do anything," Esther caustically observes. "She would only reason with me sweetly, like one intelligent mature person with another." Also examined and found wanting in every respect are, among others, Olive Higgins Prouty, the author of *Stella Dallas*, who was Plath's benefactor (she was the sponsor of Plath's freshman scholarship at Smith, paid for her hospitalization after her suicide attempt, and became a lifelong friend of Aurelia's); Plath's college boyfriend, Dick Norton; and his mother. Plath therefore published the book under the pseudonym Victoria Lucas. In January of 1963, after two American publishers had turned it down, it came out in England under that name and then, after her suicide, under her own name. When *The Bell Jar* was finally scheduled for publication in America, in 1971, Aurelia Plath was beside herself. In a letter to the publisher she wrote:

> Practically every character in *The Bell Jar* represents someone—often in caricature—whom Sylvia loved; each person had given freely of time, thought, affection, and, in one case, financial help during those agonizing six months of breakdown in 1953. . . . As this book stands by itself, it represents the basest ingratitude.

The shade of Plath must have read these words with a mocking and rather satisfied smile. Mrs. Plath giving freely of time is indistinguishable from Mrs. Greenwood reasoning sweetly. However, Mrs. Plath didn't end matters there. In 1975, to make good her claim that the not-nice persona of *Ariel* and *The Bell Jar* was Plath's sick "false self," and that her healthy "real self" was a kindly, "service-oriented" good girl, she asked for and received permission from Ted Hughes, Plath's literary executor, to publish a book of Plath's letters to her written between 1950 and 1963. The idea was to show that Plath was not the hateful, hating ingrate, the changeling of *Ariel* and *The Bell Jar*, but a loving, obedient daughter. The shade's smile of satisfaction must have faded when the letters appeared, in a volume called *Letters Home*. "Mother, *how could you?*" would be any daughter's anguished response to an act of treachery like the publication of these letters: letters sloppily written, effusive, regressive; letters written habitually, compulsively, sometimes more than one a day; letters sent in the secure knowledge that they were for a mother's uncritical eyes alone. It is one thing when some "publishing scoundrel" somehow gets hold of a cache of your most private and unpremeditated letters after your death and prints them, and another when your own mother hands you over to posterity in your stained bathrobe and unwashed face; it is quite beyond endurance, in fact. It seems simply never to have occurred to Mrs. Plath that the persona of *Ariel* and *The Bell Jar* was the persona by which Plath wished to be represented and remembered—that she wrote this way for publication because this was the way she wished to be perceived, and that the face she showed her mother was not the face she wished to show the reading public. One cannot blame the poor woman for her innocence. When a child commits suicide, the parents may be forgiven anything they do to dull their pain, even (or perhaps especially) acts of unconscious aggression.

The publication of *Letters Home* had a different effect from the one Mrs. Plath had intended, however. Instead of showing that Sylvia wasn't "like that," the letters caused the reader to consider for the first time the possibility that her sick relationship with her mother was the reason she *was* like that. Previously, the death of Plath's father, Otto (a German-born professor of entomology, who died when she was barely eight), had been thought of as the shadow-event of her life, the wound from which she never recovered. But now it looked as if the key to Plath's tragedy might all along have lain buried in the mother-daughter relationship. What Plath, with an artist's indirection, had only suggested about its pathology (in such poems as "The Disquieting Muses" and "Medusa" as well as in *The Bell Jar*) now leaped off the pages of *Letters Home*. In the last line of "Medusa"—a poem in the form of a daughter's angry speech to a mother—Plath writes, with chilling double meaning, "There is nothing between us." The crushing too-closeness of Sylvia and her mother (and its concomitant terrifying alienation) is everywhere documented in *Letters Home*. Critical commentary about the unnatural bond between mother and daughter (Harriet Rosenstein and Lynda Bundtzen are among the most distinguished contributors to this literature) could hardly have cheered Mrs. Plath. But something even more momentous than her painful miscalculation—her utter failure to convince the world of how wonderful everything was with Sylvia and between her and Sylvia—resulted from the publication of *Letters Home*. This was the release into the world of a flood of information about Plath and the people in her life, most notably Ted Hughes—a flood that could be likened to an oil spill in the devastation it wreaked among Plath's survivors, who to this day are like birds covered with black ooze. Before the publication of *Letters Home*, the Plath legend was brief and contained, a taut, austere stage drama set in a few bleak, sparsely furnished rooms. Alvarez's artful memoir established its anxious tone and adumbrated its potential as a feminist parable. Now the legend opened out, to become a vast, sprawling movie-novel filmed on sets of the most consummate and particularized realism: period clothing, furniture, and kitchen appliances; real food; a cast of characters headed by a Doris Dayish Plath (a tall Doris Day who "wrote") and a Laurence Olivier–Heathcliffish Hughes. In exposing her daughter's letters to the world's scrutiny, Mrs. Plath not only violated Plath's writer's privacy but also handed Plath herself over to the world as an object to be familiarly passed from hand to hand. Now everyone could feel that he "knew" Plath—and, of course, Hughes as well. Hughes had retained the right of final approval of the book, and he was criticized for its editing; it was felt that he had taken out too much, that there were too many ellipses. But in fact *Letters Home* is remarkable not for what it leaves out about Hughes but for what it leaves in.

Plath's hysterically ecstatic letters to her mother about Hughes when she first fell in love with him and her only slightly calmer ones during the good years of the marriage give us—even with the elisions—a remarkably close look at the man. Of course, it is Plath's vision of him that we receive—other people who knew Hughes at the time have suggested that her version is a reflection of her tendency toward exaggeration and excess—but it is one we cannot easily erase. With the instincts of the novelist she was trying to become, Plath drew Hughes's character for her mother with a few sure, bold, stylized strokes. He makes his first appearance in a letter of March 3, 1956:

> Met, by the way, a brilliant ex-Cambridge poet at the wild *St. Botolph's Review* party last week; will probably never see him again (he works for J. Arthur Rank in London), but wrote my best poem about him afterwards—the only man I've met yet here who'd be strong enough to be equal with— such is life.

On April 17, she writes:

> The most shattering thing is that in the last two months I have fallen terribly in love, which can only lead to great hurt. I met the strongest man in the world, ex-Cambridge, brilliant poet whose work I loved before I met him, a large, hulking, healthy Adam, half French half Irish, with a voice like the thunder of God—a singer, story-teller, lion and world-wanderer, a vagabond who will never stop.

April 19:

I shall tell you now about something most miraculous and thundering and terrifying and wish you to think on it and share some of it. It is this man, this poet, this Ted Hughes. I have never known anything like it. For the first time in my life I can use *all* my knowing and laughing and force and writing to the hilt all the time, everything, and you should see him, hear him!

He has a health and hugeness . . . the more he writes poems, the more he writes poems. He knows all about the habits of animals and takes me amid cows and coots. I am writing poems, and they are better and stronger than anything I have ever done.

April 29:

Ted is incredible, mother . . . wears always the same black sweater and corduroy jacket with pockets full of poems, fresh trout and horoscopes. . . . He stalked in the door yesterday with a packet of little pink shrimp and four fresh trout. I made a nectar of Shrimp Newburg with essence of butter, cream, sherry and cheese; had it on rice with the trout. It took us three hours to peel all the little tiny shrimp, and Ted just lay groaning by the hearth after the meal with utter delight, like a huge Goliath.

His humor is the salt of the earth.

May 3:

I feel that all my life, all my pain and work has been for this one thing. All the blood spilt, the words written, the people loved, have been a work to fit me for loving. . . . I see the power and voice in him that will shake the world alive.

Ted has written many virile, deep banging poems.

Plath and Hughes were married on June 16, 1956, and Plath continued to write to Mrs. Plath about the "rugged, kind, magnificent man, who has no scrap of false vanity or tendency to toady to inferior strategic officials," and whose mind is "magnificent, not hair-splitting or suavely politic." When Hughes took a job teaching at a boys' school, Plath wrote of her hulking Adam, "They must really admire him; he is such a strong, fascinating person, compared to the other sissy teachers they get," and five years later, when Plath had an appendectomy and Hughes came to the hospital bringing "huge rare steak sandwiches," Plath wrote, "He is an absolute angel. To see him come in at visiting hours, about twice as tall as all the little, stumpy people, with his handsome, kind, smiling face is the most beautiful sight in the world to me."

In Plath's journals, the representation of Hughes as an overgrown Adonis/Aryan superman is the same, although the voice of the journal writer is a different one, often sharper and darker than that of the letter-home writer. On February 26, 1956, Plath set down a now famous account of her first meeting with Hughes at the *St. Botolph's Review* party that she wistfully ("will probably never see him again" wrote about to her mother. In the journal Plath tells of drinking and talking too loud and dancing and getting drunk. Then:

> That big, dark, hunky boy, the only one there huge enough for me, who had been hunching around over women, and whose name I had asked the minute I had come into the room, but no one told me, came over and was looking hard in my eyes and it was Ted Hughes.

Hughes takes Plath to a back room, and

> bang the door was shut and he was sloshing brandy into a glass and I was sloshing it at the place where my mouth was when I last knew about it. . . .

> And I was stamping and he was stamping on the floor, and
> then he kissed me bang smash on the mouth [omission]. . . .
> And when he kissed my neck I bit him long and hard on the
> cheek, and when we came out of the room, blood was run-
> ning down his face. [Omission.] And I screamed in myself,
> thinking: oh, to give myself crashing, fighting, to you.

I quote the passage as it appears in the published *Journals*. A
fuller text—in which Hughes, along with kissing Plath, rips
off her red hairband and pockets her silver earrings—was
subsequently published elsewhere and is held up as proof of
Hughes's self-servingly suppressive editing. But even in its
censored version the passage is extraordinarily intimate, and
one can only wonder why Hughes permitted any part of it to
be published. In fact, if he was so keen to preserve his privacy
why did he sanction the publication of *Letters Home* and *The
Journals* at all?

An unpublished letter that Hughes wrote to Mrs. Plath
seven years after Sylvia Plath's death offers a possible answer.
The letter is in the Plath archive in the Lilly Library, at Indiana University at Bloomington—a huge repository of letters
by Plath and to her, as well as family correspondence written
after her death. (Mrs. Plath sold this collection to the Lilly in
1977.) In the letter, dated March 24, 1970, Hughes tells Mrs.
Plath of a house that he wants to buy on the North Coast of
Devon—"an unbelievably beautiful place"—for which, however, he hasn't the money. He doesn't want to sell a house he
bought recently in Yorkshire ("a first class investment"), nor
does he want ("for sentimental as they say reasons") to sell
Court Green, which he moved back into with the children
after Plath's death (and where he lives now, with his second
wife, Carol). "Therefore," he tells Mrs. Plath, "I am trying to
cash all my other assets and one that comes up is *The Bell
Jar*." He asks Mrs. Plath how she would "feel about U.S. pub-

lication of this now," adding that in a few years the book will "hardly be saleable," a mere "curiosity for students." Mrs. Plath, of course, hated the book, and she wrote Hughes a strong letter of protest: she does not want *The Bell Jar* published in America. But at the end of the letter, "like one intelligent mature person with another," she defers to Hughes. "As the right to publish is yours, so too must be the decision," she says, with lame primness. So in 1971 *The Bell Jar* was published in America. Mrs. Plath endured it, and presently she exacted her pound of flesh: she asked Hughes's permission to publish Plath's letters to her. Hughes could hardly refuse.

One of the unpleasant but necessary conditions imposed on anyone writing about Sylvia Plath is a hardening of the heart against Ted Hughes. In one way or another, for this reason or that, the writer must put aside pity and sympathy for Hughes, the feeling that the man is a victim and a martyr, and resist any impulse to withdraw from the field and not add further to Hughes's torment. A number of writers have, in fact, left unfinished manuscripts. In a letter to Andrew Motion, Linda Wagner-Martin's British editor, Hughes speaks of these fallen aspirants with a kind of bitter triumph:

> [Wagner-Martin is] so insensitive that she's evidently escaped the usual effects of undertaking this particular job— i.e. mental breakdown, neurotic collapse, domestic catastrophe—which in the past have saved us from several travesties of this kind being completed.

Hughes's letter to Mrs. Plath about cashing in on *The Bell Jar* allowed me to see Hughes for the first time with the requisite coldness: he had evidently exchanged his right to privacy for a piece of real estate. For if he had not published *The Bell Jar* against Mrs. Plath's wishes she would surely not have felt impelled to publish *Letters Home*, and Hughes, in his turn, might not have felt impelled to administer a corrective to her corrective by publishing *The Journals*.

In a letter that appeared in *The New York Review of Books* on September 30, 1976, written in response to a review of three books about Plath, Olwyn Hughes complains that the reviewer, Karl Miller, "treat[s] Sylvia Plath's family as though they are characters in some work of fiction." She says, further, "It is almost as though, writing about Sylvia, some of whose work seems to take cruel and poetically licensed aim at those nearest to her, journalists feel free to do the same." Of course they do. The freedom to be cruel is one of journalism's uncontested privileges, and the rendering of subjects as if they were characters in bad novels is one of its widely accepted conventions. In Mrs. Plath, Ted Hughes, and Olwyn Hughes journalism found, and continues to find, three exceptionally alluring targets for its sadism and reductionism.

When *Bitter Fame* appeared, and raised the stakes of the game, I decided to become a player. Like all the other players at the table, I have felt anxious and oppressed by the game. It is being played in a room so dark and gloomy that one has a hard time seeing one's hand; one is apt to make mistakes. The air in the room is bad; it is the same air that has been breathed there for many years. The windows are grimy and jammed shut. The old servant's hands shake as he brings watery drinks. Through a door one sees an open coffin surrounded by candles. A small old woman sits in a straight-backed chair reading a manual of stenography. A very tall man with graying hair, dressed in black, comes through the doorway, having to duck his head, and stands watching the players. The door to the street suddenly opens, and a tall woman bursts in. She whispers something into the tall man's ear; he shrugs and returns to the room with the coffin. She looks after him, then gives the card table a malevolent little shove, so that drinks spill and cards scatter, and leaves, slamming the door. I look at my cards and call the bet.

VI

ON February 11, 1991, I sat eating lunch with Olwyn Hughes in an almost empty Indian restaurant in London's Camden Town. London itself had a hushed, emptied-out feeling. The Gulf War had begun a few weeks earlier; terrorism was feared, and travel had halted—my hotel was three-quarters empty. The weather was contributing to the city's mutedness. A spell of snow and freezing weather, for which the nation was unprepared, had set in, a siege of cold like the one that England was undergoing at the time of Plath's death, which Alvarez unforgettably rendered in his memoir:

> The snow began just after Christmas and would not let up. By New Year the whole country had ground to a halt. The trains froze on the tracks, the abandoned trucks froze on the roads. The power stations, overloaded by million upon pathetic million of hopeless electric fires, broke down continually; not that the fires mattered, since the electricians were mostly out on strike. Water pipes froze solid; for a bath you had to scheme and cajole those rare friends with centrally heated houses, who became rarer and less friendly as the weeks dragged on. Doing the dishes became a major operation. The gastric rumble of water in outdated plumbing was sweeter than the sound of mandolins. Weight for weight, plumbers were as expensive as smoked salmon and harder to find. The gas failed and Sunday roasts were raw. The lights failed and candles, of course, were unobtainable. Nerves failed and marriages crumbled. Finally, the

heart failed. It seemed the cold would never end. Nag, nag, nag.

Now, twenty-eight years later, the English were still stubbornly clinging to their notion that severe winter weather comes so infrequently to their green and pleasant land that preparing for it is not worthwhile, and I was thus able to experience at first hand some of Plath's frustration and feeling of stuckness during the winter of her suicide. I had sat for hours in an unheated train—grounded at a local station because the doors had frozen shut—and observed my fellow passengers, who sat docile and expressionless, incurious about their fate, in a kind of exaltation of uncomplaining discomfort. I had walked through the city covered with treacherous hard-frozen snow and recalled Plath's "humorous" essay "Snow Blitz," written shortly before her death, in which her American impatience with English passivity and its attendant moral superiority kept breaking through the surface tone of amused detachment.

"Sylvia died this month," I said to Olwyn in the Indian restaurant. "On which day was it?"

"It happens to be today," she said. "I realized it yesterday, when I was dating a letter to you. It's strange."

"The house on Fitzroy Road where she died is near here, isn't it?" I said. "After lunch, would you walk over there with me?"

"Darling, I don't think I want to do that," Olwyn said. She lit a cigarette, and as I looked at her through the smoke I recalled an entry in *Letters Home*, dated November 21, 1956, which gives Plath's first impression of her new sister-in-law:

> Olwyn, Ted's sister, stopped by this weekend on her way from a stay at home to her job in Paris. She is 28 and very startlingly beautiful with amber-gold hair and eyes. I cooked

a big roast beef dinner, with red wine and strawberries and cream. She reminds me of a changeling, somehow, who will never get old. She is, however, quite selfish and squanders money on herself continually in extravagances of clothes and cigarettes, while she still owes Ted 50 pounds. But in spite of this, I do like her.

Plath's sense of Olwyn as a fey creature who would never grow old was brilliantly prescient. Although Olwyn today "looks her age"—isn't one of those astonishingly young-looking older women the modern world is full of—neither does she look like the usual woman in her sixties. There is something of the schoolgirl about her, an atmosphere of daring and disobedience, a hint of bohemianism. The hair is still amber-gold; the face is handsome and cared for. At the same time, there is something forbidding and imposing about her. Like Hughes (and Plath), she is large-boned and tall, and as she sat in the restaurant with her coat over her shoulders, in a hunched posture that unsettlingly fused willfulness and dejection, I thought of Dürer's allegorical rendering of Melancholy. In person, as in her letters, Olwyn is magnificently indifferent to the question of what her interlocutor does or doesn't know about the outrages that writers about Plath have committed or will commit. She simply pours out anger at and contempt for the people she has had to deal with in her position as literary agent to the Plath estate. She is like the principal of a school or the warden of a prison: students or inmates come and go, while she remains. A rowdy new class of freshmen was about to arrive. Ronald Hayman and Paul Alexander were soon to publish their defiantly unauthorized biographies, and Jacqueline Rose was about to come out with a literary study that would impertinently challenge the editing of *The Journals* and *Letters Home*. But Olwyn had by no means forgotten the misdemeanors of the alumni, or those of the recently matriculated Anne Stevenson. I had only to touch the sore spot to send her into an aria of derision whose first notes I had heard a few months earlier, and which I would continue to hear throughout our acquaintance. "Let's face it, Anne was a mistake," she had said at our first meeting. "I regret I didn't get somebody brighter, somebody like Hilary Spurling. Sylvia was an intellectual—Anne is not. I had to nanny her along. She wasted a year of my life." And (in a later recital): "Anne is a good little poet. She's a little literary lady. She did some good things; there are one or two chapters that are quite nice. She's a passionate little writer. But she doesn't have a lively hungry mind. I hadn't realized that. I was misled by her sober demeanor and her nice tweeds and the fact that she taught. She never quite grasped Sylvia's nature. She got her wrong. She was always imagining she was this sweet emotional girl. But she wasn't." Now, in the Indian restaurant, Olwyn returned to the theme. "Anne left all the interesting things out and put the dull things in," she said. "She had to put her stamp on everything. She kept one dancing about with her silly little notes. I was exasperated by this rubbish. I wanted the facts to be on record. I didn't know she would write her little personal musings on Sylvia Plath. Biography isn't a poem, it isn't a novel, it's a document."

"Why didn't you write your own book?" I asked.

"I'm not a writer. And, as Ted's sister, I wouldn't have been believed."

"*Bitter Fame* isn't believed, either," I said. "If you had written a sister's frank account, it would have been read as such. People would have known where they stood. This way, they are suspicious. They feel something is being hidden from them and put over on them."

"Yes, people can't bear to think that there's something they can't see. I've been sent a manuscript by an awful woman, a Jacqueline Rose. It's another attack on Ted. It builds its theory on Ted's cutting things out of Sylvia's journals. People have this idea that Ted watches over everything. Ted is a very sweet-natured man. A very nice guy. I've written twenty pages of notes on Rose's book—I'll send them to you. Do you know this woman?"

"I am going to meet her in a few days." I had heard of Jacqueline Rose's project—it is now the book *The Haunting of Sylvia Plath*—and a couple of months earlier I had spoken with her on the telephone about it and about the prospect of meeting with her when I came to England. The conversation had been brief. Rose told me that she had delivered her manuscript to her publisher, Virago, and was waiting to find out how a "situation" that had developed between Virago and the Plath estate would come out. If things went well—if the difficulties were ironed out and the book went uneventfully to press—she would have nothing to speak to a journalist about. If things did not go well, she would have a great deal to talk about. Evidently, things had not gone well: I had an appointment to meet Rose.

The waiter started clearing the table, and Olwyn reached into her handbag and gave me a sheet of paper. It was the letter to me that she had mentioned dating the previous day; she had decided to hand it to me rather than mail it. Most of it consisted of three passages written by relatives of three famous dead writers—Virginia Woolf, John Middleton Murry, and Sylvia Plath—expressing anger and bitterness toward biographers and/or critics. The relatives were Quentin Bell, writing to Olwyn; Katherine Middleton Murry (J.M.M.'s daughter), writing in the *Independent*; and Ted Hughes writing to Jacqueline Rose. The Hughes passage was the one that interested me most. It read:

> Critics established the right to say whatever they pleased about the dead. It is an absolute power, and the corruption

that comes with it, very often, is an atrophy of the moral imagination. They move onto the living because they can no longer feel the difference between the living and the dead. They extend over the living that licence to say whatever they please, to ransack their psyche and reinvent them however they please. They stand in front of classes and present this performance as exemplary civilised activity—this utter insensitivity towards other living human beings. Students see the easy power and are enthralled, and begin to outdo their teachers. For a person to be corrupted in that way is to be genuinely corrupted.

"That's a remarkable piece of writing," I said, putting the letter in my handbag. Then—joining the crowd of wretches begging for crumbs from the table—I added, "May I quote it?"

"I'll ask Ted," Olwyn said indifferently.

She lit another cigarette, and I ventured a question to which I felt I already knew the answer. "What was it like to know Sylvia?"

She hesitated for a moment and then said, "There was no girl-to-girl between us. She was very absorbed in Ted; she wasn't interested in me."

"Do you feel that she came between you and your brother?"

"That's rubbish," Olwyn said. "That's cultist nonsense. I was full of my own life in those days."

If all our relationships are founded on imagination as much as reality, circumstances dictated that Olwyn's relationship to Plath be more interior than most. Because Olwyn lived and worked in Paris during the six years of the Plath-Hughes marriage (two of them spent in America and four in England), she and Plath were brought together, all told, only five or six times. It could be fairly said that Olwyn's "real" relationship with Plath began only after Plath's death, when

Olwyn left her job in Paris to live at Court Green with Hughes and help him take care of the motherless children. During Plath's lifetime, Olwyn evidently thought of Plath—when she thought of her at all—as the woman she wished her brother had not married. Support for this reading of Olwyn's mind lies in three scenes recounted in *Bitter Fame*. Each of them shows something unpleasant happening between the sisters-in-law, and each of them was retailed to Anne Stevenson by Olwyn to illustrate flaws in Plath's character. In each case, the reader knows that he is hearing only one side of a quarrel, and, as with the Dido Merwin memoir, is arrested by the innocence of the narrator's belief in her power of persuasion. Reporting ill of another is one of the most difficult and delicate of rhetorical operations; to be persuasive, to leave the reader with an impression of X's badness and of one's own disinterestedness and goodness, requires great skill. One cannot just blurt out—as Dido and Olwyn blurt out—how awful X is. All this achieves is to arouse the reader's sympathy for X.

The most unpleasant of the unpleasant scenes recounted in *Bitter Fame* took place in Yorkshire, in the home of Ted and Olwyn's parents during the Christmas holidays of 1960:

> As far as Olwyn can recall [Anne Stevenson writes], it began with a remark she made in response to some rather "malicious" account of Sylvia's on the behavior of someone Sylvia knew but Olwyn didn't. Olwyn said, "I say, you're awfully critical, aren't you?"—ignoring for once the unwritten rule that one just did *not* criticize Sylvia in any way. The reaction was immediate. Sylvia glared accusingly with a half-terrified, half-furious look and drew Ted into the room, having whispered Olwyn's remark to him. Olwyn, losing her temper, asked Sylvia why she didn't behave more normally, why she was so rude, why she so often showed little consideration for others. To these questions Sylvia made no reply but kept up her unnerving stare. Olwyn, who immediately

regretted she'd said a word, remembers thinking, "Why doesn't she *say* something?"

Olwyn ended the confrontation with relief by stroking Frieda's silky hair (the baby was sitting on her knee throughout) and saying, "But we shouldn't talk like this over her sweet head." Frieda was ready for bed, and Sylvia silently seized her and went upstairs, not to reappear. Olwyn went to bed later, feeling very contrite. She was wakened at dawn by the departure of her brother and his family.

One notices that it is Plath's *silence* that unnerves Olwyn. We remember Hughes's association of authenticity—"the real self"—with dumbness. But here dumbness is perceived (as Lear perceives it in Cordelia) as aggression. Olwyn verbally attacks Plath, but Olwyn's words are only words; it is Plath's (Medusan) speechlessness that is the deadly, punishing weapon. In a letter Olwyn wrote to me a year and a half ago she returned to this incident, underscoring the threatening character of Plath's silence:

> It was, I guess, an exasperated telling off. She never said a word, but mutely glared. It is the only tiff I have ever had in my life where the other person hadn't a word to say for themselves. Looking back, it seems quite aggressive of her to have left at dawn the next day. Taking away from me the opportunity to "make it up," which I intended to do, and putting me firmly in the wrong.

Below the surface of Olwyn's story of the Yorkshire confrontation, with its anxious score-settling atmosphere, lie deep wounds, and one of them is surely the wound from which survivors of suicides never recover. Plath, as we know, "left at dawn" on another day, in 1963. The suicide "goes away," and the survivors are forever in the wrong. They are like the damned, who can never make amends, who have no prospect of grace. Olwyn's "Why doesn't she *say* something?" expresses the anguish and anger of those who have been left without a word in a lake of fire.

Of course, Plath did "say something." On January 1, 1961, she wrote to her mother about the incident, quoting the unpleasant things Olwyn had said about her, and making some unpleasant observations of her own about the relationship between Olwyn and Ted, even, outrageously, suggesting incest. The letter is mentioned in *Bitter Fame* ("Sylvia complained in characteristically extreme language about the scene with Olwyn"), but it is not quoted. Anne Stevenson had intended to quote it—passages from it appear in a draft of her book—but Olwyn couldn't bear to hear herself spoken of in this way, and insisted that the passages be removed, reproaching Anne, in a letter of December 12, 1987, for her "unaffectionate wish to slander me in Plath's words." Stevenson felt that the quotation spoke for itself—that it was so intemperate and out of control that it would actually create sympathy for Olwyn, as Dido Merwin's intemperate lashings out at Plath only created sympathy for her victim. But Olwyn couldn't see this. Plath had refused to engage with Olwyn during her life, and now, in death, was compounding the injury by talking about her behind her back. Olwyn, understandably, found this intolerable.

Olwyn's recollection of this unpleasant scene and of two similar scenes reads like a single recurrent dream of infantile diminishment. In each, Plath is rendered as a silent, powerful, uncanny antagonist, whose aggression leaves Olwyn stunned and baffled. Freud speaks in one of his technical papers of how the analytic patient's secrets leak out from every pore without his knowledge. The warily silent Hughes has protected his secrets better than his sister has: no one can use his words against him. But everyone can—and does—speculate about his motives. "They can no longer feel the difference between the living and the dead," he complains about the biographers and critics and journalists who write about him and his family when writing about Plath. "They extend over the living that licence to say whatever they please." Milan Kundera, in his novel *Immortality*, has a passage of commiseration for the dead. Under the ground, they are "even lower than the old," he writes. "The old are still accorded human rights. The dead, however, lose all rights from the very first second of death. No law protects them any longer from slander, their privacy has ceased to be private; not even the letters written to them by their loved ones, not even the family album left to them by their mothers, nothing, nothing belongs to them any longer." What Hughes is protesting is being treated as if he were dead. The issue between the Hugheses and the public hostile to them is whether or not the Hugheses are dead. They have compromised their claim to being alive by their financial gains from the dead poet's literary remains. They have eaten the pomegranate seeds that tie them to the underworld. Plath's advocates have watched with malicious satisfaction as the Hugheses vainly struggle to assert their rights as live people. Hughes's acceptance of the odd job of Poet Laureate has only further worsened his prospects as a live person. The Poet Laureate is no longer quite mortal. He has ascended to the pantheon of the belaurelled dead. He has also descended into the cesspool from which sensationalist journalism draws its lurid narratives about celebrities. "SECRET LIFE OF THE POET LAUREATE — 'TED CANNOT HIDE FOREVER'" was the headline of a particularly low specimen in the *Mail on Sunday*, on February 1, 1987. But a paradox hedges the struggle between the Plath advocates and the Hugheses. The advocates, whom Olwyn calls "libbers," because many of them are feminists, are, in this struggle, not representatives of women's liberation so much as representatives of a kind of dead lib. They want to restore to Plath the rights she lost when she died. They want to wrest from Hughes the power over her literary remains which he acquired when she died intestate. They want to remove the gag of censorship from her journals and letters. But by so doing, by restoring Plath to the status of the living, they simply achieve a substitution: they send the Hugheses and Mrs. Plath down to take Plath's place among the rightless dead.

VII

OLWYN and I left the dark, warm restaurant for the bitterly cold street. Olwyn began to tell me how to get to Plath's house on Fitzroy Road, but the directions were complicated, and when she learned that I had no street guide with me she said, "Oh, all right—I'll walk with you. You'd never find it."

We walked what seemed like a long way, having to pick our path slowly through the hardened snow. "It's strange going to Sylvia's house on the anniversary of her death," Olwyn said. We had reached the pleasant neighborhood of Primrose Hill and had crossed a square that Olwyn identified as Chalcot Square, where Plath and Hughes had lived between February of 1960 and the summer of 1961. She pointed out a handsome five-story row house where they had had a tiny apartment on the fourth floor. Dido Merwin had found the apartment; she and William Merwin, who lived in the neighborhood, had become the helpful—probably too helpful—older friends of Hughes and Plath. In her memoir Dido writes of the "literary string-pullings and introductions" that William performed on Ted's behalf, and of her own efforts in "fixing up the very pregnant Sylvia with the right National Health Service doctor." She then reports Plath's ingratitude, her "summary and unexpectedly graceless rejection" of Dido's suggestion that she buy furniture and appliances for the flat from local secondhand shops. It was, Dido writes, "like a warning shot across the bows: things, it seemed, were not going to be such congenial plain sailing as I had supposed. But if the Hugheses elected to go splurging on a posh cooker, refrigerator, and bed, what the hell? Never mind if it made no sense to a couple of flea-marketeers like Bill and me. It would have made complete sense, of course, had we any inkling of the besetting insecurity that was the root cause of Sylvia's need for morale-boosting toys." The American reader can only stare at the puritanism that conceives of the desire for a decent bed and a new stove as decadent and pathological.

The passage affords another glimpse of Plath's alienation in England. Interestingly, this was never a theme for Plath. She occasionally permitted herself a few words to her mother or to American friends about the uncleanliness and dismalness of English kitchens and bathrooms, but she seemed determined to accept the discomforts of her adopted country with good grace. After the separation from Hughes, there was nothing keeping her in England, but she never considered returning to America. In harsh England Plath had found a refuge from (as she called it in *The Bell Jar*) "the motherly breath of the suburbs" of Eisenhower America. Here her wicked wit could flourish and her writing could break out of the caul of obedient mannerism that encased its early examples. The emergence of the "true self" as a writer was a shedding of Plath's American identity along with the other "false" identities she cast off. She did not write—and could not have written—*The Bell Jar* or *Ariel* in her native Massachusetts. The pitiless voice of the *Ariel* poet was a voice that had rid itself of its American accent.

When Plath arrived in England on a Fulbright to Cambridge, in the fall of 1955, the accent was still strong. A fellow American graduate student, Jane Baltzell Kopp, recalls Plath's conspicuous "Americanisms" with the air of a sibling who has herself learned how to appear in public and not trot out the family's tacky little habits. She singles out for special scorn Plath's "full set" of white-and-gold Samsonite luggage, which (Kopp reports) inspired "much amazement, incredulity, and humor among the British" when they saw her with it on drab railway platforms. Kopp's memoir appears in *Sylvia Plath: The Woman and the Work*, an anthology of writings about Plath, edited by Edward Butscher, and published in 1977. Another contributor, the late Dorothea Krook, who was Plath's favorite teacher at Cambridge, and whose memoir is tenderly sympathetic, also, however, points out Plath's exoticism as a girl who was "always neat and fresh, wearing charming, girlish clothes, the kind of clothes that made you look at the girl, not the garments; hair down to the shoulders still, but ever so neatly brushed and combed, and held back in place by a broad bandeau on the crown. . . . This charming American neatness and freshness is what I chiefly recall about her physical person." The photographs of Plath in the various biographies and in *Letters Home* and *The Journals* show her as Krook described her. With her shining blond hair and her soft, rounded face, she evokes the soap and deodorant advertisements of the 1940s and '50s, in which the words "dainty" and "fresh" never failed to appear. Contrast this picture with Álvarez's description of Plath on the night of his last meeting with her, on Christmas Eve, 1962, two months before her death. Plath is no longer blond (the earlier blondness had been artificial) and no longer conspicuously clean. Álvarez writes:

Her hair, which she usually wore in a tight, schoolmistressy bun, was loose. It hung straight to her waist like a tent, giving her pale face and gaunt figure a curiously desolate, rapt air, like a priestess emptied out by the rites of her cult. When she walked in front of me down the hall passage and up the stairs to her apartment—she had the top two floors of the house—her hair gave off a strong smell, sharp as an animal's.

Another index to the transformation may be found in two recordings of poetry readings that Plath made—one in Massachusetts in 1958, and the other in London in late 1962, for the BBC. In the Massachusetts recording, she reads in a young, slightly declamatory voice, with a Boston accent. The reading is pleasant, a little dull. The BBC recording is extraordinary; no one who hears it can fail to be jolted by it. Elizabeth Hardwick has written a definitive description of this rare document:

> I have never before learned anything from a poetry reading, unless the clothes, the beard, the girls, the poor or good condition of the poet can be considered a kind of knowledge. But I was taken aback by Sylvia Plath's reading. It was not anything like I could have imagined. Not a trace of the modest, retreating, humorous Worcester, Massachusetts, of Elizabeth Bishop; nothing of the swallowed plain Pennsylvania of Marianne Moore. Instead these bitter poems— "Daddy," "Lady Lazarus," "The Applicant," "Fever 103°"— were "beautifully" read, projected in full-throated, plump, diction-perfect, Englishy, mesmerizing cadences, all round and rapid, and paced and spaced. Poor recessive Massachusetts had been erased. "I have done it again!" Clearly, perfectly, staring you down. She seemed to be standing at a banquet like Timon, crying, "Uncover, dogs, and lap!"

And yet when we think of Plath's death at dawn in an indifferent London it is homely Massachusetts that somehow comes back into view. The idea of death far away from home has a special pathos; embedded in it is the fantasy that the foreign place contributed to the death, perhaps was even the cause of it. Foreignness is threatening, dangerous: if only he or she had stayed home and not drunk that water, not taken that ancient bus over the pass, never ventured into that evil café. Again, it is Alvarez's memoir that sets the "if only" terms of the narrative of Plath's suicide. Plath's first suicide attempt, in 1953, took place literally at home, in the crawl space under her mother's house, and she survived it. Far away from home, she died. Alvarez believed that Plath had not meant to die, that her death "came carelessly, by mistake and too soon," and was "'a cry for help' which fatally misfired." A deadly concatenation of events—for which the relentless cold, the frozen pipes, the lack of a phone, the children's and Plath's viral infections were a kind of rancorous background music—plucked her from a world she had not intended to leave. She left it abjectly. As Alvarez remembered her from his last visit to her flat and imagined her on the eve of her death, she was a pathetic, diminished figure.

Bitter Fame further sharpens the contrast between the large, powerful panzer-woman of Ariel, who eats "men like air" and "adores a Fascist," and the little defeated American girl in the chilly white, sparsely furnished flat, who places bread and milk at her children's bedsides and then turns on the gas taps and lays her head in the oven on a folded cloth she has placed there. The folded cloth is a new detail, as is a letter from Plath's doctor, John Horder, writing of Plath's dire mental condition in the weeks before her death; and so is the testimony of Jillian Becker, a new English friend, who took Plath and her children into her house on her final weekend and tried to keep her from returning to Fitzroy Road. Paradoxically, the vividness with which Bitter Fame evokes the pathos and horror of Plath's death only contributed to the outrage that its publication provoked—only strengthened the narrative of a Plath mistreated in death by a hostile sister-in-law, as she had been mistreated in life by a faithless husband. "There she still is, a fragile, lovable creature, in danger of being crushed," Ronald Hayman, one of the most persistent of the Hugheses' harriers, wrote of Plath in the *Independent* on April 19, 1989. Ludicrous as this description of the author of *Ariel* and *The Bell Jar* is, it reflects a popular fantasy about Plath: it expresses the public's need to see Plath as victim, its desire to impose a Jamesian structure of American innocence versus European corruption (Plath as Isabel Archer, let us say, and Hughes and Olwyn as Gilbert Osmond and Madame Merle) on the struggle between the vivid dead girl and the ghostly English relations.

As I write the word "ghostly," I feel closer to the center of the mystery of why the weight of public opinion has fallen so squarely on the Plath side and against the Hugheses—why the dead have been chosen over the living. We choose the dead because of our tie to them, our identification with them. Their helplessness, passivity, vulnerability is our own. We all yearn toward the state of inanition, the condition of harmlessness, where we are perforce lovable and fragile. It is only by a great effort that we rouse ourselves to act, to fight, to struggle, to be heard above the wind, to crush flowers as we walk. To behave like *live people*. The contest between Plath and Hughes invokes the contest between the two principles that hedge human existence. In his poem "Sheep" Ted Hughes writes of a lamb that inexplicably died soon after birth:

> *It was not*
> *That he could not thrive, he was born*
> *With everything but the will—*

That can be deformed, just like a limb.
Death was more interesting to him.
Life could not get his attention.

Life, of course, never gets anyone's entire attention. Death always remains interesting, pulls us, draws us. As sleep is necessary to our physiology, so depression seems necessary to our psychic economy. In some secret way, Thanatos nourishes Eros as well as opposes it. The two principles work in covert concert; though in most of us Eros dominates, in none of us is Thanatos completely subdued. However—and this is the paradox of suicide—to *take* one's life is to behave in a more active, assertive, "erotic" way than to helplessly watch as one's life is *taken away* from one by inevitable mortality. Suicide thus engages with both the death-hating and the death-loving parts of us: on some level, perhaps, we may envy the suicide even as we pity him. It has frequently been asked whether the poetry of Plath would have so aroused the attention of the world if Plath had not killed herself. I would agree with those who say no. The death-ridden poems move us and electrify us because of our knowledge of what happened. Alvarez has observed that the late poems read as if they were written posthumously, but they do so only because a death actually took place. "When I am talking about the weather / I know what I am talking about," Kurt Schwitters writes in a Dada poem (which I have quoted in its entirety). When Plath is talking about the death wish, she knows what she is talking about. In 1966, Anne Sexton, who committed suicide eleven years after Plath, wrote a poem entitled "Wanting to Die," in which these startlingly informative lines appear:

But suicides have a special language.
Like carpenters they want to know which tools.
They never ask why build.

When, in the opening of "Lady Lazarus," Plath triumphantly exclaims, "I have done it again," and, later in the
poem, writes,

> *Dying*
> *Is an art, like everything else.*
> *I do it exceptionally well.*
>
> *I do it so it feels like hell.*
> *I do it so it feels real.*
> *I guess you could say I've a call,*

we can only share her elation. We know we are in the presence of a master builder.

VIII

OLWYN and I finally reached the house on Fitzroy
Road where Plath killed herself. I recognized it immediately—it is an obligatory photographic subject of the Plath
biographies, and its oval blue ceramic plaque reading "William Butler Yeats, 1865–1939, Irish poet and dramatist, lived
here" is a compulsively mentioned (and yet oddly inconse-
quential) detail. No. 23 was part of a row of three-story brick
houses, with white stucco around the windows and at the
basement and first-floor levels. Plath had rented the second-
and-third-floor duplex, and lived there a bare two months,
alone with her children. "Ted had been told late in September
to leave Court Green. Early in October he came to collect his
things," Stevenson laconically writes in *Bitter Fame*, and two
months later Plath moved to London with the children. The
period of the breakup of the Plath-Hughes marriage is the

radioactive center of the Plath biographical enterprise. Here is lodged the precious ore that the biographers struggle to wrest from the Hugheses. If the journals of this period, which Hughes destroyed or lost, are out of their reach, there remain the crazed letters that Plath wrote to her mother and to friends in her misery and jealousy and fury over Hughes's faithlessness. There is also the testimony of two friends, Elizabeth Sigmund and Clarissa Roche, who were confidantes of Plath's during her time of Medean trouble. They have come forward as defenders of the "fragile, lovable" Plath against the heartless Hughes. Each has published a memoir, and both have incurred the Hugheses' undying enmity and contempt for purveying lurid stories to grateful biographers and journalists. Sigmund, who lived in North Devon and saw more of Plath than Roche did, has contributed a famous set piece:

> Then suddenly, late one evening, Sylvia arrived with Nick in his carry cot, and the change in her was appalling. She kept saying "My milk has dried up, I can't feed Nick. My milk has gone."
>
> At last she told me that Ted was in love with another woman, that she knew Assia and was terrified of her. She wept and wept and held onto my hands, saying, "Help me!"
>
> What could I do? I have never felt so inadequate in my life. She claimed, "Ted lies to me, he lies all the time, he has become a *little* man." But the most frightening thing she said was, "When you give someone your whole heart and he doesn't want it, you cannot take it back. It's gone forever."

It was at Alvarez's suggestion that Sigmund wrote her memoir, for publication in *The New Review*, then edited by Alvarez's friend Ian Hamilton. It was republished (in a slightly different version) in Butscher's anthology. Roche (whose memoir also appears in Butscher's book) recalls a sim-

ilarly distraught Plath during a visit to Court Green in November, 1962: "The strong, passionate, sensitive Heathcliff
had turned round and now appeared to [Plath] as a massive,
crude, oafish peasant, who could not protect her from herself
nor from the consequences of having grasped at womanhood.
She cursed and mocked him for his weakness, and she called
him a traitor."

There is no reason to doubt the bare truth of these reminiscences. As we know from the crazed letters, Plath said all
kinds of things about Hughes in those days. And, as we all
know from our own brushes with sexual jealousy, being
crazed is the chief symptom of the malady. But what few of
us have experienced during the progress of the illness is a
surge of creativity, empowering us to do work that surpasses
everything we have done before, work that seems to be doing
itself. It was in a brief two months in the autumn of 1962,
when Hughes had left Devon, and Plath, unable to eat or
sleep, was running actual high fevers as well as figurative ones
of jealous rage and bathetic self-pity, that she wrote the ma-
jority of the *Ariel* poems. She was taking sleeping pills, and
when they wore off, at about five in the morning, she would
get up and write until the children awoke. In a letter to her
friend the poet Ruth Fainlight (which begins with the obligatory abuse of Hughes) Plath wrote, "When I was 'happy' do-
mestically I felt a gag in my throat. Now that my domestic
life, until I get a permanent live-in girl, is chaos, I am living
like a Spartan, writing through huge fevers and producing
free stuff I had locked in me for years. I feel astounded and
very lucky. I kept telling myself I was the sort that could only
write when peaceful at heart, but that is not so, the muse has
come to live here, now Ted has gone." To her mother, Plath
wrote (in a letter in which she also said, "I hate and despise
him so I can hardly speak"), "I am a genius of a writer; I have
it in me. I am writing the best poems of my life; they will

make my name." In late October, Plath began to look for an apartment in London—this was the period of her friendship with Alvarez—and on November 7 she wrote ecstatically to her mother:

> I am writing from London, so happy I can hardly speak. I *think* I have found a place. . . . By an absolute *fluke* I walked by *the* street and *the* house (with Primrose Hill at the end) where I've always wanted to live. The house had builders in it and a sign, "Flats to Let"; I flew upstairs. *Just* right (unfurnished), on two floors, with three bedrooms upstairs, lounge, kitchen and bath downstairs *and* a balcony garden! Flew to the agents—hundreds of people ahead of me, I thought, as always. It seems I have a *chance!* And guess what, it is *W. B. Yeats' house*—with a blue plaque over the door, saying he lived there! And in the district of my old doctors and in the street [where] I would want to *buy* a house if I ever had a smash-hit novel.

This was the house that Olwyn and I now stood before. It had an air of prosperity and well-being. I had expected something less ample and nicely tended; Alvarez's memoir had prepared me for something pinched and melancholy. It is a commonplace of visits to places where something bad happened that no trace of it remains; the visitor is struck by the absence of what he has come to "see." Claude Lanzmann begins his film *Shoah* with a view of beautiful green countryside. He and a survivor of the Chelmno Nazi death camp are seen strolling on the camp's site, now a poetic meadow beside a stream. In an ordinary voice, as Lanzmann questions him in an equally ordinary voice, the survivor tells of horrors that defy belief. The film is poised on the tension between time and history. Time heals all wounds, smooths, cleanses, obliterates; history keeps the wound open, picks at it, makes it raw and bleeding. In his film, Lanzmann makes the point over and over again. In Tel Aviv, he interviews a barber who survived Treblinka. The barber is cutting a customer's hair. Business as usual. As Lanzmann presses him for more specific details about the camp, the barber, now in tears, can't go on. "You must go on," Lanzmann sternly tells him. "You have to." The barber resolutely picks up his scissors and resumes his extraordinary oxymoronic performance of forgetting the past (cutting hair, cutting the connection to Treblinka) and remembering it (obeying Lanzmann's command to speak, saying the unsayable).

Imaginative literature is produced under the pressure of an inner interrogation like Lanzmann's. Poets and novelists and playwrights make themselves, against terrible resistances, give over what the rest of us keep safely locked within our hearts. Ted Hughes, in his introduction to a collection of Plath's short prose writings called *Johnny Panic and the Bible of Dreams*, writes of the "strange conflict between what was expected of her and what finally was exacted." What was expected of Plath was the obedient A student's genteel achievements of the 1950s; what was exacted was the dire poetry of *Ariel*. In "Daddy" Plath writes:

> *I thought every German was you.*
> *And the language obscene*
>
> *An engine, an engine*
> *Chuffing me off like a Jew.*
> *A Jew to Dachau, Auschwitz, Belsen.*
> *I began to talk like a Jew.*
> *I think I may well be a Jew.*

"Daddy" has had a mixed reception. There are critics who condemn Plath for appropriating the Holocaust for private purposes. "Whatever her father did to her, it could not have

been what the Germans did to the Jews," Leon Wieseltier
writes in *The New York Review of Books* (1976). "The metaphor
is inappropriate. . . . Familiarity with the hellish subject must
be earned, not presupposed." The late Irving Howe, in his
book *The Critical Point* (1973), writes, "There is something
monstrous, utterly disproportionate, when tangled emotions
about one's father are deliberately compared with the historical fate of the European Jews; something sad, if the comparison is made spontaneously." Seamus Heaney writes in his
book *The Government of the Tongue* (1989), "A poem like
'Daddy,' however brilliant a tour de force it can be acknowledged to be, and however its violence and vindictiveness can
be understood or excused in light of the poet's parental and
marital relations, remains, nevertheless, so entangled in biographical circumstances, and rampages so permissively in the
history of other people's sorrows that it simply overdraws its
rights to our sympathy." On the other side, George Steiner
honors Plath for her "act of identification, of total commu-
nion with those tortured and massacred." In his essay "Dying
Is an Art" (1965) Steiner writes of her as "one of a number of
young contemporary poets, novelists, and playwrights, themselves in no way implicated in the actual Holocaust, who have
done most to counter the general inclination to forget the
death camps." He calls "Daddy" "one of the very few poems
I know of in any language to come near the last horror." And
yet, after saying this, after calling "Daddy" the "Guernica" of
modern poetry, Steiner is troubled. Something doesn't sit
right with him. "Are these final poems entirely legitimate?"
he asks, and then, in a turnaround—one that Howe pounces
on and sees as "devastating to his early comparison with
'Guernica'"—asks, "In what sense does anyone, himself un-
involved and long after the event, commit a subtle larceny
when he invokes the echoes and trappings of Auschwitz and
appropriates an enormity of ready emotion to his own private

design?" Three years later, writing of "Daddy" in the *Cambridge Review*, Steiner is still fretting about the question: "What extra territorial right had Sylvia Plath—she was a child, plump and golden in America, when the trains actually went—to draw on the reserves of animate horror in the ash and the children's shoes? . . . Do any of us have license to locate our personal disasters, raw as these may be, in Auschwitz?"

Steiner's ambivalence, his "yes, but" verdict on "Daddy," is a characteristic response to Plath's work and to her persona. We praise her (those of us who do not condemn or dismiss her), but then we draw back. We retract some of our praise. Like Steiner, we're not sure where we stand with her. "Why doesn't she *say* something?" Olwyn asked. Like the life, the work is full of threatening silences. It is beautiful and severe and very cold. It is surrealistic, with surrealism's menace and refusal to explain itself. We stand before the *Ariel* poems as Olwyn stood before the stone-faced Sylvia. We feel humbled and rebuked, as if we were the "little, stumpy people" Plath saw in the hospital or the herbivores she writes of in her poem "Mystic," "whose hopes are so low they are comfortable." To speak of Plath's overdrawing her right to our sympathy isn't accurate. Plath never asks for our sympathy; she would not stoop to it. The voice of the "true self" is notable for its high notes of disdain—and its profound melancholy. The "tortured and massacred" are never far from Plath's thoughts. (She is reported to have said to the Scottish poet George MacBeth, "I see you have a concentration camp in your mind, too.") To say that Plath did not earn her right to invoke the names of Dachau, Auschwitz, Belsen is off the mark. It is we who stand accused, who fall short, who have not accepted the wager of imagining the unimaginable, of cracking Plath's code of atrocity.

In *The Bell Jar* Plath conveys what it is like to go mad. In the *Ariel* poems she gives us what could be called the waste products of her madness. The connection that art draws between individual and collective suffering is drawn by Plath's art in a way that not every reader has found convincing. Howe, for example, extends his criticism of "Daddy" to the whole of *Ariel*. "What illumination—moral, psychological, social—can be provided of either [extreme situations] or the general human condition by a writer so deeply rooted in the extremity of her plight?" he asks. And yet what was exacted from Plath was so far beyond what was expected of the gushing girl with the Samsonite luggage that we must all agree on the singularity of the achievement. How the child, "plump and golden in America," became the woman, thin and white in Europe, who wrote poems like "Lady Lazarus" and "Daddy" and "Edge," remains an enigma of literary history— one that is at the heart of the nervous urgency that drives the Plath biographical enterprise, and of the hold that the Plath legend continues to exert on our imaginations.

PART TWO

I

A FAST train was bearing me to Durham, in the North of England, where Anne Stevenson lived. I had met Anne earlier, a year after the publication of *Bitter Fame*, and the meeting had been depressing. I spent two hours with her at the University Women's Club, in London, where she was staying—she had come to town to give a lecture—and although the serene literary figure I had imagined for so many years occasionally came into view, it was mostly obscured by an upset, beset, wound-up woman pouring out her grievances. Public hostility toward Anne had not abated. She was still being pilloried—and she was still under the delusion that she could persuade the press that her punishment was unjust. She had been telling journalists—I was only the latest in a series—of the intolerable pressure Olwyn Hughes had put on her during the writing of the biography, how a gun had been held to her head, how she had been forced to produce and publish a book that was not her own. But the press had used Anne's complaints about Olwyn only to embellish its original narrative; to have done otherwise would have been to disobey a fundamental rule of journalism, which is to tell a story and *stick to it*. The narratives of journalism (significantly called "stories"), like those of mythology and folklore, derive their power from their firm, undeviating sympathies and antipathies. Cinderella must remain good and the stepsisters bad. "Second stepsister not so bad after all" is not a good story. Anne Stevenson had to remain bad in the scandal of *Bitter Fame*. Her fight with Olwyn had to be shrugged off as a falling-out among thieves—a distasteful spectacle, and nothing more.

Anne appeared defeated and ground down, and there seemed to me to be something peculiarly English in the atmosphere of her abjection. The lobby of the University Women's Club, where we sat at a little, wobbly table, only accentuated my sense of the complicity of England in the downward movement of Anne's life. The room had a dour and pinched character; its faded beige wallpaper and sagging brown armchairs seemed gratuitously dismal. Anne herself, who had come out of the elevator with a mackintosh over her arm, wearing sensible short boots and silver-rimmed glasses that gave her face a somewhat prim and severe look, also seemed unnecessarily drab. At fifty-seven, she was still a beautiful woman, and whenever she took off her glasses her face was transformed. Her eyes were extraordinary: very blue, with heavy lids like Virginia Woolf's. There were moments, too, when the torrent of defensive words would abate and flashes of irony would lighten the tense, heavy atmosphere of the interview. After telling me of her sense of the deep injury and injustice done her by a very unpleasant review in the *TLS* of her new book of poems, *The Other House*—a review that accused her of being envious of Sylvia Plath, and that wounded her more than all the reviews of *Bitter Fame*—Anne smiled and said, "But it doesn't kill anyone to be bitterly hurt from time to time. It's not as if I were being tortured and my nails pulled out." She added, "But it does make me very touchy and very vulnerable," and this touchiness and vulnerability dominated her discourse, giving it its weak and unpersuasive character.

As it happened, she did not need to persuade me. I was already on her side. My narrative would be revisionist—not only because of my idealization of her as a literary artist but because of an experience of my own that paralleled hers. A short time earlier, I, too, had written an unpopular book, and I, too, had been attacked in the press. I had been there—on the helpless side of the journalist-subject equation. Now my journalist's "objectivity" was impaired. I arranged to see Anne again, and I was pretty sure that further meetings would restore her image to the privileged place it had occupied in my imagination for so many years. But I took careful note of the bad impression she made on me at our first encounter. I felt there was something here that illustrated a problem of biography—the problem of how to write about people who can no longer change their contemporaries' perception of them, who are discovered frozen in certain unnatural or unpleasant attitudes, like characters in tableaux vivants or people in snapshots with their mouths open. As a journalist dealing with a live subject, I had an advantage over the biographer dealing with a dead one: I could go back to Anne again (and again and again and again, if necessary) to draw my portrait of her. I could get her to move, to let her arm drop, to close her mouth. I could actually ask her the questions the biographer only wishes he could ask his subject. The journalist's subject, for his part, is aware of the advantage of not being dead, and glad of the opportunity for further sittings.

In the following months, in correspondence with both Anne and Olwyn, the issue of contingency would come up repeatedly: "I said this then, but I wouldn't say it now. Don't hold me to this, don't use that, don't think that this is the whole truth about me." After our meeting at the University Women's Club, I had received a letter from Anne whose opening sentence was a kind of herald of the theme that would be a leitmotif of her (and Olwyn's) letters to me. "After last night's conversation," Anne wrote, "I do want to clarify certain things I said or counter-said. Since life is an ongoing process, most people, certainly myself, contradict themselves constantly, according to time and mood. My feeling about the 'truth' in human exchange can perhaps be expressed only in 'fiction'—poetry or prose." This was counterbalanced by a letter from Olwyn disclaiming what she had said in the Indian restaurant: "Talking, I express, probably too frankly, whatever aspect of this or that is running in my mind at the time—which can give false impressions of varying kinds—and whatever one says seems to be seized on and immediately deformed by the cultists. Phrases I wrote in haste years ago have been taken out of context and misunderstood (they were doubtless pretty imprecise as they were written), then used and quoted as my entire attitude on various points."

My entire attitude. At the end of Borges's story "The Aleph," the narrator goes to the cellar of a house, where he has the experience of encountering everything in the world. He all at once sees all places from all angles: "I saw tigers, pistons, bison, tides, and armies; I saw all the ants on the planet. . . . I saw the circulation of my own dark blood." Writer's block derives from the mad ambition to enter that cellar; the fluent writer is content to stay in the close attic of partial expression, to say what is "running through his mind," and to accept that it may not—cannot—be wholly true, to risk that it will be misunderstood. I, too, have spent days fruitlessly hanging around the door to that forbidden cellar. I have looked at my revisionist narrative and found it wanting. I have found every other narrative wanting. How can one see all the ants on the planet when one is wearing the blinders of narrative? On the train to Durham, however, I was still free of the (philosopher's) disease, and read with fascination and admiration the typescript of a lecture Anne had given in Toronto the previous October. It was entitled "The Making of *Bitter Fame,*" and in it the inchoate ramblings of the interview at the University Women's Club had been gathered into a coherent and vivid narrative. Here the voice was strong and clear, the tone assured.

The lecture begins with a discussion of parallels that Anne sees between herself and Plath. "Plath and I were born within months of each other, in the autumn and winter of 1932 and 1933," she writes. "We had in common American parents of German descent, though her background, unlike mine, was undilutedly Teutonic. Our fathers were both university professors. As children, we attended similar public elementary schools, and as teenagers we graduated in the same year (1950) from middle-class, 'college-oriented' American high schools." Anne goes on:

> We also shared ideological and social assumptions. We were both brought up in a protected, academic environment in which success at school, followed by a liberal-arts education in college, appeared to guarantee us a future of bustling personal happiness and usefulness to society. Our attentive mothers encouraged us to think of ourselves as "special." In college (I entered the University of Michigan the same year Sylvia started at Smith), while assuming that life would provide us with a happily-ever-after marriage and untroublesome children, we were fiercely determined to make the most of our talents. I am still coming to terms with my youthful, self-centered, characteristically American ambition to be "great." . . . Which brings me back to an aspect of Sylvia I thought I recognized when I first read her *Letters Home*. What Sylvia Plath and I had unequivocally in common in the 1950s was, of course, marriage to an Englishman and transplantation, as naive young women, from open-minded, prosperous America to class-ridden, war-depleted England. Like many, when I first began looking at Plath's life, I assumed that Plath's troubles stemmed from the difficulty of making that adjustment—particularly as a woman. I realized that my own numb misery in England after marriage was in good part due to what is commonly known as "culture shock." Even in the 1950s, American women were streets ahead of their British counterparts in terms of what they expected of and for themselves. . . . I supposed that Sylvia Plath, while imagining she was at home in British society,

had in fact underestimated her own defensive naiveté, especially among British intellectuals.

After this prologue, Anne gets down to the business of
confessing her own defensive naïveté and relating how she
allowed herself to be caught in the web from which she was
still trying to disentangle herself. It all began quietly and un-
portentously, as these things do. In 1985, Anne accepted a
commission to write a short biographical study of Plath
(about a hundred pages) for a Penguin series called Lives of
Modern Women. By the fall of 1986, she had completed a
rough draft, and decided to send the first and last chapters to
Ted Hughes for his comments. She knew Hughes slightly
from the world of English poetry. Hughes was abroad, however, and his wife, Carol, telephoned Anne and suggested
that she send her chapters to Olwyn. Anne did so, and Olwyn
was soon on the phone herself. "She said what I had written
was largely misconceived but she liked my cool, terse style,
and wouldn't I come around one day the following week and
talk about the book over lunch?"

At the lunch, in a French restaurant in Camden Town,
Olwyn did her customary growling about the Plath myth and
the "libbers" and "cultists" who had caused Ted Hughes his
sufferings, but flatteringly exempted Anne from her portrait
of Plath's biographers as a breed of malignant incompetents.
On parting, she gave Anne a sheaf of letters that Dido Merwin had written to Linda Wagner-Martin about Plath.
Wagner-Martin, while working on her biography, had been
in the habit of sending chapters to her sources for comment.
Dido, on reading the chapters based on her letters, withdrew
permission for their use. "*You* have your reasons for not wanting to acknowledge the crucial fact that Sylvia was a pathological *punisher* and Ted a constitutional *forgiver*," she wrote
Wagner-Martin. "*I* have my reasons for not wanting to have

anything to do with a book that attempts to cover this up." Anne writes, "Olwyn thought I should see the Merwin letters; they would show me a Sylvia Plath very different from the victimized martyr of the myth," and goes on:

> When I read Mrs. Merwin's letters, I confess I burst out laughing. Their bite, their wit, their unmistakable tone of bitchy, scornful, sophisticated English superiority, decked out with French phrases and trenchant literary allusions, substantiated much that I had already surmised about Sylvia's bewilderment among the English literati. Where I had shrunk into myself in England, Sylvia had come out fighting. Dido Merwin's letters—a pungent foretaste of what was to come in her memoir—accused Sylvia of monstrous behaviour: rudeness, selfishness, insensitivity, social blindness, but most of all jealousy. The letters were clearly an invaluable source of anti-cultist information, though I thought they threw at least as much light on Dido's character as on Sylvia's.

At a second meeting with Anne, a few weeks later, Olwyn delivered her spider's invitation. She proposed that Anne withdraw her hundred-page study from the Penguin series and expand it into a book, for which she, Olwyn, would negotiate contracts with American and English publishers. (Olwyn ran a small literary agency in addition to her work as Cerberus to the Plath estate.) She offered to act as Anne's agent and promised to get her large advances. Moreover, she would give the signal to friends of Ted Hughes, who had loyally kept silent for almost twenty-five years, that it was finally safe to tell what they knew to a trusted new biographer. In the meantime, Hughes had returned to England and written Anne a long letter about the two chapters she had sent him. Unlike the fifteen-page list of laconic and scornful comments he had sent to Wagner-Martin on reading her manuscript a

few months earlier ("page 201, line 4: delete 'making love'";
"page 200, line 6: delete 'and ripped . . . cheek'"; "page 273,
line 27–28: To mention these petty details at all sounds like
burlesque; delete"), Hughes's seven-page letter to Anne was
friendly, respectful, and (considering his policy of reserve) remarkably forthcoming in details about his life with Plath. As
it turned out, this letter was not only the first but the last of
Hughes's letters to Anne during the writing of *Bitter Fame*.
At the time, however, it acted as a powerful inducement; to
have the brother's flattering attentions added to the sister's
made the offer impossible to resist.

Anne entered the web. By the end of November, Olwyn,
acting with characteristic dispatch and efficiency, had negoti-
ated contracts with Houghton Mifflin in America and Viking
in England, which yielded the promised substantial advances
($40,000 from Houghton Mifflin and £15,000 from Viking).
She lined up the promised friends; there was seemingly nothing she couldn't or wouldn't do to help. She gave Anne the
use of her large Plath library. She interviewed witnesses. She
shared her own reminiscences of Plath. She wrote analyses of
Plath's poetry. She read drafts of chapters as Anne wrote
them, and offered criticism. She acted as an emissary to Ted.
Anne already shared Olwyn's view of Plath as a brilliant poet
but a trying and unlovable person, and she and Olwyn would
meet in Olwyn's house (at that time Anne was living in London with her husband-to-be, Peter Lucas) and talk about
Plath with the sort of delicious malice one permits oneself
with close, like-minded friends. In all probability, it was this
trace of Anne's negative feelings about Plath, rather than her
"cool, terse style," that had first captured Olwyn's interest
and made her feel she had finally found the right biographer—the biographer who would draw the likeness of Plath
that was needed to counteract the libbers' idealized portrait.
Olwyn regaled Anne with stories of Plath's unattractive be-

havior, and Anne listened without protest, if not entirely without skepticism. Then, in the early summer of 1987, with an outline of the expanded biography in hand, Anne flew to Boston to meet Peter Davison, the book's editor at Houghton Mifflin, and to work with him on it, chapter by chapter. Davison approved the early chapters but felt—and Anne agreed—that the final two chapters were thin and incomplete. "In the absence of any more information from Ted Hughes," her lecture continues, "I decided to fly to Indiana and spend a week combing the archives of the Lilly Library there."

At the Lilly, Anne had a revelation. "I discovered Sylvia Plath in her own, unexpurgated letters and in letters to her from her friends and lovers. . . . These letters, these breathing pieces of paper, brought [her] to life for me as the memoirs of the witnesses I had talked to had not." Anne goes on:

> Perhaps I was responding to the unselfconsciousness of the evidence, none of it trimmed for production to biographers, all of it conveying the contingent, as-yet-unfictionalized, still-happening present. . . . I came to feel in Indiana that I had finally met Sylvia Plath; that I was fonder of her because I knew her. I went back to her journal and re-read it with renewed understanding. . . . I began to understand, I think, why she had to become the extremist, uncompromising poet she was. Nothing in the middle lane would do. . . . Evening after evening, I emerged, dazed, from the air-conditioned library into the oppressive humidity of dripping Indiana nights. (I had forgotten the heavy, adhesive clasp of mid-western summers.) Living Sylvia's life instead of my own, I began to experience for the first time that intense feeling of identification with my subject that most biographers feel before they even begin their research. I realized sadly that I admired but had never liked Sylvia. Even before I began working with Olwyn Hughes, I had re-

coiled from what seemed to me her crude self-absorption and aggressive ambition. Now, I thought, I was beginning to see her in the round. I decided to go back to London and pick *Bitter Fame* to pieces once again. This time I was sure I could put together a critical biography myself.

Back in London, Anne set to work on her newly conceived biography. She was on course now, and no longer needed a genie. She knew what she was doing, and would work alone. She commanded Olwyn back into the lamp. Naturally, Olwyn refused. For the next two years, Anne and Olwyn were locked in mortal, uneven combat over the book. Anne's attempts to reclaim it—to be the author of her own book— were unsuccessful; she had lost control of the text when she made her devil's pact with Olwyn. Olwyn maintained her iron grip. Anne was always forced to retreat, compromise, give up something she wanted to use, put in something she wanted to leave out. Olwyn would not allow Anne to reject her offerings of hostile testimony. Anne's weak struggles on the pin, her attempts to stand up to Olwyn, only invited Olwyn's contempt and wrath. By 1988, things had reached such a pass that the "collaborators" were not speaking. Then, as the book was about to go the way of all the other failed Plath biographies, Peter Davison stepped in, and his offer to act as the final arbiter of what was to go into the book was accepted by both women. In 1989, a text was finally produced—one that Anne was not sure she wanted to publish under her name: "I had serious reservations as to whether I could allow the book to be represented as my work alone, rather than as the joint work of Olwyn Hughes and myself." Davison assured her that the book was "essentially mine (as indeed most of the writing still was)," and persuaded her to let the book appear as her own. She agreed, but wrote an Author's Note to apprise the reader of Olwyn's presence in the text. When Olwyn read the note ("admittedly a sotto-voce disclaimer on my part," Anne writes, "the ambiguity of which she was quick to pick up"), she would not have it: "On pain of instantly withdrawing permission to quote from Plath's writings, published and unpublished, she at the last minute substituted the present Author's Note, which encourages the reader to believe that the book appeared after Olwyn's revisions and improvements had been gratefully received."

II

THE train to Durham was a powerful express, and, unlike the sickly trains I had been stuck on earlier (and was to be stuck on a few days later), it made its way to Durham through the snow-covered country without incident. But the trip lasted nearly four hours, and I had time to read and reread various other writings by Anne in preparation for my interview with her at her house. One of these was a blue aerogram I had received from her at the end of January, a few days after a telephone call:

> . . . We never touched on the subject of victims. I do believe Sylvia's suicide has had a devastating effect on all associated with her—including her biographers. . . . all of us suffered a trauma of associated guilt. My argument with Sylvia is essentially a moral, philosophical one: to me, no art, no "great poem" is worth that much human suffering. After all, there is suffering enough in the world without creating it for the purpose of an interior psychodrama. I believe Sylvia, encouraged perhaps by her Freudian and well-meaning therapist, Ruth Beutscher, found her own psychodrama (a word I prefer to "mythology") so intoxicating and such an

inspiring source of poetry, that she lost all perspective. The notion that "perspective" has any place in Great Art is anathema, of course, to latter-day Romantics. But belief in "Art" of this kind, in the so-called "risk" of Art and the existential dilemma of the artist (give me genius or give me death) is, for me, akin to the beliefs of fundamental religious fanatics. In the end it leads (via Nietzsche, Weininger, and other German-Austrians of the decaying Hapsburg Empire) to the rise of Hitler; or the Ba'athist dictators (Saddam is only one), who threaten the whole fabric of society with intolerable absolutes. I disagree with Alvarez, with Plath, with Ted Hughes (perhaps) when they contend that the pursuit of the absolute has anything to do with the pursuit of truth. Truth is, in its nature, multiple and contradictory, part of the flux of history, untrappable in language. The only real road to truth is through doubt and tolerance. Unfortunately, philosophical skepticism can also become a mannerism; and the doubting leader is usually a bad one.

One more thing. Although I never contemplated suicide, for a long time in the 1970s I was, through my weakness and misery, to all intents and purposes an alcoholic. I have never confessed this to anyone outside the family; but I think you ought to know that my life has not been that of a nice bourgeois wife and mother. I left my children in Oxford (no, in Glasgow) in 1971, to the care of their father and grandparents, and went to live with a poet in a sort of desperate bid for my "real" self. I don't know if it was the *time* that was responsible (the infectious counterculture) or my own New England puritan upbringing. In any case, I spent ten or so years "in the wilderness"—writing "Correspondences" of course. But—and this is the point—*divided.* I now try to forget, as far as possible, those nightmare years. But I do know firsthand something of what Sylvia suffered, and Ted also. . . . I cannot believe that a biographer who does not understand the pervading madness of S.'s time can possibly understand her despair. Alvarez, of course, does; but he *admires* the extremism, self-indulgence, narcissism that I, after long experience, deplore.

While I had been astonished by Anne's candor when I first read the letter, I was not surprised by the revelation itself. *Correspondences*, although not autobiographical in any literal sense, had prepared me for it. Indeed, I would have been surprised if Anne *had* been a nice bourgeois wife and mother and had only imagined the pain and mess she wrote about in her poem. In another document I had taken with me on the train, an autobiographical sketch published in 1989 in a series called Contemporary Authors, Anne had set down the literal facts of her life—citing the actual parents, siblings, husbands, lovers, children, and moves from place to place (usually university towns) on both sides of the Atlantic. Here, again, the sense of an unconventional, unsettled life was rendered. But it was a fourth piece of writing—an essay called "Writing as a Woman," which appeared in a feminist anthology (*Women Writing and Writing About Women*, 1979)—that brought Anne into the sharpest focus for me, and made me feel I understood something about what had reduced her, a woman of substance and achievement, to the condition of helpless abjection that marked her encounter with Olwyn Hughes.

At my meeting with Anne at the University Women's Club I had asked her if there had been other relationships in her life like her relationship with Olwyn. Anne shook her head firmly and said, "No, I have never had a relationship anything like this before. I have never met anyone like Olwyn in my life." But now I saw that Anne had perhaps not looked closely enough. She had also said, "The image I have of myself and Olwyn is of me sitting happily at my desk writing, with Olwyn looking over my shoulder. Every time she doesn't like what I write she shoves me off the chair and takes up the

pen herself." In "Writing as a Woman" Anne studies herself
and her twenty-five-year-long efforts—only intermittently
successful—to stay in her writer's chair, and not be shoved
off by some Olwyn-like force. The first of these forces, she
says, was the pressure of "what used to be called 'womanli-
ness'—sex, marriage, children, and the socially acceptable
position of wife." Anne writes that she had not been willing
to sacrifice her life as a woman in order to have a life as a
writer, as Jane Austen, Emily Brontë, Stevie Smith, and Mari-
anne Moore, among other spinster writers, had done. "Surely
in the twentieth century, when society allows so much, it
ought to be possible to be a fulfilled woman and an independent writer without guilt. . . . As I look back over my own
experience, I see, however, that I have only *just* managed to
survive." She speaks of the traditional opposition between
domesticity and creativity: "Writing poetry is not like most
jobs; it can't be rushed or done well between household
chores—at least not by me. The mood of efficiency, of checking things off the list as you tear through a day's shopping,
washing, cleaning, mending, and so forth, is totally destructive of the slightly bored melancholy which nurtures my
imagination." But a few pages later Anne rejects this theory
of her failure to write during the unhappy five years of her
first marriage (to Robin Hitchcock, a well-meaning and
rather baffled young English businessman, who is the father
of her daughter, Caroline). She sees that she was unconsciously following the pattern set by her mother, who had
also wanted to be a writer but had been prevented by guilt
toward her family. "I began to realize that guilt could also be
an *excuse*. If I had really wanted to write, I would have done
so. So would my mother. . . . There is always time. No
amount of housework or baby-tending takes time from writing if you really want to write. Sylvia Plath wrote her great

last poems in the early morning before her babies were awake."

In the early seventies, now divorced from Robin and married to Mark Elvin, a scholar, and the mother of two more children, Anne began work on *Correspondences*, the earnest of her desire to write and the tour de force that was to be the centerpiece of her poet's career. Through letters written by the members of a single family over many generations, the book-length poem tells its story—of the iron hold of the puritan ethic in eighteenth- and nineteenth-century America, of its gradual loosening in the mid-twentieth century, and of its dissolution during the 1960s. The letters spell out the toll this ethic took of the lives it ruled—the lives of men no less than of women, though the women seem more crushed. A yearning that cannot be acted upon but is never absent from the margins of each correspondent's consciousness pervades the poem and gives it its pathos.

As the book comes closer to the present, the lives of three women come into prominence: Maura, who yearned to be a writer but lives out her life as a wife and mother; her daughter, Ruth, who wrote poetry and had a lover whom she sacrificed to remain a wife and mother; and Ruth's daughter, Kay, who is permitted by the counterculture of the 1960s to finally make the break with convention that the others have not dared to. But the price of Kay's emancipation proves to be as high as, perhaps higher than, the price of living bowed under the puritan order. Kay becomes an alcoholic and has a mental breakdown before she finds a kind of peace as an expatriate poet in England. Anne points out in "Writing as a Woman" that although the portrait of Kay is "a version of myself," it is not autobiographical. "All that I had suffered in my first marriage, all that I had felt about my child, my husband, my mother, came together in it. . . . And yet Kay is not me either. . . . I have never had a breakdown in a museum or lived in Westchester County or been married to a fashionable psychiatrist. Kay's *feelings*, her mixed love and hatred for her child, her sense of imprisonment in her house, her impulse to fly, to escape to drink or to an anonymous city—these feelings *have* been mine."

The work is brilliant, the voices of the letter writers are distinct, various, true. It has a poetic inventiveness, a sureness and confidence, along with a risk-taking nervousness, that bear the reader along as if he were reading a novel. How did Anne do it? How did she pull off the feat of breaking out of her mother's pattern and reconciling the claims of domesticity with those of self-expression?

Well, she didn't. As she wrote in her letter to me and in her autobiographical sketch, she had to leave her children and her second husband and go off with a poet—Philip Hobsbaum—to bring *Correspondences* to fruition. Like Plath, like so many women writers, she had to leave the daylight world and go underground to find her voice. Writing is a fraught activity for everyone, of course, male or female, but women writers seem to have to take stronger measures, make more peculiar psychic arrangements, than men do to activate their imaginations. Plath's own writing life, as we know from her journals and letters, from the testimony of Hughes and the writings themselves, was, until the final period, a painful struggle, a repeated, bloodying beating of the head against a wall. She started writing and publishing very early. (A poem was published in the *Christian Science Monitor* and a story in *Seventeen* when she was seventeen herself.) She had a great will to write (fuelled by the ambition of her real and internalized mother), and her capacity for rejection was apparently limitless: she received forty-five rejection slips from *Seventeen* before that first story was finally accepted. But she herself rejected as unworthy most of what she wrote—poetry or prose, published or unpublished. In Ted Hughes's introduction to *Johnny Panic and the Bible of Dreams*, he tells us that "her story-writing . . . always took place in an atmosphere of locked combat." The introduction—another variant on the true-self/false-self theme—sets forth the painful history of Plath's humiliating defeat by the genre she had chosen as her means of artistic and professional autonomy:

> Her ambition to write stories was the most visible burden of her life. Successful story-writing, for her, had all the advantages of a top job. She wanted the cash, and the freedom that can go with it. She wanted the professional standing, as a big earner, as the master of a difficult trade, and as a serious investigator into the real world. . . . "For me," she wrote, "poetry is an evasion from the real job of writing prose."

But she failed with her stories (her ambition to publish fiction in *The New Yorker* and the *Ladies' Home Journal* was never achieved), and, in Hughes's view, she had made a bad miscalculation in trying to write them. Her true vocation, like her true self, lay elsewhere. Throughout his essay Hughes quotes the self-denigrating comments Plath wrote in her journal: "Read over the stories written in Spain. They are so dull. Who would want to read them?" and "My Shadow story reads mighty thin, mighty pale," and "Disgust with the seventeen-page story I just finished: a stiff, artificial piece . . . none of the deep emotional undercurrents gone into or developed. As if little hygienic trap-doors shut out the seethe and deep-grounded swell of my experience. Putting up pretty artificial statues. I just can't get outside myself."

Hughes argues, "It was only when she gave up that effort to 'get outside' herself, and finally accepted the fact that her painful subjectivity was her real theme, and that the plunge into herself was her only real direction, and that poetic strate-

gies were her only real means, that she suddenly found herself
in full possession of her genius—with all the special skills that
had developed, as if by biological necessity, to deal with those
unique inner conditions." But this theory of Plath's art, beau-
tifully articulated though it is, doesn't satisfy. It restates what
we already know—that Plath's *Ariel* poems are successful and
the short stories are not—and it misstates the character of
the achievement of *Ariel*, in which Plath did nothing if not
"get outside" herself. If she hadn't, we wouldn't be reading
the poems; they would simply be the inarticulate cries of an
anguished woman. Which, in a sense, the stories are. There
is one, called "The Wishing Box," written in 1956, that illu-
minates the problem of the stories in an especially arresting
way. It is one of the weakest and most artificial of them all,
but it comes to riveting life when it is read—as it begs to
be—as a coded message about the predicament Plath felt
herself to be in as a writer. Although Hughes does not discuss
"The Wishing Box" in his introduction, he makes a general
comment about the stories that cannot but affect our reading
of it: "The themes she found engaging enough to excite her
concentration all turn out to be episodes from her own life;
they are all autobiography."

"The Wishing Box"—which may have been one of the
"dull" stories written in Spain, where Hughes and Plath spent
a long honeymoon—begins with a scene at the breakfast
table of a couple named Harold and Agnes. Agnes "smol-
dered in silence over her coffee, wrestling with the strange
jealousy which had been growing on her like some dark, malignant cancer ever since their wedding night only three
months before when she had discovered about Harold's
dreams." Harold's dreams are maddeningly rich and interesting and abundant, in contrast to Agnes's, which (when she
dreams at all) are prosaic, tedious, and fragmentary. As Harold obliviously regales Agnes with his marvellous dreams, she

feels more and more inadequate and envious and left out. One day, she confesses her dreamer's block to Harold. He is sympathetic—in his superior way—and proposes a mental exercise to stimulate her imagination, involving the closing of her eyes as she imagines an object. But the exercise doesn't work—it only adds to her feeling of insufficiency—and as time goes on she feels more and more miserable, takes to drink and to watching television, and finally, sunk in despondency, swallows fifty sleeping pills. The story ends ludicrously when Harold comes home from work and finds her lying dead on the living-room sofa, dressed in her emerald taffeta evening gown.

We note how closely Agnes's low estimate of her dreams resembles Plath's low estimate of her stories. But the most conspicuous feature of "The Wishing Box"—its emotional matrix—is the wife's hostility and envy. Until she found out about her husband's extraordinary dreams, her own prosaic dreams did not disturb her. Only after Harold has displayed the "royal baroque splendor" of his nightly productions do Agnes's own productions seem to her so pathetic and wanting. The premise of the story—that a woman's life can be poisoned, and even ultimately destroyed, by her feelings of inadequacy in the face of a man's superior achievements—is as farfetched and remote from observable experience as the Freudian concept of penis envy. And as true. (Freud's concept, of course, is not simply about anatomical difference but about what that difference connotes; it is a *description* of phallocentrism, not a recommendation of it.) The awful mixture of self-loathing and loathing and envy that Plath expresses in "The Wishing Box" is a central concern, perhaps *the* central concern, of contemporary feminism. But in 1956 there was no feminist movement or feminist theory, and relations between men and women were at a nadir of helpless transferential misprision. That Plath's struggles with writing should have become fused with her envy and resentment of men is not surprising. Many women who were trying to write in the fifties and sixties—women like Plath and Anne Stevenson and me—found themselves playing a kind of Harold-and-Agnes game with the men they were involved with. Writing got all mixed up with men. It was in some way the man's fault when the writing didn't go well, as it was Harold's fault when Agnes's dreaming didn't go well.

The smug, hateful Harold (he is a certified accountant "with pronounced literary leanings") would appear to be as far from the large-souled Adam of the *Letters Home* as one could come. (Harold resembles, if anyone, the smug, hateful Buddy Willard of *The Bell Jar*.) In November, 1956, Plath wrote to Aurelia, "We have such lovely hours together. . . . We read, discuss poems we discover, talk, analyze—we continually fascinate each other. It is heaven to have someone like Ted who is so kind and honest and brilliant—always stimulating me to study, think, draw, and write. He is better than any teacher, even fills somehow that huge, sad hole I felt in having no father. I feel every day how wonderful he is and love him more and more." And yet Ted-as-Harold was there, too, evidently. The testimony of the story when it is read together with that of the *Letters Home* gives us a powerful sense of the anarchy of mental life: in the unconscious we can comfortably love a person and hate his guts. It is only in conscious life that we feel we have to choose a side to come down on, decide one way or the other, surrender or fight, stay or go. In the case of Plath, it wasn't that she was more divided than the rest of us but only that she left such a full record of her ambivalences—which is why the study of her life is both so alluring and so disturbing, and why the predicament of her survivors is so dire. However, we cannot fail to notice a common denominator in the two visions of Hughes: he is a brilliant, kindly, lovable teacher or he is a stupid, smug, hateful one, but in both cases he is the *teacher* and she the pupil; she looks up to him, and she seeks help from him in filling the "huge, sad hole" of her inadequacy.

On the train, as I read over Plath's biographer's writings about her own struggle to be a literary artist, and pondered her many inevitably troubled relationships with men, on whom she had conferred more responsibility for the working out of her artistic fate than they could know what to do with, I began to obscurely make out a pattern to which the mired history of *Bitter Fame* belonged. In her autobiographical sketch, Anne writes of a period (1973–75) when, *Correspondences* completed, "I finally plucked up courage to go it alone." Having left the poet for whom she had left husband and children, she spent "two fruitful, independent years" as a writer-in-residence at the University of Dundee. But when, a decade later, the Plath biography confronted her with a literary project that was new and full of uncertainty, she once again drifted into a relationship of dependency, a sort of marriage of literary convenience, formed along familiar lines. That the new co-parent of Anne's literary progeny-to-be was a woman made no difference: the unconscious is no respecter of gender. But that the woman was who she was, with a special interest in the progeny, made all the difference in the world. Anne's previous "collaborators" had been willing to go away and leave custody of the work to her; Olwyn fought for custody tooth and nail. The fierceness of her involvement in *Bitter Fame* was apparent to me from Anne's Toronto lecture, and it would become even more apparent when I read the letters Olwyn wrote to Anne during their struggle for the book's authorship. But what I was most aware of now was the feeling of having stumbled across a key to the mystery of why Anne had walked so obliviously into Olwyn's web: she may have been too intent on weaving one of her own to notice where she was going.

III

O N March 9, 1956—thirteen days after her momentous first meeting with Ted Hughes at the *St. Botolph's Review* party, and three months before her marriage to him— Plath wrote to Aurelia:

> Oh, mother, if only you knew how I am forging a soul! . . . I am making a self, in great pain, often, as for a birth, but it is right that it should be so, and I am being refined in the fires of pain and love. You know, I have loved Richard above and beyond all thought; that boy's soul is the most furious and saintly I have met in this world.

Richard? Who is this man? A slip of the pen? No, he is Richard Sassoon, of whom Plath goes on to write:

> All my conventional doubts about his health, his frail body, his lack of that "athletic" physique which I possess and admire, all pales to nothing at the voice of his soul, which speaks to me in such words as the gods would envy.

The day after she bit Hughes, Plath wrote of him in her journal as "the one man since I've lived who could blast Richard," but Hughes went back to London without attempting to see Plath again, and Sassoon remained the unblasted love of Plath's life for another month. As Anne Stevenson shrewdly surmises in *Bitter Fame*, "although Sylvia had been violently attracted to Ted, the whole experience was too dreamlike to build hopes on, and, in any case, she still held to the habit of longing for Richard Sassoon." Of all the men in Plath's biography, Richard Sassoon is the most elusive and, in many ways, the most beguiling. The habit of longing for him has passed from Plath to the community of her biographers. Not one of them has been able to find him; he has disappeared without a trace. Not only his whereabouts but his entire post-Plath history is unknown. As Hughes has been trapped and imprisoned in the Plath legend, so Sassoon has flown out of it like a bird of summer.

He arrives in the story on April 19, 1954, in a letter from Plath to Aurelia: "Met Richard Sassoon (whose father is a cousin of Siegfried Sassoon)—a slender Parisian fellow who is a British subject and a delight to talk to." Plath was back at Smith after her breakdown of the previous summer and fall, and Sassoon was at Yale. On May 4, Plath wrote again to her mother about Sassoon, expressing the ambivalence that was to mark her idea of him throughout his two-year sojourn in her life: "A good Saturday with Sassoon up here—most unique—another bottle of exquisite Bordeaux wine and a picnic of chicken sandwiches in a lovely green meadow. Strange and enchanting evening spent in farmhouse while waiting for Sassoon and tow truck to get his car out of quagmire on rutted dirt road." The man is wonderful at Bordeaux and chicken sandwiches but can't get his car out of a rut. A Smith roommate of Plath's, Nancy Hunter Steiner, recalls in her memoir *A Closer Look at Ariel* a stunningly cruel remark Plath made about Sassoon's small size: "When he holds me in his arms, I feel like Mother Earth with a small brown bug crawling on me." Steiner recalls Sassoon himself as "a dark, brooding, passionate Gallic type whose brilliance and imagination were the equal of [Plath's]," and whom Plath endowed with "the qualities of a Byronic hero: an air of mystery and an almost sinister melancholia that she found fascinating." Steiner resolves the contradiction between Plath's views of Sassoon as a Byronic hero and as a crawling insect by attributing it to her "creativity."

As it happened, however, Sassoon, though he was "thin, nervous, little, moody, sickly" (in Plath's description of him in her journal), did not repel her, as other boyfriends she wrote about did. In fact, Plath's feelings about him, as they emerge from her writings, are movingly tender. His lack of physical attractiveness for her is something she regards with rue rather than resentment. If Plath actually permitted herself her bluntly mean comment to Steiner (the quotations of contemporary witnesses recollected after many years must always be regarded with skepticism), Sassoon emerges everywhere else in his Plath dossier as a sympathetic and appealing figure. As I read the intense, mannered love letters that Plath wrote to him in the winter of 1955–56—and made copies of for her journal—I was taken back to my own youth, and to the Sassoons I myself was in love with and loved to write ardent, pretentious letters to. Anne Stevenson told me that she, too, had had Sassoons in her life. The type flourished with special vigor in the Eisenhower fifties—it was a kind of joint creation of both sexes, a collaboration between bookish misfits, fulfilling each other's yearnings for romance. The boys invented themselves out of literary cloth (brooding, Gallic, Byronic, etc.), and the girls "read" them as if they were novels.

We do not have Plath's journals for her last year at Smith—she either didn't write them or didn't preserve them—and it isn't until the fall of 1955, when she was in Cambridge and Sassoon was studying at the Sorbonne, that the journals resume and we get the full flavor of her feeling for "this boy in France," as she spoke of him to the too young male undergraduates, to fend off their attentions. Sassoon, for his part, was fending Plath off. We don't know why—we don't have his letters from this period—but it appears that the emotional obstacles he put between himself and her (in her journal and letters she alludes to Sassoon's "ferocious, cold, and almost platonic scrupulosity," as well as to a Swiss mistress) only, or inevitably, kindled her passion. "I got a letter from my Richard this afternoon which shot all to hell but my sudden looking in myself and finding what I feared and fought so hard not to find: I love that damn boy with all I've ever had in me and that's a hell of a lot," she wrote in her journal. "Worse, I can't stop. . . . I love him to hell and back and heaven and back, and have and do and will. Somehow, this letter killed finally all those niggling doubts: you're as tall as he; you weigh more than he; you're physically as strong and healthier; you're more athletic." Just as Plath never wrote about Hughes without referring to his herculean hugeness, so Sassoon was never allowed to appear without his leitmotif of Proustian (or Ralph Touchettian) frailness. To Sassoon himself she wrote, "I love you with all my heart and soul and body; in your weakness as in your strength; and for me to love a man even in his weakness is something I have never all my life been able to do before." She then (the letter is extremely long) wanders off into an extraordinary vision of her woman's destiny:

> I feel I cannot really ever live with another man; which means I must become (since I could not be a nun) a consecrated single woman. Now, if I were inclined to a career as a lawyer or journalist that would be all right. But I am not. I am inclined to babies and bed and brilliant friends and a magnificent stimulating home where geniuses drink gin in the kitchen after a delectable dinner and read their own novels and tell about why the stock market is the way it will be . . . —well, anyhow, this is what I was meant to make for a man, and to give him this colossal reservoir of faith and love for him to swim in daily, and to give him children; lots of them, in great pain and pride. And I hated you most, in my unreason, for making me woman, to want this, and making me your woman alone, and then making me face the very

real and terribly immediate possibility that I would have to live my life chastely as a schoolteacher who sublimated by influencing other women's children. More than anything else in the world I want to bear you a son, and I go about full with the darkness of my flame, like Phèdre, forbidden by what austere *pudeur*, what *fierté?*

During Christmas vacation of 1955, Plath travelled in the South of France with Sassoon (this was when he evidently began to back away from her), and in the spring vacation she went to Paris to throw herself at him. "I feel I somehow must just walk to Richard's early one morning and stand there, strong and contained, and say: hello," she writes in her journal three weeks before the trip. She adds, "Oh, yes, I still think I have power: he may be sleeping with his mistress, leaving orders for me not to be admitted, or not there, or if there, worse, refuse to see me." He is not there. In her journal entry of March 26 Plath writes of arriving on Palm Sunday at Sassoon's house, at 4 rue Duvivier, after "preparing my opening speech," and being told by the "dark and suspicious" concierge that Sassoon was away and would not be back until after Easter. "I had been ready to bear a day or two alone, but this news shook me to the roots," Plath writes, and goes on:

> I sat down in her living room and wrote an incoherent letter while the tears fell scalding and wet on the paper and her black poodle patted me with his paw and the radio blared: "Smile though your heart is breaking." I wrote and wrote, thinking that by some miracle he might walk in the door. But he had left no address, no messages, and my letters begging him to return in time were lying there blue and unread. I was really amazed at my situation; never before had a man gone off to leave me to cry after.

This is where the published journal entry ends. The unpublished original entry, in the Smith archive, continues:

Dried tears, patted poodle, & asked where could find restaurant; wandered through fruit stalls in Champ-de-Mars
through flowers & crowds bearing palm sprays (not like ours
but all green small sprigs of leaves) and found large Brasserie. . . . Ordered Assiette Anglaise and coffee (which came
black & sour) and read Anouilh's *Antigone*, that magnificent
part the chorus does about tragedy. Gradually, amazingly, a
calm stole over me. A feeling that I had as much right to
take my time eating, to look around; to wander & sit in the
sun in Paris as anyone; even more right. I felt downright
happy when I ordered another cup of coffee with cream &
it was much better.

When *The Journals* were published, in 1982, they were
ungratefully received. Like *Bitter Fame*, they arrived in a state
of dishevelment that aroused the suspicions of reviewers.
Hughes's revelation in his introduction that he had destroyed
the last journal struck the first wrong note; the second was a
preface by the book's editor, Frances McCullough, about cuts
she made in the work. McCullough wrote:

> Because it is very early—in terms of the ages of Plath's
> survivors—to release such a document, there has been spe-
> cial concern for those who must live out their lives as char-
> acters in this drama. There are quite a few nasty bits
> missing—Plath had a very sharp tongue and tended to use
> it on nearly everybody, even people of whom she was inordi-
> nately fond. . . . So some of the more devastating comments
> are missing—these are marked "[omission]" to distinguish
> them from ordinary cuts—and there are a few other cuts—
> of intimacies—that have the effect of diminishing Plath's
> eroticism, which was quite strong.

McCullough's statement had an unfortunate result. By her
bringing attention to what wasn't there, what was there was

devalued. There is a belief abroad now that the published journals are some sort of censored and "suppressed" version of what Plath wrote, created by Hughes to protect himself. But in fact *The Journals* render a remarkably intimate portrait of Hughes, and have, if anything, a notably intrusive tendency; as with *Letters Home*, one is struck much more by what has been allowed to stand about "those who must live out their lives as characters in this drama" than by what has been taken out. The cuts that concern Hughes seem pathetically modest: excisions of embarrassing encomiums to his "banging virility" or of an occasional wifely complaint about things like the state of his nails. Mrs. Plath also had a hand in the removal of the "nasty bits," and here, too, more was left in than one might have expected. The "ordinary cuts"—which are the large body of the cuts—were made by McCullough, in the unsinister interests of making a readable book out of a mass of writing of uneven quality. Her cutting was in aid of moving the narrative of Plath's life along. In this, she was assisted by Plath herself, for Plath indeed wrote about herself and the people she knew as if they were characters in a novel. The journals are a kind of furiously written first draft of a bildungsroman into which the writer pours everything, knowing there will be time later on to revise and cut and shape and order. Plath writes about people with a novelist's noticing eye, and the journals' atmosphere of intrusive intimacy derives from this. We "know" Hughes and Sassoon and Dick Norton and Aurelia and Plath herself in the way we "know" characters in novels, which is more deeply and clearly than we know anyone in life except our closest intimates. Because the Annas and Vronskys and Holden Caulfields and Humbert Humberts do not exist outside the pages of their novels, we are unembarrassed by our voyeurism, by the abashing amount of personal information we receive about them. With the characters of Hughes and Sassoon and Norton and Aurelia, who have counterparts in life, we lose our feeling of comfortable omniscience; we feel we should look the other way—as in that moment of embarrassment when we meet our analyst on the street. As the analyst doesn't "belong" there—he should exist only in the consulting room—so the characters in Plath's journals become displaced persons of a sort. The character of Ted Hughes gives us the most trouble of all, since his real-life counterpart is so prominent—we keep fetching up against it in letters to newspapers, in publications of his work, in reviews of his work, in his activities as the executor of Plath's literary estate. With Sassoon, things are better: by obligingly disappearing from real life, he gives us leave to unanxiously enjoy his literary representation. Aurelia, for her part, foreshadows the eventual leaching of the traces of everyone "real" from the "fiction" of Plath's life; she is in her eighties and ill.

Plath's account of her spring vacation in France provides some of the journals' most vital moments, and has been little cut by McCullough. Her excision of the brasserie passage was a mistake, I think. Plath's recording of the calm stealing over her after she left Sassoon's house, and of her sense of her entitlement to the pleasures of Paris, wonderfully evokes the lability of feeling for which youth is famous (but which is not exclusive to youth; one recalls Proust's anecdote about Swann's father, who leaves his beloved wife's death chamber in tears, and then finds himself exclaiming over the beauty of the day and the pleasure of being alive). The two coffees, the first black and sour and the second with its transforming cream, underscore the point. But I can also understand McCullough's eagerness to get on with the story, which Plath herself tells with a headlong impatience, as if racing to beat a deadline.

The story, which covers journal entries from March 26 to April 5, is a meditation on Plath's fate as a woman. Finding herself alone in Paris, she is seized by a sense of crisis, a feeling that she has come to a turning point in her life among men. As Plath goes on to write of the new men she meets in Paris (an Italian journalist named Giovanni, whom she picks up on the street the night of her arrival, and who lends her the Olivetti on which she types the journal; an Oxford man named Tony with whom she goes to bed but who gets cold feet when it comes to the point), of the men she knows who happen to be in Paris at the time (Gary Haupt from Cambridge and Gordon Lameyer from America, both good-looking and dull), and of the absent Richard and Ted, she works herself into a fever of longing and dread, defiance and shame, resolution and vacillation. Hughes is now (rather shakily) installed in Plath's life. A few weeks after the *St. Botolph's* party, we learn from the journal, he returned to Cambridge and, late one night, with a Cambridge friend, threw stones at a window they thought was hers; Hughes returned to London without seeing her, but the friend, Lucas Myers, invited her to supper and then proposed that she meet him and Hughes in London on her way to Paris; she did this, and spent the night with Hughes, to her present vexation. "He does not know how much I could rip past here and be tender and wise, for now I am become too easy too soon and he will not bother to discover," she writes on Giovanni's Olivetti. In Cambridge, her timeless love for the diminutive Sassoon had not prevented her from aspiring to a crumb of attention from the magnificent Hughes. "Please let him come," she begged in her journal four days after writing Sassoon that she wanted to bear him a son. "Let me have him for this British spring. Please, please. . . . Please let him come, and give me the resilience and guts to make him respect me, be interested, and not to throw myself at him with loudness or hysterical yelling; calmly, gently, easy, baby, easy. . . . Oh, he is here, my black marauder; oh hungry hungry. I am so hungry for a big smashing creative burgeoning burdened love."

We know, though Plath doesn't as she sits typing in Paris, that she got Hughes for her British spring and after; she knows only that the weeks of her vacation stretch before her like the remaining years of a life (she can't go back to her dorm at Cambridge, which is closed for the vacation), and that neither of the two men she wants (at this point, Ted and Richard are almost interchangeable objects of desire) wants her. So she is reduced to filling the remaining vacation time in Europe travelling with the dreary Gordon. "I would rather be alone with my typewriter than with Gordon," she writes, "and his stupid stammering French and inability to make himself understood here, his utter lack of rapport, of that intuitive sensing of mood disgusts me." But what is a girl to do? As if in a precognition of feminist consciousness, Plath pauses to ask, "Is it some dread lack which makes my alternatives so deadly? Some feeble dependence on men which makes me throw myself on their protection and care and tenderness?" She rambles on incoherently about the men who are now her "alternatives." Sassoon, although unavailable, continues to haunt her with his "dark image"—and to displease her with his diminutive size. She contrasts his "slight, undisciplined body" and his "snail-and-wine taste" with "the orange-juice-and-broiled-chicken solidity" and "plain-steak-and-potatoes-with-nothing-done-to-them taste" of Gary and Gordon. (The huge Hughes has not yet sufficiently settled in Plath's imagination to be the only foil to Sassoon.) She considers telegraphing Hughes in London and asking if she can live with him in his flat until her dorm reopens but is inhibited by the thought of the bohemian friends who wander in and out of the flat, one of whom apparently walked in on her and Hughes in bed. In writing of her schoolgirl's dilemma of how to spend the rest of her vacation, Plath uses language like "Yes, all the auguries are for departure"; "And now the alternatives revolve in a fatal dance"; "It is the historic moment; all gathers and bids me to be gone from Paris." The Paris journal—like her journals in general—constitutes a kind of anatomy of the romantic imagination at work.

Plath's relentlessly humorless vision of herself as the heroine of a great drama gives her journal a verve and a lustre that the journals of more restrained, self-depreciating, classical (as opposed to romantic) writers lack. We all invent ourselves, but some of us are more persuaded than others by the fiction that we are interesting. Probably because Plath felt the chill of the void with such unnerving intensity did she need to put so many layers of heated self-absorption between herself and what lay outside. Stevenson begins *Bitter Fame* with an incident from Plath's young life, an anecdote about a poem called "I Thought That I Could Not Be Hurt," written when Plath was fourteen, about some terrible wound and grief, which turned out to be Plath's grandmother's accidentally smudging one of Plath's pastel drawings. Already, at fourteen, Plath knew that if she didn't care too much she might not care at all. She articulates this knowledge in a letter to Sassoon of December 11, 1955: "Perhaps when we find ourselves wanting everything it is because we are dangerously near to wanting nothing." The *Ariel* poems trace the short trajectory from being close to wanting nothing to wanting nothing. In the final poems, written in the terrible English winter of her death, Plath, like a feverish patient throwing off a blanket, sheds the ragged mantle of her rage and calmly waits for the cold of her desirelessness to achieve its deadly warmth. The journals and letters are the record of Plath's struggle against clinical and (if the two may be separated) existential depression by means of the various manic defenses offered by the romantic imagination.

IV

I N her own house, Anne Stevenson was not the person she had been at the University Women's Club. She sounded different—her speech was less clipped and British, and she spoke more slowly, more quietly, less compulsively— and she looked different: in a plaid skirt and red sweater, she had reacquired the coltish aspect I remembered from my glimpse of her in Michigan. At the University Women's Club, she had sat in a kind of dejected slump; at home, she was always in motion—jumping up to refill a teacup, dashing up the stairs to fetch a document, darting about the kitchen as she cooked the dinner she had invited me to stay for. She was a touchingly eager hostess. The house—two miners' cottages joined into a single two-story dwelling—was a maze of little rooms. I would wander into a room I thought I had been in before, and find I had not. There were at least two parlors, with fireplaces and books and pictures and sofas, each having the aspect of being *the* parlor. The rooms were separated by vague hallways into which dog-food and cat-food dishes and other unambiguously utilitarian objects (like a washing machine and a dryer) had found their way. The parlors were pleasant, inviting, slightly shabby, with pride of place given to books. The cat and the dog—two quiet, friendly beasts— slept companionably by the fireside in the room where we sat, Anne in a bentwood rocker and I on a sofa. At my behest, she was turning her thoughts to the still painful subject of her collaboration with Olwyn on *Bitter Fame* and what she herself had done to contribute to the debacle, where she had gone wrong. Characteristically, she alighted on an "other man" who might have bailed her out. "I now wish I had gone to see Alvarez," she said. "I should have said to Olwyn, 'I want to talk to Al Alvarez and see what he thinks of this.' He is not a stupid man. He is the only person in the opposition I respect, and if I could have talked to him frankly about what Olwyn was doing I think he would have said, 'Of course. Olwyn is always like that. She makes everybody cry.' But I didn't talk to him, and I would cry all night. I had no heart, I was so crushed. Because Olwyn was so sure that I was stupid and not getting it." Anne paused to pour me another cup of tea. Then she spoke of another "other man." "I wished all the time that Ted had been willing to work with me. I wrote to him several times and talked with him on the telephone. But Olwyn guarded him very carefully."

"You never saw him alone?"

"I never saw him at all."

"Do you think Olwyn only does what Ted tells her to do?"

"You mean, is he playing the good cop and she the bad cop? That is Peter Davison's theory, but I'm not sure. I think Ted is a passive guy. He's a very shy man, more comfortable with men than with women. One thing you must understand about Ted is that he was and still is an electrically attractive man, and that women throw themselves at him. Ted is not always able to say no. I'm pretty sure that all the time he was married to Sylvia—until Assia came along—he was faithful to Sylvia. But that doesn't mean women didn't throw them-selves at him constantly. So Sylvia had some reason—prob-ably more reason than I let on in *Bitter Fame*—to be jealous."

Anne then told the horrifying story of Assia Wevill's death. Wevill was the preternaturally beautiful and sexually mag-netic woman who precipitated the Plath-Hughes breakup. In 1967, she had a child by Hughes, a girl named Shura, and, in 1969, in a bizarre gesture of imitation, she, too, gassed her-self—adding the new twist of gassing the little girl as well. Hughes's sufferings may be (or, rather, can hardly be) imag-ined. The story of Assia Wevill's suicide does not appear in

Bitter Fame. (At the time of our talk, it had already been told in the English press, and was soon to be retailed in Ronald Hayman's and Paul Alexander's biographies.) "I'd known about Assia's suicide for years," Anne went on. "All the poets knew about it—but out of pity for Ted no one ever spoke of it. Ted didn't demand that people be silent, but he asked me to keep what I said about Assia to a minimum, and I obeyed. I didn't dream of disobeying Ted. He isn't bullying. He has this authority. When he says 'Please don't,' you obey. He always says 'Please.' Ted had ten years of absolute hell after Sylvia died. I was heartbroken for him, and I certainly wasn't going to scrounge around for dirt to throw at him. But Ted must have a dark side. Read his books *Crow* and *Gaudete*— they're clues to how he felt. *Gaudete* especially. Women are demon spirits in the poem. They're Racine's Phèdre. He felt he was being devoured. Ted was in the wilderness for ten years. I think he was, in a way, mad during this period. He is certainly not mad now. I am not an alcoholic now."

The short winter afternoon was waning, and I followed Anne into the kitchen to help prepare dinner. She had already made some of the elements of a lasagna; grating the cheese, chopping the mushrooms, and assembling the parts were still to be done. We worked together and continued to talk. Suddenly, in a somewhat desperate voice, Anne asked if I would mind going and reading in the other room. She needed to be alone so she could concentrate on her cooking. She couldn't both talk and cook.

I said "Of course" and withdrew. In the parlor next to the kitchen, I leafed through a pile of correspondence that Anne had gathered for me. Most of the letters were between Anne and Olwyn, but there were also a few from Peter Davison; from Anne's husband, Peter Lucas; and from Ted Hughes. The letters from Hughes immediately drew me, as if they were the electrically attractive man himself. As I looked at the pages of dense, single-spaced typing, punctuated by x-ings-out and penned-in corrections, I had a nostalgic feeling. The clotted, irregular, unrepentantly messy pages brought back the letters we used to write one another in the 1950s and '60s on our manual Olivettis and Smith Coronas, so different from the marmoreally cool and smooth letters young people write one another today on their Macintoshes and IBMs. Reading the letter giving Hughes's response to the chapters Anne had sent him of her short biography, I felt my identification with its typing swell into a feeling of intense sympathy and affection for the writer. Other letters of Hughes's that have come my way have had the same effect, and I gather that I am not alone in this reaction; other people have spoken to me with awe of Hughes's letters. Someday, when they are published, critics will wrestle with the question of what gives them their peculiar power, why they are so deeply, mysteriously moving.

Anne, having put the lasagna in the oven, rejoined me and again took up the subject of the collaboration with Olwyn. "At first, I liked Olwyn," she said. "I didn't dislike her until she began treating me as if I were a recalcitrant sixth-former: 'Why aren't you doing the homework I assigned you?' I'm not a very forceful character myself. But I am very, very stubborn when it comes to being pushed around in something I think I can do. When I came back from Indiana, I said, 'Look, Olwyn, really now, thank you, but I want to work on my own.' She saw it as an absolute insult. She was taken completely aback when this nice, gentle girl she had been having lunches with, and who had been so amenable and completely at her feet, suddenly became uppity. My husband had warned me, 'If you try to break off with her now, she won't let you.' He was right. I had fallen into a trap. There was no way out. *Bitter Fame* would have been an extremely good book if I had been able to follow my own bent. It was very painful to be interfered with at every turn. I really don't know why I published the book. My husband thinks I shouldn't have." She paused, and then asked me, "What do you think? Should I have published it?"

I didn't know what to say. I finally said that I had liked the book and that of course she should have published it. But I added that I thought the conditions under which it had been produced were horrendous, and that not every writer would have been able to accept them.

Anne said quickly, "I wasn't able to accept them. But I finally couldn't bring myself to let four years of work go down the drain. And there was something else. I was very poor, and I could never have paid back my advance."

Peter Lucas came home and joined the conversation. He is an old *Bitter Fame* hand, who had lived through all the bad years of the book with Anne, and had even intervened a few times with letters to Olwyn and Peter Davison. He is a bearish, bearded, gray-haired, young-looking, very pleasant man, who has a lawyer's leashed intellect, and who plays the role of sensible, protective husband to Anne's nervous artist. They are an affectionate couple, very amiable with each other. (Anne and Peter had met and fallen in love twenty years earlier but had not come together then.) He brought out wine, and he and I sat at the kitchen table while Anne moved about finishing the preparations for dinner. She opened the refrigerator door and let out a groan. "I forgot to put the white sauce in the lasagna," she said in a stricken voice. The omission was too late to correct; the lasagna would have to continue baking as it was. When we ate it, half an hour later, it tasted good, but Anne was critical of it and repeatedly apologized for it. As with the publication of *Bitter Fame*, she had no choice but to serve it, but she felt it to be an imperfect, compromised thing. I understood her anguish and felt for her.

V

W HEN I returned to Anne's house the next day, I found her still further transformed from the tense, plainly dressed matron of the University Women's Club. She had a calm and mild air about her, and she was wearing a pair of handsome tweed trousers and an interesting embroidered jacket. With her gleaming light-brown hair and her Virginia Woolf eyes (the glasses had disappeared without explanation), she personified the idea of the timelessly beautiful woman artist. Over lunch, we reminisced about our Michigan days and looked back with rue at the way things were for young American women college graduates in the 1950s. In a passage in *The Bell Jar* which is like a madeleine for bookish women of my generation, Esther Greenwood says:

> My mother kept telling me nobody wanted a plain English major. But an English major who knew shorthand was something else again. Everybody would want her. She would be in demand among all the up-and-coming young men and she would transcribe letter after thrilling letter. The trouble was, I hated the idea of serving men. . . . I wanted to dictate my own thrilling letters.

Anne's solution to the problem of being a B.A. without shorthand was to go to England. "I was very Anglophile," she said. "I had read Jane Austen and Charles Dickens and Henry James, and I expected England to be the book I had always wanted to live in. The crudeness of America appalled me. I thought all those crew-cutted boys I had to go on dates with were disgusting." But England turned out to be another book altogether. Anne expanded on the theory that, like her, Plath was neither prepared nor cut out for the fast track of English poets' society. "The bohemian world of English poetry would have been antagonistic to Sylvia's tidy puritanism—as it was antagonistic to mine," she said. "In this world, who you went to bed with was not a matter of much importance. Sylvia and I thought we could handle this, and of course we couldn't. Sylvia couldn't handle Ted acting like an English poet. She had always found it uncomfortable. There was some kind of Jamesian morality here. Neither of us was a natural bohemian, though I think I made a bigger stab at being one than Sylvia did." Anne went on, with her moving candor, to speak of the difficulties that attended her own literary maturation. "I think I told you, I used to drink a lot, the way women did. I couldn't get through the evening without quite a lot of drink. I had to break myself of that. I think Sylvia took up suicide the way I took up drink. It was something that bit at you. I have thought, Suppose you hadn't reached for the whiskey—suppose you had reached for the gas tap? Almost every writer I know has severe depressions."

"It's part of the work."

"Yes. It's when you know you're not fulfilling yourself, when you know you're letting yourself down. To be an artist, you have to grant a certain authority to yourself. The critical world wants to deprive you of this authority. A lot of critics—perhaps because they're failed artists themselves—love nothing so much as shooting down writers who *are* authentic artists. And if you're having a bad time in your life in order to produce this art the pain can produce an intolerable strain—which can come out as alcoholism or deep depression, or both. It's a most painful thing. I've never contemplated suicide, but there have been years in my life when I wished I were dead—years, anyway, when I thought the best part of me *was* dead."

"When was this?"

"At various times. One time was at the end of my first marriage. It was quite clear that I was a terrible wife for a businessman, and that I was never going to make it in the circles my husband thought it was important to move in. I had to summon a lot of energy to say that we had to be divorced. Neither of us had another partner. After that, I tended to have affairs with poets. Somebody would think I was a good poet and could be published, and I would go way up. Anyone who came along and told me that what I was writing was important—I loved him and went off with him. I think Sylvia would have left Ted if someone had come along who she thought was better for her poetry than Ted. I know this because I left my husband to live with Philip Hobsbaum when I was writing *Correspondences*. Philip was a poet. He was enormously helpful to me. I needed someone with whom I could talk about poetry all the time. Creating the book was something that was much bigger to me than my family." In her autobiography Anne had written:

> That winter I left Mark and the two boys in the care of a housekeeper and went to live with Philip Hobsbaum. Philip was as generous to the Glaswegian poets in those days as he had been, in former years, to the young Irish poets in Belfast. Seamus Heaney, for instance, was one of his discoveries. Like Mark, Philip was fond of children, and our living arrangements, though unconventional, were not uncivilized. When Mark moved into town, nearer to us and the university, I usually went for lunch with the children; Philip and I enjoyed them at weekends and took them for holidays.

Now Anne said, "That kind of arrangement wasn't unusual in the seventies; many people were leaving husbands or wives and living with other people, and everyone was being very civilized about it. I think we had this notion that once we were adults we could live with whomever we wanted to, but we still had responsibilities toward children. I think we all subscribed to a rather crazy sense of what was possible for a human being to do. I now look back on it all, I must say, in horror. It was not a happy time. But I did finish *Correspondences*." Anne went on to say that she had been hurt by the indifference with which *Correspondences* was met. "It came out about the time that Ted's *Crow* came out. *Crow* was a grand success, and no one paid any attention to *Correspondences*." The defeated note had crept back into her voice.

Peter Lucas, who had tactfully disappeared so that Anne and I could be alone, returned, and he and Anne drove me to the station. He joined our concluding conversation about *Bitter Fame*—again in a grimly knowledgeable way, as a sort of fellow survivor (barely) of a catastrophe. When we said goodbye, I felt a pang of affection and pity for this pair of decent and honorable people who had somehow strayed into a nightmare. Yet I was also conscious of a somewhat impatient unasked question: Why, when Anne, like her namesake in *Persuasion*, was finally safely reunited with her Wentworth, had she had to go and take up with Olwyn, yet another "other man"?

On the train back to London, I took out the packet of letters Anne had given me, and read through the correspondence between Anne and Olwyn in the years 1986 through 1989. I read with rapt fascination. I was being made privy to a lovers' quarrel. The letters rang with accusations, recriminations, resentments, grievances, threats, insults, shows of pitiableness, rage, petulance, contempt, injured pride—the whole repertoire of bad feeling that people who have got under each other's skin trot out and fling at each other like buckets of filthy water. The letters were abashingly real. They brought the story that Anne and Olwyn had told me back to its emotional source. I felt like the possessor of a great prize—the prize that the narrator of *The Aspern Papers* goes to such extreme lengths to try to get. Letters are the great fixative of experience. Time erodes feeling. Time creates indifference. Letters prove to us that we once cared. They are the fossils of feeling. This is why biographers prize them so: they are biography's only conduit to unmediated experience. Everything else the biographer touches is stale, hashed over, told and retold, dubious, unauthentic, suspect. Only when he reads a subject's letters does the biographer feel he has come fully into his presence, and only when he quotes from the letters does he share with his readers his sense of life retrieved. And he shares something else: the feeling of transgression that comes from reading letters not meant for one's eyes. He allows the reader to be a voyeur with him, to eavesdrop with him, to rifle desk drawers, to take what doesn't belong to him. The feeling is not entirely pleasurable. The act of snooping carries with it a certain discomfort and unease: one would not like to have this happen to oneself. When we are dead, we want to be remembered on our own terms, not on those of someone who has our most intimate, unconsidered, embarrassing letters in hand and proposes to read out loud from them to the world.

The conflict between one's relish, as a reader, of other people's secrets and one's dread, as a private person, of having one's own secrets get out came to a curious head in a lawsuit that the writer J. D. Salinger brought against the writer Ian Hamilton in 1986. Hamilton had written a short book about Salinger—entirely without Salinger's cooperation and against Salinger's wishes. His original plan, he says in his book, had been to write a tour de force, "a kind of 'Quest for Corvo,' with Salinger as quarry. . . . The idea—or one of the ideas—was to see what would happen if orthodox biographical ideas were to be applied to a subject who actively set himself to resist, and even to forestall them. It would be a biography, yes, but it would also be a semi-spoof, in which the biographer would play a leading, sometimes comic, role." But things had not worked out as amusingly as Hamilton had hoped. Salinger had obligingly not replied to the letter Hamilton wrote to him about his book ("Not getting a reply was an essential prologue to my plot"), and had even, on cue, written Hamilton a letter of protest and entreaty to be left alone when he learned that Hamilton was writing to family members. But, this done, the actual Salinger disappeared from the scene. Worse yet, as Hamilton pursued his researches into Salinger's childhood and youth, his own role as comically thwarted biographer was pulled out from under him; far from being thwarted, he was amassing a great deal of information about his subject. Although Salinger has been a recluse for over twenty-five years, he had lived in the world until the mid-sixties, and had left the usual traces. Thus, in due course, friends, colleagues, teachers, and others emerged who were willing, sometimes even eager, to talk to Hamilton. Then caches of Salinger's letters began to turn up in libraries, archives, and publishers' offices.

Presently, the self-reflexive scheme was abandoned and a regular, if somewhat bare and patchy, biography came into being. Its progress toward publication had reached the stage of bound galleys when the publisher, Random House, received a letter from Salinger's lawyer demanding, under threat of an injunction, that Hamilton remove the many passages he had quoted from Salinger's letters. Hamilton (and the Random House lawyers) had believed the quotations were permissible under the fair-use doctrine. But Salinger made the point—one that no subject of a biography had hitherto thought to make, probably because he was dead—that unpublished private letters were different from published writings, and therefore not covered by the fair-use doctrine. At first, Hamilton prevailed: Federal Judge Pierre Leval ruled that he was entitled to a sparing use of quotations from Salinger's letters. But then Leval's decision was overturned by an appellate court, which upheld Salinger's right to suppress letters written forty or fifty years earlier which now made him cringe. One would have thought that he had this right beyond dispute, once one had thought the matter through, even though the letters had been deposited in public archives, and even though he himself was a sort of public monument about which there was a lot of curiosity. I say this now, but I remember feeling peeved with Hamilton at the time for having spoiled things for the rest of us publishing scoundrels. If he hadn't had the dumb idea of writing about Salinger—who *of course* would sue—we could have gone on with our quiet snatch-and-run operations, and the lawyers at magazines and publishing houses could have gone on pretending that everything was all right if the number of words we had stolen wasn't excessive. Now the party was over.

Hamilton rewrote his book—which came out in 1988 under the title *In Search of J. D. Salinger: A Biography*—to exclude the contested quotations and to include a chapter about the lawsuit. When I read the book, a year ago, I found my crossness with Hamilton dissolving. I still thought (and think) the idea of writing about Salinger against his wishes a dismal one, but I was disarmed by Hamilton's awareness of the mess he had gotten himself into, and by his candor about the financial necessity that had kept him from walking away from it. Like Anne Stevenson, he had no nowhere else to go. He describes his feelings when he got Salinger's letter of protest and entreaty:

Here was this letter, obliging me to face up to the presence of the man himself. He wanted to be left alone. He'd kept his side of the bargain: by not publishing, by refusing all interviews, photographs, and so on. He hadn't gone quite so far as to withdraw his books from circulation, but perhaps it wasn't in his power to do so. He had, it would appear, behaved with dignity and forbearance whenever some eager college student had turned up at his door. Didn't he have the same right to his privacy as you and I?

Hamilton answers the question, "Well, yes. But then again, not quite." To express the ambivalence he feels toward his project, he divides himself into two people, a "me grappling feebly with the moral issues" and "my biographizing alter ego, now my constant companion, merely eager to get on with the job." There is a charming moment in one of the research libraries where Salinger's letters are on deposit: as Hamilton sits waiting for the Salinger file to be brought to him, he idly thumbs through the library's card index of its holdings. "Needless to say, the first name I looked up was HAMILTON, IAN (1938—). . . . To my horror, more than a dozen letters were listed under my defenseless name. Why, anyone could just walk in and. . . . My companion indicated that the Salinger dossier was now sitting on Desk Three."

The journalist works under the same curse as the biographer. As I sit with my treasure of Olwyn and Anne's letters, contemplating my next move, I feel the tug of the two selves, just as Hamilton did. On first sight, the Hamilton decision appears to do away with the moral anxiety of the writer who proposes to use substantial excerpts from letters in his text: he either gets permission to quote or he doesn't. So where can he go wrong? Everywhere. For if he receives permission to quote—as I have received permission from Olwyn and Anne—it means only that the author of the letters (or his literary executor) has become an accomplice; he has consented to violate his own privacy, to betray himself. Occasionally, the reasons behind this complicity have something to recommend them, but the letter writer's participation only tempers the transgression; it does not let the biographer or journalist off the moral hook. On the other hand, when a writer is refused permission to quote, his moral salvation is no better assured; in fact, his scope for immoral action may be even greater. Since he cannot unread what he has read, unsee what he has seen, unimagine what he has imagined—and since he is not a discreet lawyer carefully guarding his clients' secrets but a professional blabbermouth and tattle-tale—the denial of permission to quote may act as a spur not only to his ingenuity but to his malice. Hamilton's para-phrases of the passages in Salinger's letters that he was not allowed to quote are tinged with irony and unfriendliness. Two biographies of Plath that came out in 1991—Ronald Hayman's *The Death and Life of Sylvia Plath* and Paul Alexan-der's *Rough Magic*—employ paraphrase in a way that is a chilling object lesson in its use as an instrument of tenden-tiousness.

VI

LEAFING through the Olwyn-Anne correspondence, I have the sense of being in the company of an old and all too familiar presence, and suddenly, in an intuitive flash, I know what it is. I recognize Olwyn as a personification of the force—sometimes called the resistance—that can keep the writer from writing. She is the voice that whispers in your ear and tells you to put down your pen before she knocks it out of your hand. In letter after letter she tells Anne the withering things that writers tell themselves as they try to write. Seen as a dialogue between the writer's inner voices—the one abu-sive and scornful, the other defensive and plaintive—the Olwyn-Anne correspondence becomes something more than the trace of a quarrel between two women who should never have worked together. In a typical letter (of August 24, 1987) Olwyn says:

> Even with the written accounts by various people I've been supplying you with, the details I've rooted out, and so on, I've often been surprised by your lack of grasp of what they represented as biographical material and your reluctance to put them to use. I've also been disappointed that you have never (as far as I can recall) gone back to any of these sources with further questions or requests for any clarification. It has been as though you've been hoping only that there isn't any *more* stuff to evaluate and that the book will be finished SOON. You have been working doggedly—at least on the purely biographical level—toward the END of the book, not the final CREATION of the book. You have been to a degree resisting your material. . . . Ted's offer that if you had questions you should list them for me and he would answer them as they came up was almost totally ignored apart from a couple of queries months ago. Doubtless you were counting on a long meeting with him to clarify certain matters—but again I feel that if seeing him is going to be useful at all I shall have to make my own list of all lacunae where he could help and take notes myself during the meeting. Indeed, I think it would be better if we cobbled together a list of questions that I can put to him before the meeting and that any meeting simply serve as an occasion whereby, seeing the sort of man he is, you could brush from your mind various cobwebs you seem to have about his character and likely behavior.
>
> Now as you know I've been accepting all this and more with good grace—with a lot of sympathy for your moments of misery and no little guilt that I got you into this (though you did very willingly accept my suggestion you do the book, you clearly had no idea of what would be involved). I've been thinking "Poor Anne" and redoubling my efforts

and the hours and hours of phoning, correspondence, notes, searching through letters, journals and the rest. My own work is very behind—it's been seriously neglected. I've also stifled my own resentment at the various fits of antagonism toward me when I presented you with more material in various forms, as I understood it stemmed from your feeling of carrying too heavy a weight (and I know, none better, how depressing much of this material is). I could never understand your lack of willingness to let me help you *carry* the weight. Lately, though, I've been thinking not "Poor Anne" but "Poor me" (and even "Damn Fool Me"). . . . And such phone calls as I've had with Peter Davison have bothered me. It's almost as though he saw his role as defending you from me. I told him at one point I was sending you more notes and he actually said "Leave her alone with her writing, you'll drive the poor woman mad!" Now God knows what version of events you have been telling Peter to provoke *that* sort of message. He clearly had no conception of the method of work and was totally unaware that much of what you were "writing" sprang directly from the notes—both from the point of view of material given in them, and hints (as I've also wasted a great deal of time being positively oriental in tact, as straightforward dialogue seemed to upset you) how to interpret, select, and *use* the mass of material you have via me. . . .

You have always been quite open about your lack of real interest in the lumber of biography. But I did assume that having taken on the job you would apply yourself in a workmanlike way to marshalling all the biographical stuff I gave you and you obtained for yourself. I thought you would then become fascinated by it and handle each new piece of the jigsaw with pleasure and interest as it fell into place, slowly forming the whole picture. . . . Instead, to get this material properly represented in the book, to try to stop you cutting or avoiding the myriad relevant—and interesting for a reader—tiny brushstrokes I've had to *fight* all the way. . . .

Anne, for her part, personifies the writer at bay. She gives voice to the writer's anxiety, resentment, boundless self-pity. She writes Olwyn on December 28, 1987, "Please respect me as the author of this book and cease to persecute me with unpleasant references to my 'vapours.'" And, on February 13, 1988, "I really don't think we have much more to say to each other, so please respect my wish to be left in peace. No letters, no phone calls. You have brought me to the edge of breakdown many times in the past year." And, on March 12,

> As for the motives you attribute to me, you should know enough of my character by this time to realize that, while I detest being bullied, I wholly dislike calumny and slander. . . . I sympathize with Ted not wanting to be involved. I, too, want to go on with my life. My daughter has just given me a grandchild, I have been trying to get back to my own work after two years of sterility—Olwyn, I want a life again, not these unprofitable quarrels and vendettas!

And, on May 18, 1989,

> A person can take just so much flak, so much of being pushed into the mud, kicked, insulted, threatened, bullied, bulldozed into submission. . . . You want the world to think you "helped" me with Bitter Fame because I was too stupid to write it without you. Can't you see that half the time I was so exhausted from fighting rounds with you in the ring that I had neither the energy nor the will to give concentrated attention to the book. There are ways of "helping." If you had been capable of sitting down with me and going over the manuscript in a quiet, sensible manner; or if you had told me at the beginning that you intended to scrutinize and revise every sentence; or if you had taken over the book at an early stage and written it all yourself—well, then all

would have been different. As it is, four years of my life have disappeared in miserable wrangling. My eyesight, my digestion, my joie de vivre, the poems I might have written—all victims of your relentless persecution.

But then, astonishingly, near the end of the May 18 letter— a very long one—she writes, "In spite of my bruised feelings, I am grateful to you. All the writings and rewritings on both sides have honed the book down and sharpened its impact. In the end, with Peter Davison, we have produced a fine thing." With the work finally and actually somehow done, Anne can distance herself from the ink-stained kvetch that is her writing ego, and give the resistance its due. Now that she has defeated it, she can be generous. She can acknowledge that without Olwyn's "dissatisfactions and accusations" the work would have been a much poorer thing. On Olwyn's side, the losing side, there is no generosity. Continuing to mutter that she should have got someone else for the job, that she was misled by Anne's nice tweeds, and so on, Olwyn is the emblem of the failure that every successful piece of work also is—the ghost of the impossible ideal that gave it its life and does not survive its development and completion. The Olwyn force wins only when the writer bows to its power and puts down his pen.

VII

ON a gray afternoon, I sat with Al Alvarez in his living room in Hampstead, in a crooked little house on a street that goes down a hill. The room had wooden floors covered with Persian carpets; there were modern paintings and primitive sculptures; and in a window facing the street were flowering cyclamen, narcissi, and African violets. It was a compact, handsome, very agreeable room. Alvarez himself was very agreeable. He was older than I had expected. But everybody was older than I had expected. The characters in the Plath story are all getting on in years. Plath's contemporaries are men and women approaching sixty or just past it. Her mother is in a nursing home. Only Plath remains embalmed in her heroine's youth and angst.

Alvarez poured tea into large green, square-cut cups and spoke with a kind of grim satisfaction of his decisive role in the discrediting of *Bitter Fame.* "Everything we've ever heard about female bitchiness—a kind of permanent pressure to cut people down to size—seemed to me to be embodied in that book. But until I wrote my review, nobody had noticed it. John Updike, who is no one's fool, had done a sort of puff for the book; it came with my review copy. I think if no one had pointed out how bitchy it was, the book would have passed as the final, authoritative version." He went on, "Anne Stevenson is doing a big number, saying it's all Olwyn's fault—'Olwyn made me write the book,' etcetera, etcetera—but I think she was a very willing collaborator with Olwyn. She may say 'Olwyn pushed me into it,' but I don't think she needed a lot of pushing. She went along quite willingly." He then reiterated the theory set forth by the *TLS* reviewer, who had wounded Anne so deeply by charging her with envy of Plath. "I thought there was a huge element of unconscious envy in *Bitter Fame,*" he said. "A minor poet's envy of a major poet." I asked if he had read *Correspondences,* and he said he hadn't but had been unimpressed by the poems of Anne's that he had read. "I don't claim to be an expert on her work," he said. "She may have written some very good poems, but I just feel she's a kind of pale figure and was probably co-opted by Olwyn and Ted *because* she was a pale figure."

The conversation turned to his memoir of Plath, and Alvarez said, "When I wrote it, in the late sixties, which was quite soon after the event, I felt, perhaps misguidedly, that it wasn't anybody's bloody business what happened between Ted and Sylvia. I knew far more than I was prepared to say then. I didn't say, for instance, that when Ted left Sylvia he came and stayed with me in the studio I used to have near here. When Sylvia started dropping in on me there, I was convinced that it was to sniff around the lair where Ted had been. She also came because of poetry, of course. In those days, I was the poetry editor and critic of the *Observer*, which was *the* place to publish poetry. It was part of the literary world then, in a serious way. Lowell's *Life Studies* had recently come out, and the *Observer* was publishing him and Berryman and Roethke. I was writing a good deal of poetry myself at the time, and I was a critic who took Sylvia very seriously. What you have to realize is that in those days the stuff she was writing was in no way generally accepted. People were hardly falling over themselves to publish her poems. People didn't understand what she was getting at, or didn't like what they saw."

"You were an exception."

"She knew I could read those poems and listen to them."

In his review of *Bitter Fame* in *The New York Review*, Alvarez had also made a point of his disinclination to publicly pry into the Plath-Hughes marriage, writing, "I myself have always believed, as Robert Graves wrote of another tragic couple, 'the hazards of their love-bed / Were none of our damn business.'" But now, under the lowering influence of a journalist's visit, he grew indiscreet. "The thing about Ted is that he is a terrifically attractive man," he said. "Before my second marriage, I had an Australian girlfriend, who knew Ted, and she told me that when she first set eyes on him her knees went weak. 'He looked like Jack Palance in *Shane*,' she said. And I knew another woman, a psychoanalyst, who had such a strong reaction when she first met Ted—she told me this many years later—that she actually went to the bathroom and vomited. Ted kind of went through swaths of women, like a guy harvesting corn. Sylvia must have known that. Women really did hang around him. Of course, I don't know what happened between Ted and Sylvia, but I do know, from my own experience, that one of the things that happen in a bad marriage is that people fuck around a lot. And it's intolerable—intolerable for both."

"Wasn't that a period of bad marriages?" I said.

"Yes. Exactly. It was the period of Albee's *Who's Afraid of Virginia Woolf?* It was the period of Berryman's poem 'New Year's Eve'—which, I suspect, was about one of Hannah Arendt's New Year's Eve parties. They were marvellous parties. Did you ever go? I went to a couple. I always saw Berryman there. His poem has a marvellous line: 'Somebody slapped somebody's second wife somewhere.'"

"It brings back the time," I said.

"Doesn't it!"

Alvarez turned to his own relationship with Plath in the fall of 1962 and spelled out what he had left vague in the memoir. There, to account for his rejection of her, he had murmured about "responsibilities I didn't want." Now he confessed that it was Plath herself he didn't want. Another woman had just come into his life, he told me—the woman who was to become his second wife—but that wasn't the issue. The issue was that "Sylvia just wasn't my style—she wasn't my physical type. She was a big girl with a long face. She had wonderful eyes, marvellous live eyes, and she was so damn clever and so full of feeling. I loved her talent and her passion for poetry. I loved her the way I love D."—here Alvarez mentioned a woman we both know. "You know D. She's so clever, so full of life. Do you see what I mean?

That's what I felt about Sylvia. Do you see what I'm getting at?"

I saw what he was getting at, and it made me uncomfortable. As Alvarez had flatteringly mistaken me for someone who might have been invited to Hannah Arendt's parties in the fifties (I doubt whether I even knew who Hannah Arendt was then), so he now distressingly mistook me for someone who could listen without a pang to his discussion of women he didn't find attractive. I felt like a Jew who is tacitly included in an anti-Semitic conversation because nobody knows he's Jewish. In his review of *Bitter Fame*, discussing the feminist vision of Plath as "a great woman artist who was abused, put upon, and betrayed by men," Alvarez had written, "In every respect this is the crudest sentimentality, and I suspect Plath, who liked men and trusted them, would not have appreciated it. . . . *Bitter Fame* demonstrates in great detail that, both living and dead, Plath had a great deal more to fear from her own sex than from any man." But as he spoke of Plath now (and of D) he cast doubt on his words. Behind the smiling collegial face I showed to Alvarez—whose charm and warmth and wit I responded to—I scowled and nursed my woman's grudge. Surely the "big girl with a long face" had more to fear from men. We know from *The Journals* and *Letters Home*, and infer from the autobiographical *Bell Jar*, that Plath suffered cruel indignities at the hands of men. In the figure of Buddy Willard she created a lasting monument to an especially noxious type of self-satisfied jerk that flourished in America in the forties and fifties. Alvarez, of course, is no Buddy Willard. His words were heedlessly uttered, no doubt the product of the conversation's retrospective pull—the words of a kind of revenant. And, in all fairness to Alvarez, I should say that Plath isn't my type, either. All the photographs of her disappoint me. Over the years of the photographic archive, she changes, gradually losing the blond, dark-lipsticked blandness of her college period and the crisp, American housewifeliness of Alvarez's memoir. But of her *Ariel* persona—queen, priestess, magician's girl, red-haired woman who eats men like air, woman in white, woman in love, earth mother, moon goddess—there is no trace in the photographs. The fault may be with photography—some people never really appear in their photographs. Or it may be that Plath was only on the verge of showing herself in photographs when she died, her "true self" not yet available to the camera's vacant gaze.

At the end of the visit, I asked Alvarez about the incident of the withdrawal of the second half of his memoir from the *Observer.* He said, "When Ted wrote and said the memoir was an invasion of privacy, I didn't put up any sort of fight about publishing the second half. If it upset him that much, I thought O.K." He suggested that I go to the British Library and read the correspondence between him and Hughes about the incident—it is part of an archive of personal papers Alvarez sold to the library—and a few months later I did so. As I sat in the library's manuscript division reading the correspondence, I recognized the beginnings of the sensations I had felt in Anne Stevenson's house while reading Ted Hughes's letters. Hughes is Vronsky to Plath's Anna. He is the man on the train with the unbearable toothache. When he writes about Plath, he renders all the other writings about her crude and trivial. He writes with brilliant, exasperated intelligence and a kind of Chekhovian largeheartedness and melancholy.

In the first of two letters about the *Savage God* memoir—several pages of small, spiked handwriting—Hughes tells Alvarez that he has done something unspeakable in making public the details of Plath's suicide. "It is humiliating to me and to her mother and brother to have her last days exhumed in this way, as you do in your memoir, for classroom discussion," he writes, and goes on:

> You have supplied details and interpretations in a form that is now being taken as the official text. I thought you were sensitive to this sort of atmospheric persecution, because it is a sort of persecution. It was enough and too much before. Nobody could have written that scenario of her suicide but you (or me), and I cannot see how you persuaded yourself it was necessary. I would like to know what purpose you think it's going to serve. You kept saying you would show me what you were writing about her—why didn't you? For you, it was something you wrote, no doubt against great inner resistance, for your readers, it's five interesting minutes, but for us it is permanent dynamite.

Hughes then moves on from the atmospheric to the particular harm he feels Alvarez has done:

> For you, she is a topic of intellectual discussion, a poetic, existential phenomenon. . . . But for F. and N. [Frieda and Nicholas Hughes, then eleven and nine], she is the absolute centerpin—they have made her very important, the more so because of her obvious absence. Throughout the mess I've been making of replacing her these last years, their image of her—of what she did and was—is going to decide their lives. . . . Before your details, it was vague, it was a mystery. But now you have defined the whole thing, and handed it to the public. In a real way, you have robbed them of her death, of any natural way of dealing with her death. This will add up through every year they live. For you and everybody else, it is fading fast—you've solved the mystery of *exactly what happened, and how.* (You've given a version, anyway.) But for F. and N., it has not yet properly begun; the presiding fact

of their future will only really dawn on them when somehow they meet your memoir. . . .

They had enough of the facts and the truths living in the mausoleum Sylvia left for them. What your memoir supplies is not just facts—(so few of the facts—so many fictions and mere speculations trying to be facts)—but poison. Poison is no less poison for being a fact.

Hughes subsides into a calmer, though bitter, discussion of the situation of Plath's survivors, but then, in a kind of second wind of fury at Alvarez, he writes:

Another thing. Not even temporary insanity would explain your completely false remarks implying that there was some sort of artistic jealousy between Sylvia and me. . . . You saw little enough of us. Both of us regarded you as a friend, not a *Daily Mirror* TV keyhole, rat-hole journalist snoop, guaranteed to distort every observation and plaster us with these know-all pseudo-psychological theories, as if we were relics dug up from 10,000 B.C. Of our marriage you know nothing. . . . It is infuriating for me to see my private experiences and feelings re-invented for me, in that crude, bland, unanswerable way, and interpreted and published as official history—as if I were a picture on a wall or some prisoner in Siberia. And to see her used in the same way.

Alvarez wrote back a letter full of sense and reasonableness—a very good letter, in the ordinary course of things. But in the obliterating shadow of Hughes's emotional rhetoric it seems flat and inadequate. "You know perfectly well that the memoir is not a piece of sensationalism," Alvarez begins, and he goes on:

It was written with great care and as a tribute to Sylvia—among other reasons, to lay some of the wild fantasies which are current about her death, fantasies which I imagine you must have heard of more than I. . . . I have not intruded into your marriage or made public any intimate details about it. They did not seem to me to have anything to do with what I was writing about, or to be anybody's business. So I kept them out, although, obviously, I knew about it, and, equally obviously, Sylvia talked about it at times. Even Olwyn phoned me when she read the memoir . . . to say she liked it and thought it was tactful. She corrected me only on a couple of details. . . .

As for the children, God knows that is an appallingly difficult thing. But I would have thought it better for them eventually to see this [memoir], which is at least written with some kind of consideration and feeling for their mother, rather than a cloud of vague and malicious rumors. . . . I did not know you hadn't yet told them about it, but there is no way in which they won't eventually find out. I would have thought the pop distortions going around would be a great deal more harmful.

I will do what I can about the *Observer*. . . . I have phoned them already.

For the last 10 years or more, I have taken a lot of trouble to get both your poetry and Sylvia's read with understanding and a proper respect. I have done so not because you are friends of mine but because I think you the most gifted poets of your generation. Sylvia knew this, and knew I understood in some way what she was trying to do. That, presumably, is why she came to me with her poems after the separation. To imagine now that I am simply cashing in on her death or making a glib intellectual point is a complete distortion of everything I have written, both here and before. I am sorry you should choose to take it that way.

Hughes's reply is a very long typewritten letter—five and a half single-spaced pages. Alvarez has prodded him to an even deeper level of anger:

You say I know perfectly well the memoir is not a piece of sensationalism. Easily said. I don't know that at all—and neither do you. . . . Sylvia now goes through the detailed, point-by-point death of a public sacrifice. Her poems provided the vocal part for that sort of show. Your account, in apparently documentary style, of how she lived up to her outcry inevitably completes and concludes the performance. Now there actually is a body. The cries drew the crowd, but they came not to hear more cries—they came to see the body. Now they have it—they can smell its hair and its death. You present in the flesh what the death cries were working up to. The public isn't really interested in death cries unless they guarantee a dead body, a slow painful death, with as many signals as possible of what it is feeling like. And you present that, the thing the public really wants and needs—the absolutely convincing finalised official visible gruelling death. . . .

Whether you thought of it or not, to a sensation-watching and half-hysterical congregation (which her followers now are), your article is the ultimate sensational desired event. Only one thing could go further: that she reappear and go through the whole thing again, correcting all errors of report, on TV—stopping at intervals to answer interviewers' questions, giving her feelings and intentions. . . .

You say your article was written with care, but with what sort of care? I see only care of a very narrow technical sort—care to get the tone right and keep it right, and I can believe that was difficult, and depressing too. . . . Your care was like the care of a witness in court—this is all I know, my lord, I can't say any more than the way it appeared to me, etc.—and if you had made it clear that that is what you were presenting, at least a reader would know how to place your remarks, just how much credibility they carried. But even that would be forgetting the great point of care that really decides the whole thing—care about whether this whole project wasn't a terribly wrong thing to do at all, unethical and insensitive in every way, a wrong thing to do with the confidences of a friendship, a wrong thing to do with a keyhole view of an event that went out of everybody's grasp. . . .

How can you call it a tribute to her—to make a public spectacle of the one thing she ought to be allowed to keep to herself if nothing else—her infinitely humiliating private killing of herself. . . .

As for your article laying the wild fantasies, you know the opposite is much more likely. Before this, the fantasies were hot air, blowing each other away as fast as they were invented, all of them perfectly weightless. . . . All that nonsense is just rumor eating rumor. But now you have provided what seems to be substance, real fact and foundation—the story from one who was in the room. Between her writings and your article is a whole new world of hypothesis. And the commercial and career need for articles and theses and class material will make sure that world gets overpopulated, and your facts get turned into literary historic monuments. Nobody knows better than you that your article will be read with more interest than the poems ever were, and will be used more by the wretched millions who have to find something to say in their papers. The only difference in the fantasies now will be that they will be ten times as confident in their outrageousness.

At this point in Hughes's letter, I began to feel the excitement I had felt in another archive—in the Smith College Library's Rare Book Room, where many of Plath's typescripts and manuscripts are deposited, and where I was perusing the first draft of her poem "The Rabbit Catcher," of 1962. On the first page of the draft and on a part of the second page, the poem is unrecognizable—disconnected lines, most of them scratched out. There is the sense of a mind stirred by something, a mind activated but not able to move forward, like a car spinning its wheels in a rut, unable to get a purchase. Suddenly the car surges forward. "It was a place of force," Plath writes, and the rest of the poem follows the well-known first line essentially as we know it. The change from going nowhere to going somewhere happens so quickly that the reader of the draft is stunned, and all the more moved. In the middle of the letter to Alvarez, Hughes arrives at a moment that is like finding solid ground beneath his wheels. What has come before has been a kind of preamble—the trace of a mind repetitively whirling and straining toward the idea that finally breaks through. Hughes says:

> You didn't distinguish between two completely different kinds of writing . . . between a subjective work that was trying to reach an artistic form using a real event as its basis, and a documentary work that professes to present anything except errors—everything very purely told and impersonal—of some event that did really happen and is still an active part of some lives.

Hughes goes relentlessly on with his excoriation of Alvarez and with his analysis of the fundamental moral problem of journalism and of biography that involves living people:

> If your intentions had been documentary style, if your respect had been for what really happened, and the way things really went, you would have asked me to be co-author. And if I'd refused to cooperate, as I certainly would, you would have said, "O.K., that's one piece that can't be written." You would have done that unless you were keener to get your private account published than to get the fullest account possible and to do the human and decent thing at the same time. . . . The egoistic journalist in you . . . the publish-and-be-damned journalist (you publish and let the others be damned), it just fouled you up, it betrayed you and, incidentally, us. . . . It's only by seeing how the U.S.-ethos journalist in you rationalised you out of your real heart and your real

imagination that I can understand how that piece came to appear, and how what began by being written in a sacred way by one part of you, as a private, personal document, was grabbed and sold by the other part, sucked out into the greedy demand of that empty public.

The former friends did not speak for many years. They finally shook hands and mended the quarrel at a memorial service for Robert Lowell, at which both read Lowell poems. There has been brief, cordial, cursory correspondence between the two men since, and one near-meeting. "As I remember," Alvarez told me, "I was terribly hurt by Ted's letters, because, one, I had assumed he was a good friend and, two, he knew as well as I that I had bent over backward, almost—but not quite—to the level of falsifying the evidence, to keep the business of their marriage breakup out of my account. My impression of those letters, which I don't remember much of—I kind of skimmed them before giving them to the British Library—was that he'd gone kind of barmy, and I suspect that what was driving him crazy was the realization that, however tactfully handled, this was public-domain stuff. The death had kind of put her into public domain, do you see what I mean?"

VIII

ALVAREZ had suggested that I go speak to Elizabeth Sigmund, and a few days later I was on a train to Cornwall, where she lives, with her third husband, William. The journey was arduous. The snowstorm was over, but its effects were still being felt by the delicate British railway system, and

I arrived three hours late. William Sigmund was waiting for me at the station and seemed unexcited by the delay. He is a placid, bearded man in his forties, and, driving to his house, he talked about the work against chemical and biological warfare that he and Elizabeth have been engaged in for the last twenty years; a foundation funds it.

Elizabeth Compton (as she was then) was Plath's great friend in Devon. She knew Plath for only a year, but because it was the last year of Plath's life—the period of the breakup of the marriage and the writing of the *Ariel* poems—her testimony has assumed enormous weight and significance in the Plath legend. She is the kind of witness the dead crave, the person who speaks only well of them. In the memoir of Plath that she published in 1976 she renders her friend as an entirely remarkable, lovable, deliciously interesting, and infinitely touching person. At the end of the famous set piece ("My milk has dried up. . . . Ted . . . has become a *little* man"), she writes that Plath spent the night on the sofa in her living room, and when she came down the next morning she found Plath "bending over a box containing a cat and her new kittens." She adds, "I can see her now, wearing a pink, woolly dressing gown with a long, brown plait of hair falling into the box, turning her head and saying, 'I never saw anything so small and new and vulnerable. They are blind.' What could I do to protect and help this amazing person?"

If Elizabeth personified the entirely loving and uncritical friend, she also fulfilled the unreasonable demand we make on confidants during times of domestic discord: that they take our side completely, share our bruised feelings, and adopt our anger toward the person who has injured us as if they had been injured themselves. Elizabeth evidently never stopped blaming Hughes as she loyally blamed him in the summer of 1962. As for Olwyn, Elizabeth writes in her memoir:

The most difficult person in Ted's family was his sister Olwyn, who feared and resented Sylvia's talent and beauty, as
well as her relationship with Ted. Sylvia felt this terrible jealousy deeply, and recognized an insurmountable anger. She
often told me that Olwyn hated her, resented her position
as another daughter in the family. When I met Olwyn after
Sylvia's death, I felt that she had understated Olwyn's attitude; it was one which I found hard to tolerate even at second hand.

"I tried to explain to Sylvia the terrible, crushing class system in this country," she continues, "and how people like the
Hugheses suffered from it in ways which would be hard for
an American college girl to understand. I asked her if she
didn't think that, somewhere, Ted had a feeling of inferiority.
Her answer was a bitterly scornful laugh. 'Ted has lunched
with the Duke of Edinburgh,' she said, which of course was
no answer at all."

We arrived at the house, a small cottage deep in the country. I found Elizabeth, a portly woman in a black dress, with
a flowered shawl over her shoulders, lying on a sofa in the
middle of a small, low-ceilinged room with a large stone
fireplace. She was, like Alvarez, older than I had expected,
but what gave me a chill was the sight of her swollen feet
stretched out on the sofa. On the telephone, explaining why
she could not offer me lunch, she had told me she was suffering from a bad bout of arthritis and could not get around,
but only now did I grasp how incapacitated she was. Still, she
greeted me with a laughing reference to herself as Elizabeth
Barrett Browning and began to chatter in a way calculated to
charm and amuse rather than to invite pity. I could see why
Plath would have been attracted to this vivacious woman.
William brought a pot of tea and a plate of cookies made
from blameless natural ingredients. He then retired to his office, a room filled with computer equipment and a photocop-

ier. Elizabeth settled the shawl around her shoulders and told me stories about Plath and Hughes and Olwyn that I had already read in her memoir and in Butscher's biography, along with stories that were new to me but had taken on the subtly tainted character of stories told too many times. One of these was an account of a visit Elizabeth had paid to the flat on Fitzroy Road shortly after Plath's death: "Ted was out, and there was a little nanny there looking after the children, and she told me that Nick wouldn't eat anymore. He had been very greedy—like Sylvia, he loved food—but now he wouldn't eat, and he was absolutely silent. We talked for a while and then I asked 'Is Ted coming back?' and she said in an embarrassed way, 'Yes, but *she's* here, you know.' And I said 'Who's "she"?' and the girl said, 'Mrs. Wevill,' and I said 'Living here?' and she said, 'Oh, yes.' Then Ted came back—I heard Assia go up the stairs to the bedroom—and he looked absolutely shattered. He looked at me and just said my name, and then he went into the other room and fetched a copy of *The Bell Jar.* He was almost in tears. He said, 'This is for you—you haven't seen it,' and I said, 'Yes, thank you.' It was awful. The emotions were so powerful and so awful. And then he said—I know he didn't mean it—'It doesn't fall to many men to murder a genius.' And I thought, Poor man! How is he going to survive? We were standing in the kitchen, and he was boiling a kettle on the cooker—the one where she had gassed herself."

Stories like this regularly fill biographies and are taken to be true, because they cannot be disproved. In all the biographies of Plath, impressions and recollections of Hughes by contemporary witnesses are accorded the status of historical fact. One can imagine how Hughes must feel when he picks up one of these books and reads what someone noticed about him, or thought about him, or thought he heard him say, thirty years ago. Memory is notoriously unreliable; when it is

intertwined with ill will, it may become monstrously unreliable. The "good" biographer is supposed to be able to discrim-
inate among the testimonies of witnesses and have his
antennae out for tendentious distortions, misrememberings,
and outright lies. In his biography of Orwell, Bernard Crick
gives an instance of his own exquisite sensitivity to the problem. After quoting a lurid passage from a memoir of Orwell
by the novelist Raynor Heppenstall, he pauses to worry about
how to evaluate it. The passage tells of an incident in the thirties, when Orwell and Heppenstall were sharing a house in
Kentish Town and Heppenstall came home late one night,
very drunk. According to Heppenstall's memoir, written
twenty years later, Orwell first lectured his housemate and
then, when Heppenstall put up an argument, bloodied his
nose and finally came after him with a shooting stick. "He
fetched me a dreadful crack across the legs," Heppenstall recalls, "and then raised the shooting stick over his head. I
looked at his face. Through my private mist I saw in it a curious blend of fear and sadistic exultation." From another
source, Crick has learned that "the incident certainly occurred," but he wonders about Heppenstall's recollection,
after a lapse of twenty years, of the "fear and sadistic exultation." He speculates that Heppenstall, by the time he wrote
his account, had come to think that Orwell's writings were
"grossly overestimated" and thus "intended his account to be
a symbolic criticism of Orwell's character." Crick finds this a
more reasonable inference than "to believe that he saw the
incident in just such terms at the time." But he is still not
satisfied. In a footnote in the paperback edition of his biography, he says that Heppenstall "appears to me to crystallize,
like the accomplished novelist he is, a complicated and recur-
ring matter [a sadomasochistic streak in Orwell] into a single
significant anecdote of seemingly instant illumination." He
adds, "The complicated matter is surely evident throughout

[my book], but I may not anywhere have been explicit enough. . . . I only say that it is inexplicable, except from stock and *a priori* psychoanalytic positions. . . . I do not mean to imply that it does not exist."

Elizabeth turned from Ted to Olwyn. "I didn't meet her until Sylvia was dead, when she came to Court Green to live with Ted and the children," she said. "I got to know her very well. We played poker together. It was very alarming when you realized you had won, because you felt Olwyn might lean across the table and smack you, though she never did. She was wild in her playing. She'd risk a lot. She scared me to death when she was raging—she had a terrible temper and was incredibly sarcastic—but she was also very fascinating. She had lived in Paris, and she had all sorts of exciting anecdotes about her life. To a country mouse like me, she was very interesting. Now Olwyn talks about me as if I were stupid and disgusting. She once told somebody that I was a pig living in mud. She and Ted and Carol don't speak to me anymore. I went to hear a talk Anne Stevenson gave at Exeter last year, and there was Carol, sitting at the back. She is very dark and very beautiful. She used to be rather a timid girl—she was a nurse, and she was twenty-two when they married—but she's grown very proud and very handsome. I went up to her and said hello, and she said, 'I cannot speak to you.' It was ridiculous. It's not that I'm trying to push myself forward or trying to climb to fame on the back of the poor dead girl. I know that's how they see it, but it's not like that. Nobody can deny that when someone you knew becomes enormously famous it polishes your ego. You think, This brilliant person actually liked me, so I must be of some use. And people coming to see me, like you—of course it makes me feel something about myself. But the times when I've pushed myself forward"— Elizabeth was speaking here of calls she had made and letters she had written to newspapers—"it's always been in reaction to something outrageous that somebody had done about Sylvia."

On a low table beside her, Elizabeth had a file folder of newspaper clippings, many of which I had already seen. The characters in and chroniclers of the Plath legend collect these thin, unreliable narratives as if they were sacred writings. At no time, perhaps, is the power of the press so evident—and so troubling—as when some part of its steady dripping freezes into the stalactite known as "archival material." Newspaper stories that were originally written to satisfy our daily hunger for idle and impersonal Schadenfreude—to excite and divert and be forgotten the next week—now take their place among serious sources of information and fact, and are treated as if they themselves were not simply raising the question of what happened and who is good and who is bad.

I went into William's office and on his copier made duplicates of the stories that were not in my own archive. Over the afternoon, he had become not exactly resentful but a little less friendly; he compressed his lips and looked distracted when I spoke to him. When the visit ended, I called a taxi, and as we waited Elizabeth's bright chatter faltered. She looked tired and was probably in pain. She told me that getting from the sofa to the bathroom was a difficult feat. I felt the sadness and harshness of her life; the house emanated pathos and a certain uncanniness. My glimpse of this woman and her husband, who lived so close to the margin and worked against chemical and biological warfare, told me little more than what I have just written, and left me with a chastening sense of the effrontery of my journalist's account of my visit. What did I know about them? How inadequate and off the mark my account must be! The biographer commits the same offense when he proposes to solve the mystery that is a life with "data" no less meagre (when you consider the monstrous mass that accrues from the moment-by-moment events of a life) and interpretations no less crass (when you consider what a fine-tuned, custom-made instrument human motivation is).

The taxi arrived, and on the drive to my hotel I asked the driver if he knew anything about the problem on the railway line that had caused my three-hour delay. He said he did—a tunnel had been damaged by the snow—and predicted that I would have the same trouble leaving Cornwall the next morning. He asked me where I was going, and when I said Milverton, in Somerset, a hundred miles away—where I was to have lunch with Clarissa Roche—he named a fee for driving me there. I accepted.

IX

THE next day, a Sunday, the driver arrived at my hotel at ten; a woman and an infant were in the back seat of the taxi. I got into the front seat, and the driver said that the woman and the infant were his wife and son, but didn't introduce me. Throughout the ride, he kept up a stream of chat with me but never addressed a word to his wife. The child gurgled for a while and then went to sleep. At first, I turned to the wife to try to include her in the conversation, but she made it clear that she didn't want to be drawn. I felt I was in the presence of a husband-and-wife relationship so archaic, so out of date, that it was almost like standing in front of some extraordinary old ruin. This was the real thing, this was sexism so pure and uninflected it inspired a kind of awe, almost a sort of respect. I thought of Plath's poem "The Applicant," of 1962:

A living doll, everywhere you look.
It can sew, it can cook,
It can talk, talk, talk.

It works, there is nothing wrong with it.
You have a hole, it's a poultice.
You have an eye, it's an image.
My boy, it's your last resort.
Will you marry it, marry it, marry it.

I asked the driver if he could make a small detour, and he pulled over to the side of the road to study the map I had with me. In the hotel that morning, while looking at the map, I had noticed that the village of North Tawton was not far off the main highway to Milverton. North Tawton is where Court Green is. The driver said "No problem" (he did not consult his wife), and resumed driving. But there was a problem. The driver missed the turnoff to North Tawton and then spent over an hour—instead of the ten minutes of the direct route—finding his way to the village through the traffic-choked city of Exeter. I was now going to be seriously late for lunch at Clarissa Roche's (I had already defeated the object of taking a taxi instead of risking the train), and I deeply regretted my idea.

As we finally drove through North Tawton—a small, silent, austere old village—and I saw the spire of what must have been the church that abuts Court Green, my regret deepened. I was filled with the enormity of my misguidedness in coming here. What could I have been thinking of? What was I going to do when we reached the house? It was one thing to pay a reverent visit to the house where Plath died; it was another to go snooping around the place where Ted Hughes lives. But I was committed to my heedless course; I could not tell the driver not to bother, after all his efforts, and when we reached a house that I did and didn't recognize as

Court Green from Alvarez's description of it and from photographs in the various biographies, I told him to stop. The photographs were indistinct and had left an impression in my mind of a house with a thatched roof, rather low to the ground, surrounded by tangles of vines and wildflowers and old trees and cobblestones—a place that looked like its name and, as Plath wrote to her mother soon after her arrival, in September, 1961, was "like a person; it responds to the slightest touch and looks wonderful immediately." The house I now reluctantly stepped out of the taxi to stare at was tall, and white with black trim. It looked massive and suburban; it put me in mind of the fake-Tudor houses of the twenties and thirties in places like Riverdale and Scarsdale. At the side of the house was a picket fence that I had never seen in any photograph, and I wondered whether this was the right place after all, and when a child came down the street I asked her, "Is this the house of the Poet Laureate?" She nodded and hurried on. There was a front lawn, with a few small, bare trees. In the windows, the curtains were drawn, and I was relieved to see none of them twitching. Perhaps the Hugheses were away. Then I saw something that suggested the Hugheses were not away, that my intrusion might not be going unmarked. Hanging from one of the trees on the front lawn was a fully stocked bird feeder, around which English robins and sparrows were swarming. I felt a return of my feeling of tenderness toward Hughes—I felt his reality, his aliveness, his stuckness, and I felt shame at my complicity in the chase that has made his life a torment; I had now joined the pack of his pursuers. But I continued my inspection of the house and the grounds, stubbornly looking for some mental trophy to bear away, some impression to mark my visit to the place where, in the blue hours before dawn, the soon-to-be-dead girl had claimed her immortality. In the 1962 poem "Letter in November" Plath writes of walking around Court Green "stupidly happy, / My wellingtons / Squelching and squelching through the beautiful red." She says, almost gloating:

> *This is my property.*
> *Two times a day*
> *I pace it, sniffing*
> *The barbarous holly with its viridian*
> *Scallops, pure iron.*
>
> *My seventy trees*
> *Holding their gold-ruddy balls*
> *In a thick gray death-soup,*
> *Their million*
> *Gold leaves metal and breathless.*

This is my property. It is Hughes's bitter fate to be perpetually struggling with Plath over the ownership of his life, trying to wrest it back from her. In "Daddy" Plath writes of her dead father as a vampire whom she has finally been able to rekill:

> *Daddy, you can lie back now.*
>
> *There's a stake in your fat black heart*
> *And the villagers never liked you*
> *They are dancing and stamping on you.*
> *They always knew it was you.*
> *Daddy, daddy, you bastard, I'm through.*

Hughes has never been able to drive the stake through Plath's heart and free himself from her hold. (Who are the biographers, journalists, critics, curiosity-seekers, and libbers swarming around Hughes but stand-ins for the Undead woman herself?) He has never found the right maneuver, made the right move that would result in the "death" he seeks. "I have never attempted to give my account of Sylvia," he wrote to Anne Stevenson in November, 1989, replying to a letter in which she reproached him for publicly dissociating himself from her biography, "because I saw quite clearly from the first day that I am the only person in this business who cannot be believed by all who need to find me guilty." He continued:

> I know too that the alternative—remaining silent—makes me a projection post for every worst suspicion. That my silence seems to confirm every accusation and fantasy. I preferred it, on the whole, to allowing myself to be dragged out into the bull-ring and teased and pricked and goaded into vomiting up every detail of my life with Sylvia for the higher entertainment of the hundred thousand Eng Lit Profs and graduates who—as you know—feel very little in this case beyond curiosity of quite a low order, the ordinary village kind, popular bloodsport kind, no matter how they robe their attentions in Lit Crit Theology and ethical sanctity. If they do feel anything more vigorous, it is generally something even lower: status anxiety, their professional angst on the promotion scramble.

With rising bitterness and contempt, he went on:

> Often enough, all they feel is the opportunity to make a penny. Even yourself, Anne, you remember as I do that it wasn't any great love of Sylvia's poetry, or passion to set her story right, that brought you to this book. When you told me that you could really do with that advance promised by Penguin, my only reaction was: If someone's going to do the book (since it came up in a series), why shouldn't the cash go to Anne? But isn't it usually like that? If a struggling young lecturer wants to place an article prestigiously, will he send in something about Thomas Wyatt or about SP? I expect

you know that Paul Alexander (with little more to his name than the introduction to that book of essays) walked into— which publisher I forget— . . . and walked out with 150,000 dollars. Or have I got the sum wrong. Butscher wrote his biography [so] the publisher would take a book of his poems. A friend of Linda Wagner-Martin told me that after the success of her book she moved to a fancy new teaching post at a fancy new salary. Maybe this is a vile angle to view this business from, but what else can I see when I'm howled at to revere it above my own life and to feed it, in fact, chunks of my own life, or at least not try to snatch any of my life out of its mouth?

I've accepted all that long ago but, Anne, please don't expect me to accept it gladly. Or to make no effort, now and again, to surround the children and my wife and myself with a wall of astral fire. If old friends of mine want to defend me (if that's their motive) I don't feel I have to agree with all that they say, nor out of dumb loyalty to them do I have to let the public enter another charge against me—that I run around asking other people to give the low-down on Sylvia because it would look bad if I did it. . . . My simple wish [is] to recapture for myself, if I can, the privacy of my own feelings and conclusions about Sylvia, and to remove them from contamination by anybody else's. . . .

You must not feel too surprised at the way I do it. I wish I could think of a more effective way. But the moment you agreed to work with Olwyn you put me in this quandary of finding a way, any way, of dealing with this bizarre new twist in the situation. You made it inescapable for me.

Hughes's letter, like his second introduction to the *The Journals*, works its way toward a stunning culmination:

In all this, Anne, I am very aware that it is not likely that I shall be ever doing the right thing, or even the sensible thing, and at the very best I have ended up serving two masters. I encouraged you to let everybody tell their tale. But at the same time I know what that means to us on the inside, and start looking for defences. And your working with Olwyn simply made the dilemma infinitely more ticklish.

Just one instance will show you how far from my world your book is. I regret not deleting one phrase in particular. When Sylvia's destruction of my papers etc. has been described, it is said "this could never be forgotten or forgiven," or words to that effect. I remember that conclusion was first drawn by Dido, but it seems to have been understood by you and Olwyn as if it were self-evidently true. I don't think I altered it in Dido's text—I was so exercised trying to persuade her to understand Sylvia altogether differently.

The truth is that I didn't hold that action against [Sylvia]—then or at any other time. I was rather shattered by it, and saw it was a crazy thing for her to have done. But perhaps I have something missing. She never did anything that I held against her. The only thing that I found hard to understand was her sudden discovery of our bad moments ("Event," "Rabbit Catcher") as subjects for poems. But to say I could not forgive her for ripping up those bits of paper is to misunderstand utterly the stuff of my relationship to her. It is factually untrue, in other words. So in future, in any new edition or translation, I would like to have that phrase cut out. Let the episode speak for itself.

All those fierce reactions against her—which she provoked so fiercely—from people who thought, perhaps, sometimes, that they were defending me—were from my point of view simply disasters from which I had to protect her. It was like trying to protect a fox from my own hounds while the fox bit me. With a real fox in that situation, you would never have any doubt why it was biting you.

PART THREE

I

I GOT back in the taxi, where the man and woman and child were sitting in silence. "No one home?" the driver asked. I began to explain that I had come only to see the house and thought better of it. We drove on, and the anxiety that had been just under the surface throughout this trip to England now emerged and fastened itself to the fact of being late to lunch at Clarissa's. But when I arrived Clarissa, like a nurse applying balm to a wound, welcomed me cheerfully and waved away any question of being discommoded by my lateness. She is an American who has lived in England for over thirty years and has four grown children. Until a decade ago, she was the wife of the poet Paul Roche (he moved to Majorca after their divorce), who in his youth had modeled for the painter Duncan Grant and had then become the Watts-Duntonish friend to whom Grant left half his paintings and drawings when he died, in 1978. The rare aesthetic experience I had expected Court Green to give me was now given me by Clarissa's house. Frances Spalding, in her 1983 biography of Vanessa Bell, renders a portrait of Charleston, the house in Sussex where Vanessa lived, ostensibly with her husband, Clive Bell, but actually with Grant, with whom she was hopelessly in love, and by whom she had a daughter, Angelica. In order to keep Grant near her—and as a kind of monument to the fruitful union of the discipline of art with the chaos of unconventional domestic arrangements—she also entertained his boyfriends, one of whom, David Garnett, married Angelica when she was twenty-three. I now felt as if I had stepped into another Charleston, a place of ravishing and interesting beauty, utterly unconnected to the "English style" of decorating magazines, a product of high, willful taste derived in turn from an ingrained love of looking at the world's surfaces. Angelica Garnett, in *Deceived with Kindness*, a memoir of her childhood and youth at Charleston, gives an unhappy child's twist to the story of Bloomsbury but corroborates the portrait of Charleston:

> Though we were unbrushed, unwashed and ragged, our carpets and curtains faded and our furniture stained and groggy, appearances of a purely aesthetic kind were considered of supreme importance. Hours were spent hanging an old picture in a new place, or in choosing a new colour for the walls.

Clarissa's house was full of Grant's paintings and drawings, which had been hung with evident care and premeditation. In the hall, there was a singular sight: a Grant painting of two children on a sofa and, below it, the sofa itself. And who should happen to be in the house—spending the weekend looking at art and documents for a biography of Grant—but Frances Spalding herself. Clarissa gave me a tour of the main rooms (through French doors I glimpsed an old-fashioned walled garden), and then Frances emerged from a study: a tall, thin Diana of a young woman with boyishly cropped hair, dressed in slacks and a long striped T-shirt, everything about her orderly and nicely in place. She had a calm, clear, shy manner, and spoke in a low, quiet, murmuring voice—not speaking very much, but always to effect. As I observed her over the afternoon, she appeared to me the exemplar of the "good" biographer: one who doesn't overstep, who is respectful of the given, who is unintrusive, judicious, who evaluates wisely and evenly—and who doesn't get into the messes that Anne Stevenson and Olwyn Hughes got into.

Her appreciative biography of Vanessa Bell won her critical and popular acclaim; it is a long, well-narrated work. It convinces the reader that Vanessa was splendid—a game, kind woman and a gifted artist, who led a rich, beautiful life—and it is poised on the tension between the demented "plot" of Vanessa's existence and its serene day-to-day actualities and achievements. Angelica Garnett's memoir, in contrast, like Dido Merwin's memoir of Plath, is full of aggrievement and complaint and one doesn't like her for it—as one ultimately doesn't like *it*. We don't want to be told what vengeful memoirs like Angelica's and Dido's oblige us to consider: that our children and friends do not love us, that we are neurotic, blind, pathetic, that under the eye of God our life will be seen as a mistake, something botched and wasted. The outcry against the Dido Merwin memoir was a cry from the reader's heart about his own posthumous prospects, an expression of his wish to be remembered benevolently and not all that vividly. It was not the truth or falseness of Dido's recollections of Plath's bad behavior that hurt; it was their unseemly specificity. There is evidence in Plath's own writings that she could be extremely disagreeable when things didn't go well. She knew this about herself and could be quite strict with herself about it, as when she writes in her 1956 Paris journal of "that ridiculous tantrum last winter about our [theatre] seats not being side by side but one in front of the other, which resulted in Sassoon's sweetly humoring me and turning in the tickets," and adds, "Now that I look back, I am appalled at my spoiled, demanding behavior." When she criticizes herself, we applaud her for her honesty, but when Dido Merwin complains about the food Plath plundered from her refrigerator we only blush for Dido's small-mindedness.

Clarissa served us lunch not in the formal dining room, filled with Grants, but in a small dining room, off the kitchen, that had a fireplace, in which, English style, a few flames wanly flickered. Clarissa is a rounded, middle-aged woman with gray-blond hair and an easy, hearty, slightly vague manner. Just as my readings of books about Bloomsbury had prepared me for her house, so my readings of Plath's journals had given me a feeling of having already met Clarissa. She and Paul Roche became acquainted with Plath and Hughes when Plath was teaching at Smith in 1957–58, and Plath frequently wrote about them in her journal, though only some of what she wrote got into the published *Journals*. Frances McCullough, in writing of the "nasty bits" she removed from the published text, cites the Roches as two of the friends Plath was nasty about: "Paul and Clarissa Roche, for instance, who take some tartness in this book and yet were very close to Plath right up until the end." Plath's "tartness" in the published *Journals*—her references to Paul's "machinations" and "seed[iness]" and her descriptions of Clarissa "in a sulk of tears . . . like Miss Muffet in a private tantrum"—is but a faint aftertaste of the sourness of the full, harshly derisive portrait of the Roches that appears in the unpublished version, particularly of Paul, who had a repellent fascination for her. But the nastiness of the portrayal, unlike the nastiness of Dido and Angelica, has a detached, disinterested, almost clinical quality. She writes with the novelist's cold eye, rather than with the memoirist's still warm dislike. And she writes—as she also writes of Hughes and Richard Sassoon—with the novelist's artful economy and redundancy. A suit Roche wears—"a bright absinthe-green suit that made his eyes the clear unearthly and slightly unpleasant acid green of a churned winter ocean full of ice cakes"—is one of her recurrent figures for him (as hugeness is her recurrent figure for Hughes, and sickliness and smallness for Sassoon). "Oh, only left to myself, what a poet I will flay myself into," Plath writes, in a journal entry of May, 1958. The journals keep forcing us to engage with the idea of what a novelist she might have lived herself into. As they record her struggle to produce the inert short stories, they themselves testify to her abilities as a fiction-maker. Hughes's idea that Plath's genius for "instant confrontation with the most central, unacceptable things" could find proper expression only in verse is belied by the confrontations that appear in the journals.

In 1958, when Plath and Hughes were living in Boston (Plath had decided not to continue teaching at Smith) and trying to support themselves with their writing, she went back into therapy with Ruth Beuscher, the young psychiatrist who had attended her at McLean, where she spent three months after her suicide attempt. The journals show her working at her therapy with characteristic diligence, acquiring painful insights into the central, unacceptable thing—her relationship with her mother—in the same way she had piled up letters of encouragement from magazines for her precocious writings and A's for her schoolwork. She also "saw" that Ted was a father figure. "I identify him with my father at certain times," she wrote in her journal in December, 1958, "and these times take on great importance: e.g., that one fight at the end of the school year when I found him not-there on the special day and with another woman." The "fight," which had taken place seven months earlier, at Smith, is one of the great novelistic set pieces of *The Journals*. That it is a set piece— the shaped, premeditated work of a writerly narrator, rather than the innocent blurtings of a diarist—is established by the entry's opening line: "May 19, Monday. Only it isn't Monday at all, but now Thursday, the 22nd of May, and I through with my last classes and a hot bath and disabused of many ideals, visions, and faiths." Something has happened to cause Plath to feel disillusioned with Hughes, to believe that he has betrayed her and lied to her, but she doesn't immediately tell us what it is. She speaks, instead, of the novel she will write— "a story, like James's, of the workers and the worked, the exploiters and the exploited, of vanity and cruelty: with a ronde, a circle of lies and abuse in a beautiful world gone bad," and goes on, mysteriously, "The irony I record here for the novel, but also for the *Ladies' Home Journal*." Then she writes:

> I am no Maggie Verver, I feel the vulgar heat of my wrong enough to gag, to spit the venom I've swallowed; but I'll take my cue from Maggie, bless the girl. How the irony builds up. . . . And all this time it has been going on, on the far edges of my intuition. I confided my faith in Ted, and why is the wife the last to see her husband's ulcer?

What had Ted done? Plath continues to put off the revelation. She writes of attending a public reading of Paul Roche's translation of *Oedipus* the night before, at which Ted had read the part of Creon. Ted had not encouraged her to come, but she had gone anyway, creeping into the hall and taking a seat in the rear, and: "The minute I came in [Ted] knew it, and I knew he knew it, and his voice let the reading down. He was ashamed of something." After the reading, Plath went backstage and found Hughes sitting "with a mean, wrong face over the piano, banging out a strident one-finger tune, hunched, a tune I'd never heard before." Finally, Plath comes to the point. She writes of having arranged to meet Hughes in a campus parking lot, of his not being there, of her going to the library and still not finding him, and then:

> As I came striding out of the cold shadow of the library, my bare arms chilled, I had one of those intuitive visions. I knew what I would see, what I would of necessity meet, and I have known for a very long time, although not sure of the place or date of the first confrontation. Ted was coming up the road from Paradise Pond, where girls take their boys to

neck on weekends. He was walking with a broad, intense smile, eyes into the uplifted doe-eyes of a strange girl with brownish hair, a large lipsticked grin, and bare thick legs in khaki Bermuda shorts. I saw this in several sharp flashes, like blows. I could not tell the color of the girl's eyes, but Ted could, and his smile, though open and engaging as the girl's was, took on an ugliness in context . . . his smile became too white-hot, became fatuous, admiration-seeking. He was gesturing, just finishing an observation, an explanation. The girl's eyes souped up giddy applause. She saw me coming. Her eye started to guilt and she began to run, literally, without a good-bye, Ted making no effort to introduce her. . . . Jealousy in me turned to disgust. The late comings home, my vision, while brushing my hair, of a black-horned, grinning wolf all came clear, fused, and I gagged at what I saw.

Swept away by her sense of being wronged, Plath sinks deeper and deeper into bitter bathos, writing of "the fake excuses, vague confusions about name and class. All fake. All false. . . . It is awful to want to go away and to want to go nowhere. I made the most amusing, ironic and fatal step in trusting Ted was unlike other vain and obfuscating and self-indulgent men. I have served a purpose, spent money, Mother's money which hurts most, to buy him clothes, to buy him a half year, eight months of writing."

Which hurts most. To know what was passing through Plath's mind when she wrote this would be to understand much about her relationship with her mother. But we don't know; we can only speculate. Similarly, we don't know what to make of Plath's suspicions about Hughes. Had he actually been unfaithful to her or was she accusing him unjustly? Had she picked up something real in the encounter near the library, or was she only imagining it? In *Bitter Fame* Anne Stevenson opts for the latter interpretation. She writes:

Remarkable about this entire entry is the lightning quickness with which Sylvia made her deductions. One day Ted was her godlike father risen to be her mate; the next, he was a scurrilous adulterer hiding behind a façade of fake excuses, vague confessions, and lies. Ted was a handsome man, and no doubt girls made passes at him. Sylvia's over-reaction to seeing him once talking to a student was fueled, no doubt, chiefly by her exhaustion, but it blazed up, as always, in the theatre of her terror, her paranoia, and her ever-ignitable imagination. The girl was in fact one of Hughes's students from the University of Massachusetts who just happened to be crossing the Smith campus as he went to meet Sylvia; he had caught up with the girl only minutes before Sylvia saw them.

The alert reader will be struck by and want to challenge Stevenson's terms "overreaction" and "in fact." The source of her information about the girl from the University of Massachusetts must have been Hughes (it can't have been Plath), and is his account trustworthy? The questions raised by the passage only underscore the epistemological insecurity by which the reader of biography and autobiography (and history and journalism) is always and everywhere dogged. In a work of nonfiction we almost never know the truth of what happened. The ideal of unmediated reporting is regularly achieved only in fiction, where the writer faithfully reports on what is going on in his imagination. When James reports in *The Golden Bowl* that the Prince and Charlotte are sleeping together, we have no reason to doubt him or to wonder whether Maggie is "overreacting" to what she sees. James's is a true report. The facts of imaginative literature are as hard as the stone that Dr. Johnson kicked. We must always take the novelist's and the playwright's and the poet's word, just as we are almost always free to doubt the biographer's or the autobiographer's or the historian's or the journalist's. In imaginative literature we are constrained from considering alternative scenarios—there are none. This is the way it *is*. Only in nonfiction does the question of what happened and how people thought and felt remain open.

The journal entry of May 19, 1958 (and the following one, of June 11, in which Plath describes the violent aftermath of her un-Maggie-Ververesque confrontation of Hughes with her suspicions), once again raises an old question: Why has Hughes chosen to feed the public imagination so many tasty scraps of his life with Plath? His sanctioning of the entries of May 19 and June 11 (in the latter, Plath writes "I had a sprained thumb, Ted bloody claw marks for a week" and "I got hit and saw stars—for the first time—blinding red and white stars exploding in the black void of snarls and bitings") would seem to contradict all his anguished protests against the violation of his privacy. Why, if he is so keen to own the facts of his life, has he distributed them so freely to the reading public?

A possible explanation is so obvious that one is tempted to dismiss it out of hand: he did it because he is Plath's greatest critic, elucidator, and (you could almost say) impresario. Hughes has lived so long in the public imagination as Plath's enemy and censor that his actual role since her death has gone largely unnoticed (sometimes, it would seem, even by himself). But the more one examines Hughes's activities as Plath's literary executor, the more one is obliged to consider the possibility that he has been actuated as much by literary motives as by personal ones—that he probably felt some ineluctable *literary* necessity for needlessly exposing himself to public scrutiny. When the first part of Alvarez's memoir was published in the *Observer*, Hughes protested to Alvarez, "What makes it so much worse is that it was so totally unnecessary. And that it was written by you—the very person most likely to know that there are quite a few things more im-

portant than literature—more important even than great poetry, let alone memoirs." But this was only one part of
Hughes speaking—the self that destroyed Plath's last journal
and is represented in the second foreword to *The Journals* as
"her husband." Another self—the self that has presided over
Plath's posthumous reputation and is her fellow literary artist—knows no such thing. To this self, nothing is more important than literature, and no sacrifice in its service is too
great. Hughes's plight as a man trying to serve two masters
and knowing that it isn't ever going to come out right is, of
course, the plight of every artist. His effort to disentangle his
life from the Plath legend while tending its flame is a kind of
grotesque allegory of the effort of every artist to salvage a
piece of normal life for himself from the disaster of his calling. Although we know little about Hughes's own struggles
with writing (in *The Journals* Plath occasionally mentions that
he is depressed), we may imagine that if he had never met
Plath he would still be living the crazy, beset life of the creator rather than the peaceful, sane life of the average newspaper reader.

As I now reread the journal entries of May 19 and June 11,
it seems clearer than ever why Hughes could not bring himself to remove them from the published text. They are too
interesting, and the latter entry culminates in a scene that
someone as fascinated by myth as Hughes is could not help
wanting to publish. The scene takes place at twilight in a public park near the apartment where Hughes and Plath live and
have gone to walk at the end of a wet, misty day. As they leave
the house, Plath slips a pair of silver-plated scissors into her
raincoat pocket. It is her habit to cut a rose or two for the
apartment; she now seeks a yellow bud to replace a dark red
rose that has come into full bloom in the living room. In the
rose garden, while Plath is cutting a pink bud (the yellow

roses are all "blowzy, blasted"), three "hulking" girls emerge from a rhododendron grove. "I'll bet they're wanting to steal some flowers," Hughes says. He and Plath "stare them down," and the girls retreat; but then, walking on, Hughes and Plath are shocked and angered to come upon two huge bunches of rhododendron boughs that the girls have hidden behind some bushes, wrapped in newspaper. Presently (the exits and entrances are like those of a ballet), the girls re-appear:

> We heard muffled laughter and the cracking of branches broken carelessly. We came up slowly with evil eyes. I felt bloodlust—sassy girls, three of them—"Oh, here's a big one," a girl ostentatiously said. "Why are you picking them?" Ted asked. "For a dance. We need them for a dance." They half-thought we would approve. "Don't you think you'd better stop?" Ted asked. "This is a public park." Then the little one got brassy and fairly sneered, "This isn't your park." "Nor yours," I retorted, wanting strangely to claw off her raincoat, smack her face, read the emblem of her school on her jersey and send her to jail. "You might as well pull the bush by its root." She glared at me, and I gave her a mad wild still stony glare that snuffed hers out.

It isn't lost on Plath that she is the pot calling the kettle black. "I wondered at my split morality," she writes. "Here I had an orange and a pink rosebud in my pocket and a full red rose squandering its savors at home, and I felt like killing a girl stealing armfuls of rhododendrons for a dance." She goes on—as we somehow knew she would—to contrast her modest, seemly theft ("My one rose a week is aesthetic joy for me and Ted, and sorrow or loss for no one") with the hulking girls' gross, wanton one ("These girls were ripping up whole bushes"). Working herself up, she writes, "That crudeness and wholesale selfishness disgusted and angered me. I have a violence in me that is hot as death-blood. I can kill myself or—I know it now—even kill another. I could kill a woman, or wound a man. I think I could. I gritted to control my hands, but had a flash of bloody stars in my head as I stared that sassy girl down, and a blood-longing to [rush] at her and tear her to bloody beating bits."

Sometime later, Plath wrote a poem about the incident, called "Fable of the Rhododendron Stealers," which she didn't consider good enough to put into *The Colossus*. (She called her successful poems "book poems.") It is a pallid, stiff version of the journal entry, ending with the prim question of "Whether nicety stood confounded by love, / Or petty thievery by large." It is another poem, "In Plaster," written in March, 1961, that registers Plath's understanding of what was at stake for her in the confrontation. She was, of course, encountering the "not-nice" part of herself, the "true self" of *Ariel*, the self that was not afraid to rip up whole bushes, because this is what it is the business of the artist to do. Art is theft, art is armed robbery, art is not pleasing your mother. In "In Plaster" Plath uses the image of a body in a plaster cast (in his notes to Plath's *Collected Poems* Hughes says that she wrote the poem while she was in the hospital for an appendectomy, and a woman in a plaster cast lay in a neighboring bed) to render the opposition between her nice/false self and her not-nice/true self; i.e., "this new absolutely white person" and "the old yellow one" within it. The poem is a monologue by "old yellow." (I take the term from George Stade's very fine essay about the poem, which serves as the introduction to Nancy Hunter Steiner's memoir "A Closer Look at Ariel.") The voice is deadpan; it reminds one of Esther Greenwood of *The Bell Jar* (which, as it happens, Plath was working on at the time):

Without me, she wouldn't exist, so of course she was grateful.
I gave her a soul, I bloomed out of her as a rose
Blooms out of a vase of not very valuable porcelain,
And it was I who attracted everybody's attention,
Not her whiteness and beauty, as I had at first supposed.
I patronized her a little, and she lapped it up —
You could tell almost at once she had a slave mentality.

The originality of the poem lies in its daring, disorienting reversal of the traditional soul-body opposition, wherein the essential, irreducible soul resides in a gross, irrelevant body. Here the essential part of a person, the precious inner core, is represented by an "ugly and hairy" yellow "half-corpse," while the outer part, which doesn't matter ("not very valuable"), is the beautiful, pure, white plaster cast. Old yellow ends her speech thus:

I used to think we might make a go of it together —
After all, it was a kind of marriage, being so close.
Now I see it must be one or the other of us.
She may be a saint, and I may be ugly and hairy,
But she'll soon find out that that doesn't matter a bit.
I'm collecting my strength; one day I shall manage without her,
And she'll perish with emptiness then, and begin to miss me.

The true self is aggressive, rude, dirty, disorderly, sexual; the false self, which mothers and society instruct us to assume, is neat, clean, tidy, polite, content to cut a chaste rosebud with a pair of silver-plated scissors. "One day I shall manage without her." None of us can manage without some of the hard white stuff of social convention around us, the carapace that protects as well as hides our instinctual core. In *The Bell Jar* Plath closely observes the mental disintegration of her autobiographical heroine, Esther Greenwood, noting that she hasn't washed her hair or changed her clothes for three weeks. "The reason I hadn't washed my clothes or my hair was because it seemed so silly," Esther says. "It seemed silly to wash one day when I would only have to wash again the next. It made me tired just to think of it. I wanted to do everything once and for all and be through with it." Soon after this, Esther tries to kill herself (as Plath tried) by crawling under her mother's house and swallowing a bottle of sleeping pills. When Alvarez was struck by the smell of Plath's hair on Christmas Eve, 1962, Plath was evidently once again in a condition of wanting to do everything once and for all and be through with it. Opposing the priestess with the long, feral hair was the ultra-clean American girl of Dorothea Krook's description. In *The Journals* Plath's writing is laid out on a kind of grid of "clean" and "dirty" lines of self-representation. On the clean side, she obsessively sets down the baths and showers she takes, the times she washes her hair, the laundry she does, her housecleanings and tidyings; once, she even describes the scrubbing of a pot. On the dirty side, she writes of the clogged pores of her skin, her sinuses full of mucus, her menstrual blood, her throwings up. In an extraordinary passage, written while she was an undergraduate at Smith, Plath presages the precisely observing, perversely transgressing poet of *Ariel* as she celebrates "the illicit sensuous delight I get from picking my nose":

> There are so many subtle variations of sensation. A delicate, pointed-nailed fifth finger can catch under dry scabs and flakes of mucus in the nostril and draw them out to be looked at, crumbled between fingers, and flicked to the floor in minute crusts. Or a heavier, determined forefinger can reach up and smear down-and-out the soft, resilient, elastic greenish-yellow smallish blobs of mucus, roll them round and jellylike between thumb and forefinger, and spread them on the under-surface of a desk or chair where they will

harden into organic crusts. How many desks and chairs have I thus secretively befouled since childhood? Or sometimes there will be blood mingled with the mucus: in dry brown scabs, or bright sudden wet red on the finger that scraped too rudely the nasal membranes. God, what a sexual satisfaction! It is absorbing to look with new sudden eyes on the old worn habits: to see a sudden luxurious and pestilential "snot-green sea," and shiver with the shock of recognition.

Ted Hughes has let us know (in an essay entitled "Notes on the Chronological Order of Sylvia Plath's Poems") that there is a "twin" to "In Plaster"—a poem written by Plath in the hospital on the same day. This is the great poem "Tulips." As "In Plaster" affirms the life instinct, so "Tulips" is a hymn to the death wish. In the poem, a patient lies in a white hospital room in a state of peaceful inanition. A bunch of red tulips that has been brought to her disturbs the room's atmosphere of deadly whiteness and stillness. "The tulips are too excitable," the patient-narrator says in the opening line of her protest against the invasion by the flowers, which are emblematic of the life and movement she doesn't want.

> I didn't want any flowers, I only wanted
> To lie with my hands turned up and be utterly empty.
> How free it is, you have no idea how free—
> The peacefulness is so big it dazes you,
> And it asks nothing, a name tag, a few trinkets.
> It is what the dead close on, finally; I imagine them
> Shutting their mouths on it, like a Communion tablet.

"The tulips are too red in the first place, they hurt me," Plath writes as she coolly makes her way toward her distinguished, astonishing final stanza:

> The walls, also, seem to be warming themselves.
> The tulips should be behind bars like dangerous animals;

They are opening like the mouth of some great African cat,
And I am aware of my heart: it opens and closes
Its bowl of red blooms out of sheer love of me.
The water I taste is warm and salt, like the sea,
And comes from a country far away as health.

II

A T Clarissa's lunch table, Frances Spalding and I asked Clarissa questions about herself and her acquaintance with Plath and Hughes, but our main attention was elsewhere; it was on the food Clarissa had put on the table, which was to the food one usually eats as her house was to the houses one usually visits. This was seriously wonderful cooking, cooking that warmed, delighted, seduced. Frances and I knew we were not to see its like again for a long time, and we ate with that knowledge well in mind. Before lunch, Clarissa had grumbled that none of the Bloomsbury memoirists had taken notice of her except to mention her cooking; now it was evident why they did.

I asked Clarissa where she came from, and she said Michigan.

Then Frances, in her murmuring voice, asked, "What was your father?"

"What was my father?" Clarissa considered. "My father had an advertising agency—it just sort of happened, because he had to do something. Everything fell apart during the Depression. He was very eccentric." She added vaguely, "He did other things."

"What other things?" Frances murmured.

"He painted. He sculpted. He was a master bridge player. He used to be a good golfer."

Frances got to her point. "Is this, then, why you accepted Paul's sort of not having a job?"

Clarissa turned to me and explained, "I was saying to Frances that I couldn't think that any family but my own would have accepted a son-in-law who just lay naked in the garden and wrote poetry and lived off the fat of the land. Eventually, after Potie"—Clarissa's second child—"was born, and there were too many people in the house, my mother's sister got Paul a teaching job at Smith." I already had in my mind a picture of the jobless Paul in the garden. Plath had drawn it in her journal of May 13, 1958: "Heard how [Paul] lay naked in the rose garden at Clarissa's mansion in Saginaw, crocheted, while intently observing TV, a light blue wool cape for [a child], with PR embroidered on it in white angora and a bunny tail at the back."

As Clarissa brought to the table a tart she had made herself, I asked her how she had come to write her memoir of Plath in Edward Butscher's anthology of writings about Plath.

She gave a discursive answer, beginning with a displeased account of Butscher's visit to her during the preparation of his biography. In all complicated feuds, there tend to be small pockets of agreement between the antagonists; both sides join together in hating certain people, and Edward Butscher is such a person. No one I talked to on either side of the Plath-Hughes feud had a kind word to say about him. "Thank you for your copy of the letter to that rat Butscher," Frances McCullough wrote to Peter Davison in 1976, setting the tone of the discourse about the man. Butscher appeared on the Plath biographical scene in the early seventies, at a time when Lois Ames, an official biographer appointed by the Plath estate, was in the early stages of her research. (Her work was never completed.) Butscher nevertheless embarked on a biography of his own. He later gave a detailed account of how—with no cooperation from any of the central figures, and without benefit of any of the archival material now in the Lilly and Smith Libraries, and before the publication of *Letters Home* and *The Journals*—he amassed the material for his book. "Facts as such are relatively easy to come by in a society where growing complexity has spawned a growing network of official institutions," he wrote in the introduction to his anthology. "Schools, libraries, newspaper files, governmental agencies, and the like are there for the plundering, as every credit house and FBI investigator well knows, and the laziest of biographers can still construct a reasonable collage from the bits and pieces resurrected from these bureaucratic mausoleums." Butscher was anything but lazy, and his collage of Plath's short life is a dense and detailed one. In fact, it bears a striking resemblance to the collages produced by later biographers, who could consult the published and unpublished letters and journals and, in the case of Anne Stevenson, had the cooperation of the Plath estate. The traces we leave of ourselves are evidently so deep that every investigator will stumble upon them. If the door to one room of secrets is closed, others are open and beckoning. There is a law of human nature—let us call it the Confidant's Law—that dictates that no secret is ever told to only one person; there is always at least one other person to whom we feel compelled to spill the beans. Thus, Butscher, who did not have access to Plath's letter telling her mother of her quarrel with Olwyn in Yorkshire, was able to get "the grim details" (as he calls them) from another source—Elizabeth Sigmund, to whom Plath had also told the story. But it isn't only our secrets that survive us; evidently, every cup of coffee we ever drank, every hamburger we ever ate, every boy we ever kissed has been inscribed on someone's memory and lies in impatient readiness for the biographer's retrieval. In an almost uncanny way, Butscher's diligent soundings of Plath's teachers, friends, lovers, and colleagues in America and England brought forth a world that paralleled the world reflected in *Letters Home* and *The Journals*. The dates, the college weekends, the scenes of necking and petting, and the rows that were recorded by Plath are here recorded from the other side, but in the same intimate detail and with the same authority; the witness, as he blabs to the biographer, is himself like a person writing in his journal or to his mother, without shame, without inhibition, sometimes almost without thought.

If Butscher's book still holds its own among the five Plath biographies in regard to the scope and depth of its intrusive research, in another respect it has been superseded. The Paul Alexander and Ronald Hayman biographies have introduced a new meanspiritedness. Butscher's *Method and Madness* is a big brute of a book—shapeless, uneven, filled with maladroitly handled psychoanalytic language and presumptuous speculations about how people thought and felt. When it came out, the Hugheses were appalled by it. ("I found the portraits in the book of my parents, of Ted, of Sylvia herself, of Mrs. Plath and of others virtually unrecognizable," Olwyn wrote in a letter to *The New York Review of Books* protesting a review of the book by Karl Miller as too kind.) But if they could have looked into the future and seen the horrors that awaited them in the Alexander and Hayman books they would have sent Butscher flowers. Both writers have advertised their independence of the Plath estate—neither even requested permission to quote from Plath's writings—and, with their paraphrases and interviews with hostile witnesses, they raised Hughes's punishment by biography to a new level of excruciation. Hayman's *The Death and Life of Sylvia Plath* is as poisonous as Alexander's *Rough Magic*, but it is more elliptically and less crudely written. Hayman's contribution to the sport of tearing off Hughes's wings is to publish above- and belowstairs gossip about his relations with Assia Wevill before and after Plath's death. Alexander's book is the prize negative example. Here is his rendering of Plath's famous account of the *St. Botolph's* party:

> Eventually, Sylvia dressed in a cute "American" outfit, which she accessorized with silver earrings, a red hairband, and a pair of red shoes. After supper with Nat, she returned to Whitstead, where Hamish picked her up in a cab. At Miller's Bar, a stop they made on their way to the party, Sylvia stood at the counter and quickly downed several whiskeys. Soon the whole world floated around her. . . .
>
> By the time they reached the Women's Union, a foreboding building on campus just off Falcon Yard, Sylvia was very drunk. Still, as they entered the huge second-floor room in which the party was located, she took the scene in. . . .
>
> Guiding her into a side room, Hughes shut the door and poured Sylvia [a] drink. . . . Dreamily, Sylvia looked at his face, noticing his demure lips, his wide forehead, his soulful eyes. Then, as if to acknowledge the palpable sexual charge that had formed between them, Hughes leaned down and kissed Sylvia on the mouth. Pulling away, he tore the red hairband from her head and yanked off her silver earrings. "Ah, I shall keep these," he said.
>
> Sylvia felt pleasantly dazed. As soon as Hughes made a move to kiss her on the neck, Sylvia, ready to show that she could hold her own in such matters, reached up and bit his cheek so hard her teeth broke skin, causing him to flinch. Somehow it did not seem possible to continue, so they stepped apart.

In addition to emptying the incident of all its energy and urgency, Alexander has accessorized Plath's journal entry with details—the "demure lips," the "wide forehead," the "soulful eyes," Plath's "pleasantly dazed" feeling, and Hughes's "flinch"—that appear nowhere in the original. To further illustrate my profound dislike of Alexander's book—

whose chief aim seems to be to see how outrageously it can slander Hughes and still somehow stay within the limits of libel law—I offer the following passage:

> Only one episode, in Sylvia's account of it, marred the well-ordered, productive rhythm of their days in Benidorm. Years later, she told a close friend that one afternoon while she and Ted sat on a hillside Ted was overtaken by an inexplicable rage. As Sylvia had described it, his face whitened, his body contorted, his gaze intensified. And, according to Sylvia, before she knew it, he was on top of her—not kissing her, as he usually did, but choking her. At first, she said, she fought him. Then, eventually, she merely gave in and allowed his superior strength to dominate her, his fingers to tighten more and more around her neck. Finally, at the moment when she began to lose consciousness—the moment she said she resolved herself to die—Ted released his grip and stopped his assault as abruptly as he had started it. When Sylvia told this story, her marriage to Ted was under enormous stress, and she claimed that this episode had made her question the wisdom of her decision to marry him. Whatever the case, whatever happened on the hillside in Benidorm, Sylvia did nothing.

This is a horrible story. Who is this "close friend" who can charge Hughes with nothing less than attempted murder? How reliable a witness? We will never know. "The information for this paragraph comes from my interview with a confidential source," Alexander calmly writes.

Butscher, however, despite all that has come after, retains his special bad reputation in the Plath world. When he published *Method and Madness*, he got into trouble not only with the Hugheses and Mrs. Plath, who resented his intrusiveness into their lives, but with some of the people who gave his intrusiveness its object and opportunity—the people who blabbed to him about Plath and Hughes and Olwyn and Mrs. Plath, and then were appalled to see their words in print. One of these burned witnesses, David Compton, wrote to Butscher:

> I am very distressed at the use in your book to which you have put our conversation about Sylvia Plath. . . . Particularly on the subject of Aurelia Plath it seems to me that you have chosen only my most adverse comments—thus falsifying what I seriously believe to be the truth, and most certainly causing unjust and unnecessary hurt. . . . As for my ex-wife's recollections, these—and I positively remember warning you—are likely to be coloured (to say the least) by her vivid sense of the dramatic.

Of course, Compton hadn't a leg to stand on; Butscher was entitled to choose what he wished to quote from Compton (who could, after all, have avoided any risk of causing "unjust and unnecessary hurt" by keeping his "adverse" comments to himself), and was entitled to believe what he wished to believe of what Compton's ex-wife had said. But Butscher's unpopularity—the special dislike he has drawn to himself in the Plath biographical community—has yet another source. Butscher has figured as a kind of Leonard Bast in the community's imagination—and, I should hasten to add, in his own. When I spoke with him in New York, our conversation was dominated by his class consciousness: he would frequently use the term "lower middle class" about himself and "Wasp" and "upper middle class" about other people. A man in his late forties, with an easy, genial manner, he was at pains to represent himself as plainspeaking and unpretentious. He teaches high school in Flushing, Queens, where he has lived all his life, and has never gained (or, for that matter, seriously sought) admission into any of the higher academic, journalistic, or literary worlds inhabited by most literary biographers. Like the Jew who is fascinated with the question of who else is Jewish, Butscher is obsessed with the question of who else has lower-middle-class or working-class parents or grandparents. In Olwyn Hughes he felt he had found a comfortable fellow "Jew," with whom he did not have to put on airs. He spoke of her to me with a kind of fond spite: "I enjoyed my encounter with Olwyn. After you've spent a great deal of time interviewing Wasps in Massachusetts, you kind of hunger for some vulgarity. You hunger for this kind of Queens approach to the world of power. So I don't have the usual negative feelings about her. I get a kick out of her."

Clarissa Roche, for her part, did not get a kick out of Butscher during his visit to her house. "It's so unlike me, but I didn't ask him to spend the night," she told Frances and me. "I was perfectly decent to him. But I just didn't take him seriously. I haven't lived in America since 1956, and I know there have been great changes, but I couldn't believe that this man was an academic. Then I got a letter from him saying his tape recorder hadn't been on and would I please write and tell him what I had said. Of course, I didn't. Then, years later, he wrote again. At the time, I was building on to the house and getting all the windows changed, and there was this carpet I had got it into my head to dye dark green—almost black—and I had found out that at Wilton you could get carpets dyed any color you wanted. In his letter Butscher asked me to write a memoir for his anthology, and he offered me exactly the amount of money I needed to get my carpet dyed. So I did it."

Clarissa said she had started a long work about Plath, but "months and months and months go by and I don't do anything at all." In fact, she said, she had gone twice to a hypnotist to try to retrieve further memories of Plath and Hughes, but had failed. Throughout the afternoon, I felt in her the wish to be as hospitable with her memories of Plath and Hughes as she was with her house and food, but as the house and food were nourishing, the memories were exiguous. She was reduced to serving up insubstantial fragments of stories reflecting her dislike of Hughes. "When Sylvia was teaching at Smith, Ted was sort of indulged," she said. "People didn't dislike him, but he was just sort of nobody."

"He was good-looking, wasn't he?" Frances said.

"I could see that some people might think he was. But I never thought he was."

We left the table and returned to the now almost extinct fire. Clarissa stared into the embers and told a story; it wasn't quite clear whether she had heard it from Elizabeth Sigmund or from Y, a friend of Sigmund's whom Hughes had gone with before his marriage to Carol. "Ted had turned up at Y's house—he had run over this hare—and he went into the kitchen to dress it. He was there a long time, and finally Y opened the door. He had the hare all spread out, and there was this wild, wild demonic look in his eyes. 'Scrying' is a way of telling fortunes by entrails. Y said that when he looked up he was actually"—here Clarissa paused and lowered her voice—"*slavering*. Now, Y wouldn't make up a story like that."

III

O N March 18, 1991, a month after my return to New York from England, I wrote a letter to Jacqueline Rose:

DEAR JACQUELINE:

There was a moment during our talk in February that was like one of those moments during an analytic session when the air is suddenly charged with electricity, and what has ignited the spark is some small, casual, unconsidered action by one of the interlocutors. When you produced the passage from Ted Hughes's letter about literary criticism and the living and the dead, and I remarked on the sentence that I had not seen in Olwyn's copy of it, there was (and I will be interested to know if this description conforms with your experience) an almost palpable thickening of the emotional atmosphere. Your realization that you had unwittingly shown me something you felt you should not have shown me affected us both strongly. As I thought about the moment later in Freudian terms, it seemed to me that issues of secrets and forbidden knowledge, as well as of sibling rivalry (the image of two women fighting over something—over a man?), had been stirred up. In addition, the moment raised for me the question of the place of morality in post-structuralist discourse. You value doubt and accept the anxiety of uncertainty—but you also have very definite notions of what is right and wrong. You immediately felt it wrong to "give" me what Ted Hughes had "given" you. When you asked me not to quote the sentence I should not have seen, you used the word "ethically." Doesn't the very idea of ethics imply a standard, a norm, a canon of acceptable behavior? And isn't there some discontinuity between your position as a post-structuralist literary theorist and your attentiveness to the requirements of living in the world as a morally scrupulous person? Finally (and more directly to the point of our respective Plathian enterprises), doesn't this tiny incident of suppression in a sense reproduce the larger suppressions of the Hugheses? Now that I have seen the sentence, can I "unsee" it?

I never received a reply to this letter—or expected one—since I never sent it. After reading it over, I marked it "Letter not sent" and put it away in a folder.

The genre of the unsent letter might reward study. We have all contributed to it, and the literary archives are full of specimens. In the Plath archive at the Lilly Library, for example, there are several of Aurelia Plath's unsent letters to Hughes—letters in which she permitted herself to say what she finally decided she couldn't permit herself to say. But she carefully preserved the letters, and included them in the material she turned over to the archive. The preservation of the unsent letter is its arresting feature. Neither the writing nor the not sending is remarkable (we often make drafts of letters and discard them), but the gesture of keeping the message we have no intention of sending is. By saving the letter, we are in some sense "sending" it after all. We are not relinquishing our idea or dismissing it as foolish or unworthy (as we do when we tear up a letter); on the contrary, we are giving it an extra vote of confidence. We are, in effect, saying that our idea is too precious to be entrusted to the gaze of the actual addressee, who may not grasp its worth, so we "send" it to his equivalent in fantasy, on whom we can absolutely count for an understanding and appreciative reading. Like Anne Stevenson with Olwyn, I had been tempted by the idea of collaboration with Jacqueline Rose on the rendering of the moment between us over Ted Hughes's letter. But I feared that she would not read the scene as I had read it, that she would tell me that her own experience of the moment had been entirely different and that I had my nerve attributing motives and feelings to her that she did not have. So I tore up the airmail envelope I had addressed to her. But I did not tear up the letter itself, and as I now pluck it from its place of hibernation the thought floats into my mind that some of the early English novels were novels-in-letters.

The moment with Jacqueline Rose that had affected me so strongly and moved me to write my own epistolary fiction took place in the middle of a conversation I had with her at her very handsome flat, in West Hampstead, a few days after my return to London from Devon and Somerset. I was greeted by a small, attractive woman in her early forties, wearing a short and close-fitting skirt and a sweater, whose face was framed by a great deal of artfully unruly blond hair, and whose whole person was surrounded by a kind of nimbus of self-possession. That she was an adept of a theory of criticism whose highest values are uncertainty, anxiety, and ambiguity was a curious but somehow unameliorating facet of her formidable clarity, confidence, and certainty. During our meeting, her manner was engaging—neither too friendly nor too distant—and on a scale of how people should conduct themselves with journalists I would give her a score of 99. She understood the nature of the transaction—that it was a transaction—and had carefully worked out for herself exactly how much she had to give in order to receive the benefit of the interview. In most interviews, both subject and interviewer give more than is necessary. They are always being seduced and distracted by the encounter's outward resemblance to an ordinary friendly meeting. The meal that is often thrown around it like a cloth, to soften the edges; the habits of chat and banter; the conversational reflexes, whereby questions are obediently answered and silences too quickly filled—all these inexorably pull the interlocutors away from their respective desires and goals. However, Rose never—or almost never—forgot, or let me forget, that we were not two women having a friendly conversation over a cup of tea and a box of biscuits but participants in a special, artificial exercise of subtle influence and counterinfluence, with an implicit antagonistic tendency.

Rose teaches English literature at the University of London, and now, as if addressing a class, she gave a crisp, succinct account of the events that had led her to make public her dealings with the Plath estate. "I took careful legal advice on questions of citations and permissions," she said. "I had followed the business with Linda Wagner-Martin and Anne Stevenson, and I knew this was a potentially difficult area. After I finished a rough draft of my book, in early 1990, I wrote to Olwyn Hughes asking permission for the four poems I quote in full, and Olwyn gave it to me in a very friendly letter." But when Rose, following further legal advice, sent her manuscript to the Hugheses, all smiles ceased. Although Rose is a critic of distinction and originality, in the eyes of the Hugheses she was just another member of the pack of Ted Hughes's tormentors and pursuers, and they fought the publication of *The Haunting of Sylvia Plath* with their usual clumsy fierceness. First, they attempted to revoke the permissions for the four poems, and then, when that failed ("Legally, once you've given permission, then that is a contract, and I had paid," Rose told me), they attempted to persuade Rose to make changes in her text. What stuck in the Hugheses' craw (as Rose had expected it would) was a chapter called "The Archive," which she describes in the book as "a reading—of necessity speculative—of the editing of Plath's work," and which studies the omissions from the letters and journals with a very critical eye. It also takes some savage pokes at *Bitter Fame*: Rose characterizes the book as "something of a 'cause célèbre' in the genre of abusive biography," and she joins Alvarez in protesting the book's sternness with

Plath and indulgence of Hughes. In accordance with post-structuralist theory, Rose argues for suspension of all certainty about what happened, and thus of judgment and blame. "I'm not *ever* interested in what happened between Plath and Hughes," she told me. "My position is that you're left with a tangle of competing viewpoints, and if you try to make sense of it you'll go wrong one way or another. You have to live with the anxiety that such uncertainty generates. It's not helpful to resolve it too fast." In her book Rose says of *Bitter Fame*, "One of the strangest effects of reading this book, especially if you have read the unedited letters and journals, is that it precisely becomes impossible to know whom to believe." (In fact, it is *only* if you have read the letters and journals—or have been in other ways alerted to the controversial character of the Plath-Hughes narrative—that *Bitter Fame* seems strange. The lay reader, who knows only what the biographer tells him, reads it, as he reads every other biography, in a state of bovine equanimity.) Rose continues her argument:

> Like the child caught up in a hideous divorce case between its parents, the writing of the life of Sylvia Plath, both by herself and by those who knew her, forces you—and makes it impossible for you—to take sides. Whom to believe, how to know, what is the truth of the case? Behind the self-interest of the protagonists lies a drama about the limits and failure of knowledge and self-knowing. We can settle it, like indeed the proceedings of a divorce case, but only by entering into the false and damaging forms of certainty for which those settlements are so renowned.

What Rose leaves out of account (and what her colleagues in the academy left out of account in their anxious and contorted writings about another hideous divorce case, that of

Paul de Man and his wartime journalism) is the psychological impossibility of a writer's not taking sides. "Forces you," yes. But "makes it impossible for you," no. Without some "false and damaging" certainty, no writing on any subject is humanly possible. The writer, like the murderer, needs a motive. Rose's book is fuelled by a bracing hostility toward Ted and Olwyn Hughes. It derives its verve and forward thrust from the cool certainty with which (in the name of "uncertainty" and "anxiety") she presents her case against the Hugheses. In the "Archive" chapter, her accusations against Hughes for his "editing, controlling, and censoring" reach an apogee of harshness. If it had truly been impossible for Rose to take a side, her book would not have been written; it would not have been worth taking the trouble to write. Writing cannot be done in a state of desirelessness. The pose of fairmindedness, the charade of evenhandedness, the striking of an attitude of detachment can never be more than rhetorical ruses; if they were genuine, if the writer *actually* didn't care one way or the other how things came out, he would not bestir himself to represent them.

Rose is the libber in whom the Hugheses finally met their match, who could not be contemptuously dismissed, who was a serious and worthy opponent. In *The Haunting of Sylvia Plath* she speaks for the dead poet and against Hughes in a way no other writer has done. She objects not only to Hughes's suppressions in the journals and letters but to his presentation of Plath as a high-art poet and of *Ariel* as the tiny nugget of gold extracted from the ore of a painfully misdirected writing life. Rose rejects the distinction between high and low art, good and bad writing, "true" and "false" selves on which the Hughes view is posited. To Rose, the stories written for the "slicks" (as Plath described them to her mother) are no less worthy of examination than the *Ariel* poems. For Rose, there are no "waste products." All Plath's writings are precious to her; all the genres she wrote in, all the voices she assumed—and all the voices buzzing around her since her death—are welcomed into Rose's bazaar of postmodernist consciousness.

The Haunting of Sylvia Plath is a brilliant achievement. The framework of deconstructive, psychoanalytic, and feminist ideology on which Rose has mounted her polemic against the Hugheses gives the work a high intellectual shimmer. There are close to eight hundred footnotes. One is dazzled, excited, somewhat intimidated. The Hugheses, however, were upset and angered; they could hear only Rose's reproachful aria. They could catch only the note of hostility that Rose herself was evidently unaware of—that perhaps only they, as the subjects of her criticism, could fully hear. In a letter to Anne Stevenson, Olwyn wrote of what it felt like to be attacked in Rose's book: "I wonder if you have the slightest idea how enormously unpleasant it is to open such a manuscript as Rose's and meet that malevolent surge—from a person one has never heard of before."

As the reader knows, I, too, have taken a side—that of the Hugheses and Anne Stevenson—and I, too, draw on my sympathies and antipathies and experiences to support it. My narrative of Rose has an edge; my silver-plated scissors are ever at the ready to take snips at her. In another context—if, that is, I had read *The Haunting of Sylvia Plath* as a book on a subject in which I had no investment—I would have felt nothing but admiration for it, since I tend to support the new literary theorists in their debate with the traditionalists. But in the Plath-Hughes debate my sympathies are with the Hugheses, and thus, like a lawyer defending a case he knows to be weak and yet obscurely feels is just, I steel myself against the attractions of the opposition's most powerful and plausible witness.

In her apartment, having finished her account of the hard

time the Hugheses had given her over the "Archive" chapter, Jacqueline Rose poured tea and went on to speak of "another area of trouble with the estate," which she said she found "at least as interesting." This area was a chapter of Rose's book called "No Fantasy Without Protest," whose centerpiece is a reading of Plath's poem "The Rabbit Catcher." Ted Hughes had taken violent exception to this reading and had asked Rose to remove it. Rose had not expected Hughes to be happy with her "Archive" chapter, but she was utterly unprepared for his objections to the "Rabbit Catcher" reading, which said nothing critical of him, and, in fact, took issue with the conventional feminist reading of the poem as a parable of the domination of men over women—the snares the narrator encounters on a walk in the country being seen as the trap that conventional marriage is for women—and as a direct commentary on Plath's own marriage. Rose offers an alternative reading, which finds in the poem's arresting, enigmatic imagery a fantasy of androgyny. Although no commentator had ever found this fantasy before—it is doubtful whether Plath herself would have been aware of it—Rose's reading does not seem very remarkable in today's climate of acceptance of both enacted and imagined homosexuality; the bisexual component of human sexuality is a commonplace of post-Freudian thought. But for Hughes—perhaps for the whole pre-Freudian English nation—the idea of unstable sexual identity was unacceptable, and Rose's suggestion that Plath even thought about such things as lesbian sex (never mind doing them) struck Hughes as abhorrent beyond imagination. I speak for Hughes so confidently because he made his views public in a letter written in response to a letter by Rose and published in the *TLS* on April 10, 1992. In his letter Hughes movingly, if bafflingly, told of his concern about the injurious effect that Rose's reading of "The Rabbit Catcher" would have on his children (now in their thirties). "Professor

Rose distorts, reinvents etc Sylvia Plath's 'sexual identity' with an abandon I could hardly believe—presenting her in a role that I vividly felt to be humiliating to Sylvia Plath's children," he wrote, and he went on:

> I tried to jolt Ms Rose into imagining their feelings, seeing her book (as I have seen it) in a friend's house and assuming instantly that their friend now thinks about their mother the thoughts Professor Rose has taught. . . .
>
> Having thought it through for her in that way, I did not see how Ms Rose could fail to have full and instant knowledge of the peculiar kind of suffering such a moment induces—the little dull blow of something like despair, the helpless rage and shame for their mother, the little poisoning of life, the bitter but quite useless fury against the person who shot this barbed arrow into them just to amuse herself. And the unending accumulation of such moments, since Rose's book is now in the college libraries for good, her idea percolating into all subsequent books about their mother.

Hughes makes what Rose wrote sound so unspeakable and unprintable that I had better hasten to quote the offensive or inoffensive passage (as the case may be), so that the reader can decide for himself. It concerns the first two stanzas of "The Rabbit Catcher," which read:

> *It was a place of force —*
> *The wind gagging my mouth with my own blown hair,*
> *Tearing off my voice, and the sea*
> *Blinding me with its lights, the lives of the dead*
> *Unreeling in it, spreading like oil.*
>
> *I tasted the malignity of the gorse,*
> *Its black spikes,*
> *The extreme unction of its yellow candle-flowers.*
> *They had an efficiency, a great beauty,*
> *And were extravagant, like torture.*

In her "No Fantasy Without Protest" chapter Rose writes of this opening:

> For the sexuality that it writes cannot be held to a single place—it spreads, blinds, unreels like the oil in the sea. Most crudely, that wind blowing, that gagging, calls up the image of oral sex and then immediately turns it around, gagging the speaker with her own blown hair, her hair in her mouth, her tasting the gorse (Whose body—male or female—is this? Who—man or woman—is tasting whom?), even while "black spikes" and "candles" work to hold the more obvious distribution of gender roles in their place. For Freud, such fantasies, such points of uncertainty, are the regular unconscious subtexts—for all of us—of the more straightforward reading, the more obvious narratives of stable sexual identity which we write.

At her tea table, Rose continued her cogent account of her struggle with Ted Hughes over her reading of "The Rabbit Catcher." She said, "In my communications to Hughes I said—and I say this over and over again in my book—'Look, I'm in no sense speaking of Plath's lived sexual identity in the world, about which I know nothing. I'm only discussing fantasy.' But he says that the distinction is not viable, because the fantasy concerns very intimate aspects of their life. It's true, it is intimate and it is private. But if you cannot talk about fantasy in a discussion of the literary writings of Sylvia Plath, then you cannot talk about Sylvia Plath. Because that's what she writes about. About the psyche and about inner images. Wonderful inner images of difficulty and pain—images which implicate us all, I think. I don't accept the reading that says they demonstrate her pathology. I'm not interested in the question of whether she was pathological or not. I don't think one knows, and I think you can only make statements like 'She was pathological' if you are absolutely sure of your own sanity, which I consider a morally unacceptable position."

I asked Rose if Ted Hughes had been appreciative of other parts of her book. "No," she said. She added, allowing a note of bitterness to get into her voice, "Hughes wrote an article in which he was very critical of Ronald Hayman's reading of a poem in *The Colossus*. He said that in the classroom this kind of literal interpretation would be a joke. Therefore I thought—as it turned out, foolishly—that there might be some appreciation for my more complex readings of the poems. But I've not had one positive statement from Ted Hughes or from Olwyn Hughes."

I mentioned that I had met Olwyn a few days earlier, and Rose asked, "What did she say to you about my book?" I told her what she already knew—that Olwyn had been displeased—and when Rose pressed for details I cited the passage in the Hughes letter that Olwyn had handed me in the Indian restaurant.

Rose looked at me with surprise. "The passage about what literary critics do to the living and the dead?" she asked.

"Yes."

Rose sat still for a moment, looking thoughtful. Then she abruptly left the room, saying over her shoulder, "I want to see if it's the same passage." She returned with a sheet of paper and handed it to me. I glanced at it and said, "Yes, that's it. It's an interesting perspective, isn't it?"

"Well, it's an argument against the right to do criticism," Rose said. "This line about how critics reinvent the living— 'They extend over the living that licence to say whatever they please, to ransack their psyches and reinvent them however they please.' It implies two things. First, that I am saying I have *the* truth about the Hugheses' lives—which I never say I do—and, second, that they themselves possess it, and any interpretation beyond theirs is a violation of that singular truth."

"May I look at this again?" I said, reaching for the sheet, the better to follow Rose's discussion.

"Yes, of course. I mean, in the end he leaves no room for literary criticism. Which may be what Ted Hughes wants to say. Which is a very interesting thing to say. But it also means there's no room for reading, rereading, interpretation, and discussion of meanings in our culture. The implications of this are really quite extraordinary."

"Here's a sentence I hadn't seen. It's striking," I said, looking up from the paper in my hand. "It wasn't in the passage Olwyn showed me: 'Miss Rose thought she was writing a book about a writer dead thirty years and seems to have overlooked, as I say, the plain fact that she has ended up writing a book largely about me.'"

Rose said very quickly, "I don't think you can quote that without asking Ted Hughes. I think that would be a problem legally." (Later, I did ask for and receive permission to quote the line.) "And, in fact, I wouldn't have shown you that if I wasn't wanting to check the passage Olwyn quoted to you." In her discomposure, Rose had slipped into a more colloquial syntax: "wasn't wanting to check" was unusual in her impressive, lecturer's speech.

I began to say something further about the significance of the extra sentence—how it affected the meaning of the rest of the passage—and Rose, again uncharacteristically, interrupted. "Well, I know," she said. "But this is awkward. I don't feel I should give you communications I've received from Ted and Olwyn Hughes. They were directed to me. They were not meant for public circulation. I only showed you this because Olwyn Hughes showed you a passage from a communication to me, right? And it just so happens that you have therefore seen an additional sentence. I think this is an awkward area, ethically. And I would ask you not to quote that sentence." She thought briefly and then added, "Yes, I think I have to say that."

This, then, was the charged "moment" of my unsent letter. I render it with the help of a tape recording, which preserved the words that passed between Rose and me but did not catch any of the language of face and body by which we all speak to one another and sometimes say what we dare not put into words. Deconstructive writers use the word "aporia" to refer to a place in a text of unexpected difficulty or impasse, a passage that does not yield to the reader's usual quick, logical, frontal approaches to understanding. Rose and I had reached an aporia in our encounter—something unexpected and complicated had occurred. I remember feeling that she and I were struggling over something—were having a fight about some central, unacceptable thing—but today, two years later, much of what was going on between us has left no objective trace of itself, and I no longer have the conviction I once had that Jacqueline Rose and I were fighting over Ted Hughes. Like a biographer, I have only the evidence of texts—in this case, the "fictional" text of my unsent letter and the "factual" text of my tape recording—to guide me in my narrative. They are not guides that feel very reliable to me.

In her memoir of Plath at Cambridge, Jane Baltzell Kopp (the girl who made fun of Plath's Samsonite luggage) reported an incident that falls rather short of its intended effect. Kopp writes of being astonished by Plath's white fury on discovering that five books she had lent Kopp had been returned to her with Kopp's pencilled marks added to Plath's inked underlinings. Kopp seems oblivious of the offense she committed in writing in a borrowed book; she quotes Plath's "Jane, how *could* you?" as if it were a peculiar reaction. Plath, on the other hand, thought Kopp's act outrageous enough to mention in a letter to her mother and in a subsequent journal entry: "I was furious, feeling my children had been raped, or beaten, by an alien." Biography can be likened to a book that has been scribbled in by an alien. After we die, our story passes into the hands of strangers. The biographer feels himself to be not a borrower but a new owner, who can mark and underline as he pleases. Kopp makes the point that it was Plath's own dark underlinings that "emboldened" her to make her "few pencil marks." (In Plath's version, Kopp wrote "all over" the five books.) Writers on Plath have felt (consciously or unconsciously) something of the same sense of permission, as if they had been given the right to act boldly, even wildly, where ordinarily they would be cautious and tread delicately. In Plath's "cathartic blowup" (as she described it in her journal), she brought Kopp to her knees, shaming her into cleaning up the pencil marks. Hughes's distress over the mess the various new owners have made of the book that he once jointly owned with Plath—but which her death and fame, and his own fame, have ruthlessly taken from him—is understandable, but his efforts to get them to clean up their marks have brought him only grief; he is no longer in possession, he has no say in the matter. His attempt to meddle with Linda Wagner-Martin's biography gave her bland book a status and an interest it would not have otherwise had; his attempt to meddle with Jacqueline Rose's study gave this more substantial work a similar réclame. As Wagner-Martin had punished and triumphed over Hughes (and Olwyn) with the account in her preface of their hard dealings with her, so Rose, in *her* preface, with the composed air appropriate to such occasions, calmly laid out, one by one, the four aces the Hugheses had dealt her:

In correspondence with the Hugheses, this book was called "evil." Its publisher was told it would not appear. At one point an attempt was made to revoke previously granted permissions to quote from Plath's work. I was asked to remove my reading of "The Rabbit Catcher," and when I refused, I was told by Ted Hughes that my analysis would be damaging for Plath's (now adult) children, and that speculation of the kind I was seen as engaging in about Sylvia Plath's sexual identity would in some countries be "grounds for homicide."

Rose's book came out in England in June, 1991, to almost universal acclaim. It received substantial, largely admiring reviews in the *TLS* and the *London Review of Books*, from Joyce Carol Oates and Elaine Showalter, respectively. In the daily English press, it was reviewed together with Ronald Hayman's *The Death and Life of Sylvia Plath*, which (happily for Rose) had been published at the same time; the shallowness of Hayman's book provided a foil for Rose's scholarly seriousness, and several reviewers were quick to structure their reviews around the disparity. The Hugheses' difficulty with this distinction may be imagined. I felt for them, even as I knew the distinction to be just, beyond any argument.

After my return to New York, in February, Olwyn, in correspondence and telephone conversations, continued to voice her vexation over the Rose book. "The book is a determination to show Ted as a monster," she said to me on one occasion. "Rose reads dark Machiavellian thoughts into everything—thoughts that I assure you nobody ever had. There isn't one interesting or intelligent thing in the book. She's a structuralist, she's a feminist, she's a God knows what. Did you actually meet her?"

I said I did.

"What is she like? Does she have four eyes?"

"She's a very attractive woman, very precise and confident."

"Is she English or American?"

"She's English."

There was a long pause; Olwyn had obviously wanted Rose to be American. She resumed: "The way she goes on about Sylvia's sexual life—it's incredible, it's libellous."

"You can't libel the dead," I said.

"But, in a way, that passage libels everybody, doesn't it? It libels Ted, it libels Carol, it libels any woman he ever had anything to do with."

"This is getting very complicated," I said.

"It's appalling. It's so intended. It's so nasty. And they talk about *my* wickedness, denying permission to these angels to quote. What can one do? Should one just let them quote and let the myths get wilder and wilder—or should one try to correct them, as I have done?"

Olwyn's attempt to correct Rose—which consisted of sending her a document of twenty single-spaced typewritten pages, entitled "Notes Re J. Rose's Mss—'The Haunting of Sylvia Plath'"—only provided further grist for Rose's deconstructive mill. She coolly added the "Notes" to the hundreds of texts she cites in her footnotes and quotes from in her own text. Rose's method of citation reminds me of those prison scenes in historical movies where aristocrats and beggars, virtuous women and prostitutes, righteous men and thieves have all been thrown into one cell and are being treated by the guard with elaborate democratic sameness. In *The Haunting of Sylvia Plath*, the writings of Freud, James, Ronald Hayman, and a friend of Aurelia Plath's are all accorded the same grave attention; and Olwyn's "Notes" and Ted's letters to Rose are treated simply as interesting late-in-the-day contributions to the book, rather than as angry attacks on it. ("I found their

comments helpful, meaningful, and informative, as they repeatedly fed into and contributed to the overall argument of
the book," Rose writes.) In August, 1991—her fur sleek and
a few feathers still around her mouth—Rose wrote me a long
letter replying to some questions I had put to her (in a sent
letter) after reading the final version of her book:

> On the question of why we sent the Hugheses the manu-
> script. We (i.e., myself and Virago) were legally advised to
> do so. We knew that publishing on Plath was a difficult pro-
> cess, and both Virago's lawyer and counsel considered that
> sending the manuscript was in fact the way to secure the
> book's final publication. We would know the reaction, the
> likelihood of legal action, and how or whether to respond to
> the possibility in advance.

I had also asked Rose to explain an odd term, "textual
entities," she uses in her introduction. ("In this book, in the
analysis of [Plath's] writings, I am never talking of real
people, but of textual entities (Y and X), whose more than
real reality, I will be arguing, goes beyond them to encircle
us all.") She replied that here, again, a legal consideration had
guided her. Lawyers had advised her to use the term to make
it impossible for Hughes to sue her, she wrote, and she gave
an illustration: "Although violence is one of the repeated
themes of Plath's writing, I at no point deduce from that writing that any violence necessarily passed between them. To do
so would have been legally defamatory, and the book could
not have appeared." She added, "More important, however,
I have no desire to make such a suggestion, as it seems to
me that I have absolutely no way of knowing this, and firmly believe that writing is as much a place to explore what
did not happen but is—say—most feared or desired as
what did."

Perhaps no greater tribute could have been paid to Rose's position, and to the post-structuralist vision of writing as a kind of dream, which no one (including the dreamer-writer) ever gets to the bottom of, than the tribute Ted Hughes paid in his April 24, 1992, letter to the *TLS*, where he wrote of his shock and dismay on learning that Rose had interpreted his remark about homicide as a threat. In her own letter to the *TLS* Rose had indignantly quoted the remark: "I was told . . . that to speculate on a mother's sexual identity would in some countries be 'grounds for homicide.' If this is not illegitimate pressure (it did not—I of course checked with Virago's lawyer—legally constitute a threat), then I would like to know what is." Hughes wrote that his intention had been to arouse her "common (even maternal) sensibility":

> I cast about for some historical example, a situation in which what is perceived as a fanciful, verbalized, public injury to a mother's "sexual identity" strikes into her children with a pain that is not only violently real, but is also well recorded, documentary, believed by Professor Rose. I lit on the obvious case, and asked her to imagine how it would be, to interpret some local mother's "sexual identity," publicly (even publishing it to the world), as she had interpreted Sylvia Plath's—in one of those pride and honour societies of the Mediterranean.
>
> I was so strenuously locked into beating at her door, as I have described, simply to wake her up—it never dawned on me that all she could feel was *threatened*. . . .
>
> I was trying, rather desperately and with a sense of futility, to get her to look into her heart, but the only effect I had, as she now tells, was that she consulted her lawyer.

IV

THE game continues. The players come and go, and, as the years pass, the Hugheses seem to grow more accustomed to the unpleasant conditions of the casino. They have got better at their work; they no longer run the place as if it were a candy store. Olwyn has given up the job of literary agent to the Plath estate, though she continues her activities as the fierce and selfless protector of her brother. She writes letters to editors and speaks her mind to journalists, "in her plain Yorkshire way," as one of them put it. When, in reply to charges that the Plath estate was suppressing material, she wrote a letter to the *TLS* saying that she alone, and not she and Hughes, was responsible for "any exertion of 'pressure'" on biographers, readers could almost see her once again interposing her body to shield Hughes from gunfire. In her letters to me, and in telephone conversations, she has alternated between growling about the probability that I have fallen under "the Roche-Sigmund influence" and grudgingly acknowledging the possibility that I will not write the usual "cultist rubbish." "With these people, you can't appeal to their humanity, because they haven't any," she said during a telephone call. "You can't appeal to their wider understanding, because they haven't any. You can't appeal to their good will, because all their little futures and their little ambitions are invested in their *ill will*—so what can you do with them? One can't go on perpetually bringing up bus tickets to prove that what one said was correct. It's so insulting. It's so stupid. If people wish to believe these silly women and their hysterias, let them. I just can't be bothered anymore." Here and there, in the latter part of our correspondence, she has sounded a softer, more personal note. For example, on December 10, 1991, she wrote:

> Sylvia & I: While she was alive I just accepted her. Most of the time it was quite pleasant when she was around. She was very involved with Ted and either busy at her typewriter or in the kitchen but mostly amusing and interesting the rest of the time. . . .
> After her death, it became clear that the "Ariel" poems, however wicked, were the work of a major poet. I never doubted that for a second. Then I read the Journals and simply wept for her—that all that agony lay beneath that cool, controlled exterior was astonishing. "Letters Home" I found pretty distasteful, but I could understand at least their tone—I found myself writing pretty artificial letters, about the children, to Aurelia, too.
> It was always clear Sylvia was inclined to be selfish, was inordinately possessive of Ted, and kept one at a distance. But plenty of people have faults of one kind and another. My general feeling was [that] if they were happy together (as most of the time they certainly were) it was put-uppable with.
> Clearly with all the mess her various writings and malicious sayings have caused since, I would be a saint if I did not from time to time much dislike that side of her. But basically I just feel sad for her. . . . I think she was brave, and struggled with a bigger problem than most are handed out.

Passages like this encouraged me to expect that there would be a rapport between us a month later, when we met again. But the meeting—in another restaurant in Camden Town—turned out to be strangely chilly, almost unpleasant. On my return to New York, Olwyn wrote me:

> I was depressed by your dogged refusal to realize, seemingly, what I meant by Sylvia's lack of openness, which—

for me, at least—resulted in my feeling that I knew her so little. . . . And I would not have thought the concept difficult to grasp. This was hardly a feeling unique to me—many people who knew her better or as well as I did have made similar comments. . . .

Having one's word continually judged and doubted . . . is unpleasant and frustrating.

What had triggered Olwyn's anger was some remarks I made about a man named Ed Cohen, with whom Plath had corresponded when she was in college. At the Lilly Library, I had read Cohen's letters to her—they were wonderful, evocative young man's letters—and I had flown out to Chicago to speak with him. Cohen had written to Plath after reading a short story of hers in *Seventeen*, she had responded, and a (veiled) romance by mail had developed. Then, one day, Cohen suddenly appeared at Smith, and the romance abruptly ended. He was evidently not Plath's type, and she was not nice to him. Presently, the correspondence resumed—Cohen apparently forgave her for her rejection of his actual person and accepted his Cyrano role. In Chicago, in a beautiful, neglected early-twentieth-century stucco house, where he lives and runs a business in used electronic devices, Cohen told me a strange, complicated story about how Plath's letters to him had vanished from a file cabinet. On reading the review of *Bitter Fame* in the *Times Book Review*, Cohen wrote a letter to the editor, published six weeks later, in which he identified himself as "a close friend and frequent correspondent of Sylvia Plath in the early nineteen-fifties," and said, "Sylvia Plath was, from at least late adolescence on, at her very best what the psychiatrists refer to as a borderline personality." During my interview with him, Cohen also characterized her as "manic-depressive," "paranoid," and "practically anything else you want to pull out of the hat as far as psychological terms are concerned," adding, "She must have been a very, very difficult person to live with." Telling Olwyn of my meeting with Cohen, I suggested that his "diagnosis" of Plath was a kind of revenge for her rejection of him, and I mentioned other men she had rejected (Peter Davison is one) who had come forward after her death to pronounce on her personality problems. Olwyn, her radar always searching for crypto-libber views, had taken my defense of Plath against her stung boyfriends as an attack on her own attitude and position. I quickly wrote back a mollifying reply, and our "row" subsided. We have resumed our peaceful, odd, wary correspondence.

A very businesslike, impersonal figure at Faber & Faber, Hughes's publisher, now handles permissions. He writes terse notes to supplicants, telling them that he will forward their requests to Ted and Carol Hughes (one deals with the couple as a unit), and will write again when he hears from them. Sometimes he doesn't hear for a long time. In securing the permissions for this essay, I have collected a dossier of his brief, bloodless communications. (My negotiations with the estate were tense but fairly straightforward. The Hugheses originally wanted the right to read my manuscript in its entirety, as a condition of giving permission to quote from writings under their control. I found this proposal unacceptable. Presently, they changed their position and asked to see only the paragraphs on either side of the quotations. This condition I accepted, and the relevant permissions were granted under it.) I have formed an image of Olwyn's successor that resembles one of the pair of men in Plath's poem "Death & Co.":

> The one who never looks up, whose eyes are lidded
> And balled, like Blake's,
> Who exhibits
>
> The birthmarks that are his trademark —
> The scald scar of water,

The nude
Verdigris of the condor.

Alvarez recalls in his memoir that Plath read this poem aloud to him during his visit to her flat on Christmas Eve, and that he "argued inanely" with her about the image of the condor. "I said it was exaggerated, morbid. On the contrary, she replied, that was exactly how a condor's legs looked. She was right, of course. I was only trying, in a futile way, to reduce the tension and take her mind momentarily off her private horrors—as though that could be done by argument and literary criticism!" In mid-January, Alvarez reports, Plath wrote him a note proposing a visit to the zoo with the children so she could show him the nude verdigris of the condor. He did not answer.

V

AT noon on a mild gray day in September of 1991, I got off a train at an ugly modernized station in Bedford, a town an hour out of London, and found that Trevor Thomas, the man meeting my train, wasn't there. Thomas was the third member of the anti-Hughes axis of Elizabeth Sigmund and Clarissa Roche. He was the source of the story about the party with bongo drums in Plath's flat on the night of her funeral (for which the Independent had to apologize, and which he himself had to retract). He was the man who had lived downstairs from Plath on Fitzroy Road and may have been the last person to see her alive; he said that on the eve of her suicide Plath appeared at his door and borrowed stamps from him. In Alvarez's memoir, Thomas is the linchpin of Alvarez's theory that Plath had not meant to die but had intended to rise from her death by gassing as she had risen from her death by sleeping pills. She had, according to Alvarez, counted on "the elderly painter who lived below" (he was fifty-five) to save her. A new au-pair girl was scheduled to arrive at nine, and if all had gone according to plan Thomas would have heard her ringing the doorbell; she would have discovered Plath's still warm body, and "there is little doubt she would have been saved." But Thomas had not heard the ringing—gas had evidently seeped down to his apartment and drugged him—and by the time the girl returned with help, after an interminable wait at a telephone box, it was too late. (In *Bitter Fame*, the idea that Plath would have been saved if the girl—who, further research disclosed, was a nurse for Plath, sent by Plath's doctor, John Horder—had got into the house at nine is put into doubt. Stevenson writes, "It is Dr. Horder's opinion that even if she had been rescued while her body was alive, it is likely that her mind would have been destroyed.")

Thomas himself neither confirmed nor disputed Alvarez's account; he had moved out of London, and nothing was heard from him, or of him, until 1986, when he resurfaced in the Plath legend. A letter by Elizabeth Sigmund in the *Observer*, protesting a characterization of Plath in its columns, caught his approving eye and prompted him to write to Sigmund through the newspaper. Sigmund then passed the seventy-nine-year-old Thomas on to Roche, who persuaded him to put his memories down on paper. At her urging, he produced a twenty-seven-page typewritten manuscript—in 1989 he had it photocopied and bound in an edition of two hundred copies—chronicling his two-month-long acquaintance with Plath at 23 Fitzroy Road and recounting what he heard and saw in the house in the months following her death. The memoir, called "Sylvia Plath: Last Encounters," is a remarkable document. Like Dido Merwin's memoir, it renders an immediate and vivid self-portrait, and, like Dido, Thomas remembers Plath unaffectionately. But, unlike Dido, Thomas doesn't put Plath down in order to elevate Hughes: he speaks badly of him, too. He isn't really interested in either Plath or Hughes. He makes it clear that he is interested only in his own life. That he knew Plath at all was just another of the pieces of bad luck by which his life has been dogged. "Ever since my wife left me in September 1962 I had been desperate to find somewhere where my sons Giles and Joshua could live with me," Thomas writes on the opening page of "Last Encounters." One day in late October or early November—it was shortly before Plath wrote her ecstatic letter to Mrs. Plath about finding the maisonette on Fitzroy Road— Thomas saw the flat, too, and was equally enamored of it. The problem was the high rent: he wasn't sure he could raise the money needed to pay the required three months' rent in advance, and he asked the real-estate agent to hold the maisonette over the weekend, which the agent agreed to do. But when Thomas telephoned on Monday, to say he would take it, it was gone. The agent "told me that a young married couple with two small children, a Mr. and Mrs. Hughes, had viewed on Sunday afternoon, and because he felt their need was greater than mine he had let them have the maisonette, and he had reserved the ground-floor flat for me." Thomas continues:

I was very angry, because the ground-floor flat was too small. Also I felt sure I had been cheated in some way. Although they were now living apart, Ted Hughes was helpful, going along with her to house agents, who would be unlikely to let to a woman living alone with two children. Years afterwards, I learned that Mrs. Hughes had paid a *year's rent* in advance and signed a five-year lease. No wonder the agents thought their need was greater than mine.

Even though the ground-floor flat didn't suit him, Thomas took it. "I had to make the best of a poor deal," he grumbles. "I had my belongings brought out of store and stuffed into the flat. . . . I was having to construct bunk beds for the boys." The reason for this, on the face of it, mystifying compromise—surely he could have looked elsewhere for a larger flat—was the blue ceramic plaque with Yeats's name on it. In his youth in Liverpool, Thomas had been in charge of a production of Yeats's play *At the Hawk's Well*. He had produced, acted in, and designed the costumes for it. Thomas believed in the occult, and he felt he "had to" live in Yeats's house on Fitzroy Road. But he felt under no obligation to be helpful, or even particularly civil, to the young woman who moved into the flat upstairs, and in his memoir he relates with a kind of relish his various unhelpfulnesses and incivilities. When Plath, on the day of her arrival, accidentally locked herself and the crying children out of the flat and applied to Thomas for help, "I had to dash her hopes about the keys, as I had only those for my flat. The last thing I wanted was to become involved, so I advised her to phone the police, and I went on my way." On another occasion, during the big freeze, when there was deep snow and Plath couldn't start her car, "she wanted me to go out and swing one of those heavy handles you had to insert in the front of the car to get it started. I had to refuse, because if you didn't have the knack of it you could break a thumb, or even a wrist." Thomas reports that Plath put her garbage in his trash cans instead of getting trash cans of her own, and blocked the hallway with her baby carriage. "I think it would be correct to say that I did not positively dislike her," he writes. He adds:

> She tended to be a self-centered person, not letting herself become involved with other people's problems. Never at any time did she wonder about me and my sons and what

stress we might be under. Nor did she manifest any interest in my paintings nor in what I did. The world revolved around her. This self-preoccupation I have observed in other creative people.

Thomas presently gets to his two set pieces, the "last encounters" of his title. In the first, which takes place about 8 p.m. on a Sunday not long before Plath's death, she appears at his door and is so distressed that even he is moved:

> She stood there with red, swollen eyes, the tears running down her face, and with voice shaken by sobs she said: "I am going to die . . . and who will take care of my children?" I did not quite know what to do. I reached out and took her arm. "You'd better come in and sit down. I'll get you a drink."

Plath weepily tells Thomas that she has come to the end of her tether. Then her mood changes and she becomes

> fiercely angry with an intensity that was quite alarming as she punched clenched fists up and down. "It's that awful woman's fault. She stole him. We were so happy and she stole him away from me. She's an evil woman, a scarlet woman, the Jezebel. They're in Spain spending our money, my money. Oh! How I hate them!" She was in such a tantrum I tried to distract her by telling her that my wife was supposed to be in Spain with the man she'd gone off with; wouldn't it be funny if they were in the same hotel in Barcelona? It didn't work. As on previous occasions, she was wholly and intensely concerned only with her troubles. She had no time for mine.

In the second encounter, at 11:45 on the eve of Plath's death, she again comes to his door, this time to ask for stamps. She says she needs them to post letters to America that night. Thomas gives her the stamps, and she opens a small purse to reimburse him. "I told her not to worry, as I never took money for stamps, whereupon she said, 'Oh! But I must pay you or I won't be right with my conscience before God, will I?'" After reentering his flat, Thomas continues to see light under his front door and returns to find Plath still standing in the hallway with "her head raised with a kind of seraphic expression on her face." Thomas offers to call her doctor—she looks very ill to him—but she says, "No, please don't do that. I'm just having a marvelous dream, a most wonderful vision." She doesn't accept Thomas's offer to come into his flat or his suggestion that she go back upstairs. She continues standing in the hallway, and he finally tells her, "I'd have to go or I wouldn't be able to get up in time." As it proves, he does not get up until five o'clock the next afternoon. Because of the gas leaking down to his flat, he entirely misses the commotion of the morning: the discovery of the body, the arrival of the police and ambulance, the crying children, the shocked relatives. It is a fine stroke—worthy of a canny novelist—that the egocentric narrator of "Last Encounters" should be spared the role of ordinary appalled onlooker and given his own "death" to undergo. By the time Thomas awakens, feeling strange and his head hurting, the house is quiet, and he simply goes to his job, at the Gordon Fraser Gallery, to (oddly) apologize for not having telephoned. Only on his return—his boss sends him home—does he learn of the suicide from a neighbor.

At the Bedford station, at twenty minutes past the hour, a wan sun appeared in the gray sky. I looked nervously at my watch. Then a tall man of around seventy shambled toward me. "I'm Robbie," he said, and apologized for his lateness, which, he said, had to do with an unsuccessful attempt to buy a vegetarian pizza. "Trevor is in the car," he said. "He's been

having a bit of trouble with his leg, so he stayed in the car."
Robbie spoke slowly and calmly and evenly. He had a protu-
berant belly, weary eyes, and the steady, mildly subduing
manner of a nurse or a dog trainer. In the car, Thomas
reached out an inattentive hand and immediately began to
speak fretfully of the pizza with sausages that he had been
obliged to buy because the shop that sold vegetarian pizza
was closed on Sunday. The vegetarian pizza had been sought
on my behalf, and though I said it didn't matter in the slightest, Thomas continued to fuss about it. A distinguished-
looking man with white hair and a white beard, he was
dressed in a kind of jumpsuit made of black-and-white-
striped seersucker; a bit of turquoise shirt showed at the
throat, and a medal hung down his chest. He carried his
handsome head proudly, and his rosy lips were set in a pout.
His left leg was badly swollen.

⟨The car was a secondhand vehicle that Robbie and
Thomas had bought the day before and didn't quite have the
hang of yet. At every light, there was a fierce struggle with
the gearshift. I asked Thomas a question about his memoir,
and he started to answer and then said, "I'm too anxious
about the car to talk now. I'll talk later." As we neared a small
grocery, Thomas told Robbie to stop; he spoke to him as if
Robbie were the chauffeur. Robbie obediently pulled over to
the curb. "Get some stuffed olives and Heinz salad cream,"
Thomas said. Robbie went into the shop. While he was there,
Thomas told me a dream he had had the night before. "I was
in a landscape of pink rocks overlooking the sea. A young
hippie girl came up to me and asked for money. I said, 'I'm a
Frenchman, and I have to go home.' She said, 'I'll follow
you,' and she kept trying to push me off the pink rocks into
the sea below. I kept saying, 'Don't do it. I haven't any
money,' and she kept saying, 'I don't care.'"

Robbie came out of the store with a parcel. "Here we are,

Trevor," he said. "Now, she doesn't have any stuffed olives, but I got the two other kinds. Here's the change. Is there anything else you've thought of?"

Thomas considered and then said, "You could get some prepared French dressing for the avocados." Robbie stolidly started for the shop again. I felt the shameful, murderous impatience that maundering old people engender in those who still have time to spare. Thomas reconsidered. "Never mind," he called after Robbie. "I'll make my own dressing." Robbie impassively turned back.

When we were on our way again, I said to Thomas, "How do you interpret your dream? Do you think it had something to do with my coming to talk to you today about Sylvia Plath and Ted Hughes?"

"No," Thomas said. "It had to do with my brother going off with someone else, leaving me—"

Robbie cut in blandly, "Before you begin your story, Trevor, I think you'd better tell Janet what you have to say about the—er—legal side."

"If you could please be quiet," Thomas said. "If you talk and tell me what to do, I will make mistakes."

"All right," Robbie said.

"If you leave it to my intuition, it will be much smarter of you."

"All right."

"It's my story. I was the one who had to put up with it, and nearly go to Heaven on it."

I already knew something about "the legal side." After bringing the *Independent* before the Press Council over the bongo-drum story, Hughes had a court order issued against Thomas to ensure that the libel be permanently put to rest. The libel derived from the closing pages of "Last Encounters," covering the period after Plath's death, when relatives, friends of Plath and Hughes, and successive nannies appeared at 23 Fitzroy Road, and Thomas, from his ground-floor post, darkly observed their comings and goings. Like his early meetings with Plath, his meetings with her survivors were brief and fragmentary; in his account of them, petty aggrievement and voyeurism again struggle for ascendancy over the writer's feelings. Thomas reports several meetings between him and Hughes and Assia Wevill. He writes appreciatively of Wevill (she was "very helpful in getting an interview for Giles with the J. Walter Thompson organization, for which she worked") but presents Hughes as a haughty, menacing figure who was consistently unpleasant to him: "I knew from my first view of him he was someone I'd want to keep at a very safe distance." Later, Thomas reports, when he mistakenly thought that a burglar had broken into the Plath flat, and called the police, who roused Hughes from his sleep, the irritated Hughes "shouted down the stairs for my benefit: 'It's only that silly old fool downstairs.'" In Hughes's letter to Andrew Motion about Wagner-Martin's biography—the letter in which he wrote of the "mental breakdown, neurotic collapse, domestic catastrophe" that "saved us from several travesties of this kind being completed"—he went on to make a large, blunt point:

> The main problem with S.P.'s biographers is that they fail, at the outset, when they embark on the book they hope will sell a lot of copies, to realize that the most interesting and dramatic part of S.P.'s life is only 1/2 S.P.—the other 1/2 is *me*. They can caricature and remake S.P. in the image of their foolish fantasies, and get away with it—and assume, in their brainless way, that it's perfectly O.K. to give me the same treatment. Apparently forgetting that I'm still here, to check, and that I've no intention of feeding myself to their digestions and submitting myself to their reconstitution, if I can help it.

In the case of Thomas's memoir, Hughes had to leave Plath to Thomas's mercies, but he brought a lawsuit against Thomas and forced him to withdraw and apologize for—I quote from a legal document of 1990—the "suggestion that on the very evening of Sylvia Plath's funeral Mr. Hughes had attended a high-spirited and boisterous party, with bongo drums, which was organized and held in the flat where Sylvia Plath had earlier that week committed suicide, the stated purpose of the party being to 'cheer up' Mr. Hughes." This document, which was read in open court, also contained Thomas's acknowledgment that the suggestion was false, that "Mr. Hughes was not present at any such party as was referred to in the Memoir, and indeed he [Thomas] now accepts that he was mistaken as to whether such a party took place on the night in question."

As I started to question Thomas about his legal encounter with Hughes, we arrived at our destination: a small house on a silent street of narrow, rather bleak and pinched two-story brick row houses, the most common form of English domestic architecture. But I was not prepared for what I saw when I entered the house: a depository of bizarre clutter and disorder. We entered a narrow passageway, made almost impassable by sagging cardboard cartons stacked to the ceiling, which led to a small, square, dimly lit, windowless room. There was a round white plastic table in the center, surrounded by ruined chairs of various kinds, the largest of which faced a television set. Along the walls and on the floor and on every surface hundreds, perhaps thousands, of objects were piled, as if the place were a secondhand shop into which the contents of ten other secondhand shops had been hurriedly crammed, and over everything there was a film of dust: not ordinary transient dust but dust that itself was overlaid with dust—dust that through the years had acquired almost a kind of objecthood, a sort of immanence. Through an archway near the entrance one could see into a dark bedroom with an unmade bed, on which rumpled bedding and vague piles of clothes lay, surrounded by shadowy stacks of more objects. One looked with relief to the daylit kitchen that opened off the living room. But one's relief was short-lived. In its way, the kitchen was the most disturbing room of all. Here, too, every surface swarmed with objects—hundreds of utensils, appliances, gadgets, bottles of condiments, boxes, baskets, dishes, jars jostling one another—so that all the functions of the room had been cancelled; the place was useless for the preparation of food and the cleaning up afterward. There was nowhere to put anything down or to work, or even to cook: the gas range was out of commission and had become another surface for objects to proliferate on.

Robbie brought the boxed pizza and the parcel of olives and Heinz salad cream into the kitchen and gazed helplessly around, as if he had never seen the place before. Thomas had sunk into the chair facing the television set, but then painfully got up and began giving Robbie orders about the preparation of lunch. Robbie had found a place to work: a small section of a tiny cutting board, on which he was slicing tomatoes amid piles of old crumbs. He good-naturedly followed Thomas's imperious instructions, though he finally protested "But there's no room!" in response to some impossible command. After offering to help, and knowing I couldn't, I went back to the living room; the sight of the two old men squabbling and anxiously fumbling in the horrible kitchen was a painful one. Finally, the preparations were completed, and while the pizza warmed in one of two microwave ovens in the kitchen Robbie went upstairs to his own quarters and Thomas and I sat at the white table. Thomas started on a rambling story about his difficult and unlucky life, whose misfortunes had evidently been only compounded by the "malign, black vibrations" that "the Yeats influence" had released at 23 Fitzroy Road. I listened fitfully as he spoke of various jobs he had had that hadn't worked out, of his wife's leaving him for a rich businessman on the Isle of Wight, of one of his sons' running away from boarding school, of this person and that person by whom he felt badly used. As my eye had recoiled from the threatening multiplicity of objects in Thomas's house, so my mind retreated before the dulling incoherence of his monologue. In a note about the author at the end of "Last Encounters," R. C. Stuart (Robbie) has crisply ordered this material into a kind of job résumé— "Professor Trevor Thomas, administrator, artist, author, and actor, has had a varied and distinguished career"—citing "much praised" productions in which Thomas acted, his "uniquely distinctive" style of painting, his "revolutionary techniques of museum display," and his "impressive integrity." Now, in Thomas's peevish recital, the material was being restored to its primordial state.

Later, as I thought about Thomas's house (which I often did; one does not easily forget such a place), it appeared to me as a kind of monstrous allegory of truth. This is the way things are, the place says. This is unmediated actuality, in all its multiplicity, randomness, inconsistency, redundancy, *authenticity*. Before the magisterial mess of Trevor Thomas's house, the orderly houses that most of us live in seem meagre and lifeless—as, in the same way, the narratives called biographies pale and shrink in the face of the disorderly actuality that is a life. The house also stirred my imagination as a metaphor for the problem of writing. Each person who sits down to write faces not a blank page but his own vastly overfilled mind. The problem is to clear out most of what is in it, to fill huge plastic garbage bags with the confused jumble of things that have accreted there over the days, months, years of being alive and taking things in through the eyes and ears and heart. The goal is to make a space where a few ideas and images and feelings may be so arranged that a reader will want to linger awhile among them, rather than to flee, as I had wanted to flee from Thomas's house. But this task of housecleaning (of narrating) is not merely arduous; it is dangerous. There is the danger of throwing the wrong things out and keeping the wrong things in; there is the danger of throwing too much out and being left with too bare a house; there is the danger of throwing everything out. Once one starts throwing out, it may become hard to stop. It may be better not to start. It may be better to hang on to everything, like Trevor Thomas, lest one be left with nothing. The fear that I felt in Thomas's house is a cousin of the fear felt by the writer who cannot risk beginning to write.

Robbie returned and served lunch. He brought each of us a plate on which a slice of pizza, potato salad, and olives and tomatoes had been nicely arranged, and which bore no trace of the struggle to produce it. Thomas stared at his plate and said, "Clarissa says that Olwyn told her that Sylvia said awful things about me. I don't believe that. She couldn't have disliked me as much as that and still come to me for help, could she? She might. I don't know."

I said, "One can have many feelings about a person. You yourself didn't like her, and at the same time you felt pity for her."

Robbie said, "Moods are not the same as permanent attitudes."

I said, "Do you feel as if you'd been there, too, Robbie?"

"I've heard Trevor tell it so many times. Always the same. It never varies. He's got a photographic memory, a visual memory like a camera." Robbie spoke proudly, as if about a performing horse.

"I do," Thomas said. "When I tell you the story now, I see the scene. I see her standing there, I'm opening the door. There she is. Tears are streaming down her face. She is all red-eyed. Her hair looks awful. 'I'm going to die. Who will take care of my children?' I didn't know what to do. What would you have done? I said, 'Come in.' This was the second time. The first time was the night she rang my doorbell and said would I go start her car. There were big drifts of snow. I said, 'No.' I could have broken my wrist. 'You better phone the BBC.' Which she did—she was making a broadcast. They told her to call a taxi. While she was waiting, she said, 'I love all these old English things you have. You know, you remind me of my father. He was a professor, too, in America.' So she did know I had been a professor. But she never once asked me what I did. She never asked me if I painted, or if I drew, or was I an artist. I could have done a portrait of her if she had been cooperative."

"Did you ask her what *she* did?"

"Well, I just assumed she was a housewife," Thomas said after a pause. He added, "I didn't know she was a writer until the night she got hysterical." In the scene in his memoir where Plath comes to his flat and speaks of the Jezebel who took Hughes away, she also shows him a page in the *Observer* where there is a review of *The Bell Jar* and on the facing page, as it happens, a poem by Hughes. Plath tells him that she is Victoria Lucas. Then, "with fierce intensity," she says, "He'll be down there with our friends, receiving their congratulations about his poem, the centre of admiration, free to come and go as he pleases. And here I am, a prisoner in this house, chained to the children."

I asked Thomas if he had read *The Bell Jar*.

"Oh, yes indeed, after she died. I had read nothing of hers before she died. I have never read any of her poetry. I'm not interested in poetry. I like novels. I like memoirs. Best of all, I like biographies. I think I write rather well myself. Clarissa says the style of my memoir is very moving. She says it is a very good style. I seemed to have been inspired in some way. It's readable, isn't it?"

"Yes, it is."

"Almost everybody has said, 'I couldn't put it down.' I don't see what Hughes has to complain about in it. I don't denigrate him in any way. Robbie, don't put milk in. Janet doesn't want milk."

"I know. This is for you."

"I've already got one here."

"That's stone cold. I've made a fresh one."

Thomas stared with displeasure at the cup of tea Robbie put before him. Then he said, "When Miss Malpass rang—she's in the big law firm that represents Ted, of Nabarro Nathanson. They're Jewish, basically. They have a huge roster of solicitors. They can draw on barristers. When she rang and said, 'Why don't we try to arrange a reconciliation? It's silly, you two men getting at each other this way,' Robbie said, 'Why don't we accept? All that hassle is distressing you.' I *was* terribly distressed. I became quite ill, didn't I, Robbie?"

"Yes. It was nervous exhaustion. So much worry. All those thoughts coming vividly back into his photographic memory. Again and again. Every time he has an interview, like today—"

Thomas cut in. "Oh, I don't mind that. It was Ted Hughes's threats. I was frightened of him, I was frightened that he would sue me. A bailiff came here. My solicitor told me that Hughes could take my house, my paintings—everything I have. This sounds a bit conceited, I know, but I think it's outrageous that one literary man—if Ted Hughes can be regarded as a literary man of any standing—would take this kind of action against a man like me, who is much older, and also of a certain intellectual calibre. I mean, my entry in *Who's*

Who puts his entry to shame. His is just a catalogue of the books he wrote."

When it was time to go, the men overruled my idea of calling for a taxi and drove me to the station. Robbie managed better with the gearshift. In answer to a question from me about what he did, Robbie said that he had retired six years earlier, and described, in baffling technical detail, his work in electronics. When he finished, Thomas said, "You see, there's more to Robbie than you would think."

On the train, I read a copy of Thomas's *Who's Who* entry which he had given me. It was long, and listed many jobs in museums and universities, several of only a year's duration, and cited three publications in museum journals. Then I made notes on Trevor Thomas's house. I knew that the labyrinth of the Sylvia Plath and Ted Hughes story would eventually lead me back to it—the Aleph of my tale—and that when the time came I would want evidence that I had not merely conjured it up for the purposes of my plot but had seen it as well.

PERMISSIONS ACKNOWLEDGMENTS

PERMISSIONS ACKNOWLEDGMENTS

Collected Poems administered by Faber and Faber Limited, London. Reprinted by permission of HarperCollins Publishers, Inc., and Faber and Faber Limited.

Olwyn Hughes: Excerpts from unpublished letters to Anne Stevenson and the author. Reprinted by permission of Olwyn Hughes.

Anne Stevenson: Excerpts from unpublished letters to Olwyn Hughes and the author. Reprinted by permission of Anne Stevenson.

Wylie, Aitken & Stone, Inc.: Excerpt from letter from A. Alvarez to Ted Hughes, copyright © 1971 by A. Alvarez. Excerpt from *The Savage God* by A. Alvarez, copyright © 1971 by A. Alvarez. Excerpt from review by A. Alvarez of *Bitter Fame* by Anne Stevenson (first published in *The New York Review of Books*), copyright © 1989 by A. Alvarez. Reprinted by permission of Wylie, Aitken & Stone, Inc.

A NOTE ON THE TYPE

This book was set in a digitized version of Janson. The hot-metal version of Janson was a recutting made direct from type cast from matrices long thought to have been made by the Dutchman Anton Janson, who was a practicing typefounder in Leipzig during the years 1668 to 1687. However, it has been conclusively demonstrated that these types are actually the work of Nicholas Kis (1650–1702), a Hungarian, who most probably learned his trade from the master Dutch typefounder Dirk Voskens. The type is an excellent example of the influential and sturdy Dutch types that prevailed in England up to the time William Caslon (1692–1766) developed his own incomparable designs from them.

Composed by Graphic Composition, Athens, Georgia
Printed and bound by Arcata Graphics/Martinsburg,
Martinsburg, West Virginia
Designed by Virginia Tan